From Starr to Starrfish

From Starr to Starrfish

A non-swimmer's quest to swim the English Channel

Rob Starr

Book Guild Publishing
Sussex, England

First published in Great Britain in 2013 by
The Book Guild Ltd
The Werks, 45 Church Road
Hove BN3 2BE

Printed in Great Britain by
CPI Antony Rowe

A catalogue record for this book is available from
The British Library.

ISBN 978 1 84624 948 8

Introduction

From a paddler to a Channel swimmer in less than 12 months... hmm, it was an interesting idea. I was doing some running a few years back in the hope I'd be good enough to compete in the London Marathon. There was no particular reason for this other than I always thought I should be able to run a marathon, it looked hard for sure, but I was fit and young (ish). I secured my place, received my number and started training. The first few miles were fine although a little tiring, but each time I got to around 10 miles, my right leg felt like it was about to explode. This is the leg that I suffer with when my rheumatism plays up - always the same leg and generally in my foot. Each time after the near-explosion I would rest for a couple of weeks and try again. It was after perhaps the tenth or eleventh try that I finally figured out I had a problem. While I was sure I would still be able to run a marathon one day, I decided that perhaps a less leg-pounding sport might be better for me. Who said I didn't catch on quickly?

So into the pool I went, an endless pool that I have at home in which, until then, I had never actually swum. Twice a week before work, for three weeks, I used the pool. I built up from doing one minute without a rest to a staggering twenty minutes. It was during my third week of being an Olympic endless pool swimmer that I thought there was a challenge here for me instead of running a marathon. This thought coincided with two other things; first, my head banging heavily into the side of the (rather short) pool and second, with me needing to raise the profile of the Starr Trust, the charity I set up in 2008 in memory of my dad, Edward Starr, who died of cancer in 2006, aged 61.

Standing in the 35-degree water, rubbing the side of my head, it occurred to me that learning to swim properly and swimming the Channel would be a good plan - and surely not that tough. After all, I could now do twenty minutes without stopping! I never gave a second's thought to the cost of it, the fact that the sea can fall to below 4 degrees and is probably one of the most powerful and dangerous things in the world, or that fewer people

1

have swum the English Channel than have climbed Mount Everest.

In my blind optimism I dried myself off, went to my computer, found the Channel Swimming Association and joined as an associate member. I then read a bit more of their website, found they have a fleet of recommended out of season fishing boats and that they are booked up well over a year in advance. I quickly sent an email to reserve one as soon as I could. You would have thought that at some point between drying off and sitting at my computer I would have considered, as a barrier to this challenge, that I was dealing with three illnesses (Crohn's disease, osteoporosis and palindromic rheumatism, each of them debilitating at different times). I was also helping my wife Sharon to bring up our three young children, then all under four, running a group of three companies I owned that was in its twentieth year, and building the Starr Trust as it struggled to find its feet.

On top of all that I was now going to learn to swim in the sea and tackle an English Channel crossing. It was utter madness, both in hindsight and at the time, but that simply didn't occur to me. What mattered was raising money for the Starr Trust and raising its profile – that and that alone was enough of a driving force to get me started. The Starr Trust was set up to *Help Children Smile* and if it meant a few cold morning swims then so be it.

The Edward Starr Charitable Trust was not set up with any money in the bank, therefore everything has been achieved through the hard work of the trustees, the staff, the volunteers and our supporters. In our first four years we funded more than sixty projects in sixteen countries and helped create literally thousands of smiles around the world.

The running costs of the Starr Trust are covered by my company, Seico Group, meaning that we can give out 100% of everything we raise. We believe that *all* children deserve the chance to smile and to have the support they need to achieve their goals and we also believe that children should be encouraged to support other children and to listen to and understand each other. Sometimes a smile is worth a million pounds; it can inspire, it can create, it can encourage and it can be infectious, the world simply needs more smiles.

My 'Swim4Smiles' campaign raised more than £75,000, which we gave to twenty-one different projects (twenty-one, because that is the distance in miles across the Channel from England to France, ignoring the tides, of course).

This is my diary over two-and-a-half years, written originally as a blog that marked the days that I swam (and a few that I didn't): some good days, some not so good days, but every one most certainly a character-building day!

Day 0 - 25th April 2010

Last night at a party I was talking to my friend Nicky about my swimming idea (she thought I was nuts of course) and she said she knew this lady called Fiona Southwell who had already swum the Channel. A couple of phone calls later and tomorrow, Monday 26th April, 2010, will mark my start as a Channel hopeful (or Channel hopeless, we shall see). What have I started?

Day 1 - 26th April 2010

Today was my first day ever into the sea as a swimmer rather than a paddler. What makes me think that I can swim in the sea in April, let alone swim the English Channel? In fact what's April got to do with it? What makes me think I can swim in the sea at all? Did my 20 minutes in the endless pool waterlog my brain or something? Am I so conceited that I think I can achieve anything? Maybe I am!

The founder of Ford Motors, Henry T Ford, said: 'Whether you think you can, or you think you can't - you're right.' So here I go. Either way I'm right!

At 7a.m. I met Fiona Southwell (oldest UK female Channel Swimmer on 18th August 2009 - amazing lady) on the beach outside the Brighton Swimming Club Arch, just next to Brighton Pier. I'm extremely nervous, both about swimming this morning and about emerging from the Arch in my skimpy Speedos looking rather pale, not at all muscled and being a relative non-swimmer. Not one for the photo album!

We went in for exactly 12 minutes, which was good as Fiona said two minutes would be enough on my first day with the sea temperature just under 7 degrees. I think I have convinced myself I did well.

The waves seemed as tall as me, and were very *cold*. I had to walk in backwards because they were so high and for the first time since I was in Egypt four years ago in 50 degrees of heat I found myself unable to breathe! It seems that both extreme heat and extreme cold can take your breath away. About six other swimmers went in but most came out before us and a couple had on full body costumes.

We swam from the middle of the beach to the groyne and back, which seemed miles away but in reality was only a few metres. I'm already talking in metres, so at least I sound like a swimmer even if I don't look like one.

After the swim I had a shower in the Arch (what a charming place it's not) and then proceeded to shiver uncontrollably for about an hour - I'm told in this temperature it's not unusual to shiver for quite some time. I also found it hard to speak clearly, which apparently is very mild hypothermia. What a pleasant experience today wasn't.

Day 2 - 27ᵗʰ April 2010

I came back, so English Channel here I come. This morning was easily as cold as yesterday, if not colder. Fiona and I swam to the silver ball and back, which is maybe 25% of the way along Brighton Pier. It seemed a long, long way from the shore. The sea was very calm, unlike yesterday, and there was hardly any movement at all.

I got to the ball OK but when I turned around to come back it was really hard. I am not yet a swimmer, so what was I doing out there on Day 2? Then my goggles completely steamed up and I couldn't see a thing. I instantly got into a panic, which is a very new and uncomfortable experience for me.

By 7.45a.m. I was sitting in my car listening to Lady Gaga singing about some bloke called Alejandro and feeling rather worried. I was shaking like an old man at a disco, which is possibly due to a mixture of extreme cold and extreme panic. I urgently need sea goggles rather than the pool goggles I had on and I must learn to swim properly! The cold - although under 7 degrees and making me shiver - I can deal with. But my lack of experience to get out of a problem in the sea did unnerve me and I need to deal with that right now. I must remain calm; anything else is simply not acceptable.

Two people swam twice around the pier this morning, beach to beach to beach. How the hell do you do that? Even once seems madly impossible.

Day 3 - 28ᵗʰ April 2010

Despite yesterday being a bad day in the sea, which bugged me all through the night and into the wee hours, I have come back for more. Bob Bicknall, a really nice guy, is a member of the Brighton Swimming Club. He's been swimming for years (probably most of my life) and for 50-something he's in incredible shape. Fiona isn't here today so Bob is swimming with me, as I'm not allowed to go out into the open sea on my own yet, not as a member of Brighton Swimming Club, that is. Quite right after yesterday's nonsense!

The temperature was still under 7 degrees and there were small waves, which were quite slappy on the head. It was like Benny Hill was the sea and we were the pretty young girls running around the park. However we did swim further today than yesterday and even went under the pier and then back through the pier and back to shore. That was a very cool experience.

I used flippers and a swimming hat for the first time today and goggles which were definitely better than the others but still crap. My brand new goggles from wiggle.com hopefully come today. So was it better than yesterday? Did I panic again? Well actually, I think I enjoyed it. I felt I understood why they do it. Bob told me to relax if I got into a panic, to lie on my back and float it out, or let myself drift a bit towards shore or swim to the pier and climb up the stairs. Either way you can get out if you don't panic. As soon as he said that it made perfect sense and the fear went away. Such little and simple advice but it was like turning a corner.

I have now arranged to meet Mark Shepherd this coming Saturday. He was Fiona's swimming trainer and hopefully he will swim with me and see what I'm like and then help me to plan my training. Now it really begins.

It felt like a good day today, I'm feeling quite happy about it.

After work at 5p.m. I did a 5.4k run in 31 minutes around Hove Park, up King George Avenue and home. Is it possible I can start running as well?

Wouldn't it be mad if I ended up taking on swimming because I can't run, only to find it is good for my running?

Day 4 - 29th April 2010

I'm sitting in my car near the Brighton Pier, it's 6.50a.m. and I'm once again listening to Lady Gaga singing about that Alejandro bloke; change the tune Heart! This is fast becoming my sea swimming song. The sea is calm and the tide is low. I can see a man walking on the beach with a metal detector, which seems odd so early in the morning.

This morning it was Fiona, Bob Bicknell and Midge (really nice girl from the club and another distance athlete) and little moi! Guess what? We swam round the pier, the whole way around. What an amazing thing to do on Day 4 of my swimming career, and even more amazing considering two days ago I was panicking halfway along.

It was sunny but the sun wasn't directly on us as we swam up the pier. Then as if from nowhere the sun was on my back and all around me as we swam to the other end. It was astonishing. Looking up you can see the rides hanging off the end of the pier and heading up into the sky, and from straight ahead you can see right under the pier and the intricate weave of the stanchions as they struggle to hold up such a goliath of metal and wood above them. I can't believe I've got to over 40 years old, have always lived in Brighton and had never seen this. Coming back around the pier and down the other side, then back through the pier and to the beach seemed a huge swim to me but the others seemed to take the whole thing in their stride, and their stride is quick! I found myself breathing hard and clearly my technique is pretty rubbish but I did get around and back safely so maybe, just maybe, I'll be a sea swimmer one day soon. The whole swim only took about 45 minutes though I'm sure it would have been half that time for the others if they didn't have to keep waiting for me. What an amazing achievement so quickly on in this challenge. I really think I can do this!

Day 5 - 30ᵗʰ April 2010

I can't believe it's a whole week now. How many weeks left? Best not think about that. Yesterday the air was warm and the sea was calm. What a difference a day makes. Today the air temperature has dropped back to cold and the sea is very choppy indeed. I think they call it 'white horses', although I'm still trying to work out why as it just looks like waves to me.

The tide was out yet again which was a pain (literally) as it meant we had to walk in quite a distance to get to swimming depth. The waves were crashing over us every few seconds and the tide was dragging us towards the pier. It was so different to the calmer last couple of days that it's hard to even think of them as the same challenge. I actually enjoyed it as much, if not more, than yesterday. I certainly took more water into my stomach than before - not exactly the nicest breakfast I've ever had but the swim was really exciting and that definitely made up for the salty cereal. The whole swim, around the pier again, took maybe 35 minutes, which was a lot quicker than yesterday. I can't believe I was that much faster; those white horses must have taken me on their back for a ride. Once again I swam with Bob Bicknell, Fiona and another man. All of them are fast swimmers and sadly for them they had to babysit me yet again - give me another week and I'll be fine to be on my own, I'm sure.

After we came back around the head of the pier and under again they all headed away from the pier in a straight line until they got a distance away and then they went at an angle to the beach. It seemed such a long way to get back and I was pretty knackered so I thought, 'Bugger that,' and headed under the pier and then straight back down to the beach, almost to the head of the groyne next to the pier. They ended up on the beach very nicely and politely, whilst I ended up knee-deep in sharp shingle and cut both my legs (I look like I have been whipped on both my legs back and front with a cat o' nine tails, oooh arrgggh) and in my thrashing about I also lost my brand new goggles - what an idiot! Tomorrow I shall be following the party line. A week clearly isn't enough to understand the way this works.

Mind you, how fast are they! Fiona swims at about 500 miles an hour;

Bob follows very closely at about 450 miles an hour and then there is me, the Sunday driver doing about 0 miles an hour. I get a feeling this is going to frustrate me more and more if I don't speed up. Sure they have been doing this all their lives and I'm a week into it, but still, how slow could I go? Hey ho. I still got around the Pier again, albeit damaged and lost goggles!

Day 6 - 1st May 2010 (Saturday)

It's Saturday morning, 10.30a.m., and I'm back at the beach, this time with my wife Sharon in tow. She needs to see first-hand the madness I've got myself into. This morning I'm meeting Mark and Fiona, my first meeting with Mark. He trained Fiona on her channel swim. He is a B.I.G guy. I'm not sure how someone as stacked as him can swim so well. Last night I looked up Fiona's YouTube Channel swim. I went to bed afterwards feeling somewhat dazed by it, yet I've committed to it now and do it I will (somehow).

The three kids are with my in-laws, so Sharon is with me to meet Mark and take some photos of me swimming in my Speedos. I'm almost more nervous about that than the swim.

I'm still really annoyed about my goggles as I now have to show Mark what I can do and the replacement ones I've ordered won't be delivered until next week. Meanwhile I've had to buy a cheap £6 pair from the surfing shop. I hope they work, as I don't want to end up having to be rescued.

11.30a.m. - We swam around the pier together. It was extremely choppy but I did it with relative ease, which surprised Mark and me. The £6 goggles were amazingly OK - not perfect but definitely worth the money.

After the swim Mark told me about the challenges I face (a looong list) and he explained the two main areas we need to work on: my swimming technique and my eating. He said he thinks my mental ability will get me through to a large extent and he felt that as I can clearly handle the cold and as I have come on so quickly in my first week there is a chance, however slim it is, that I can do it. Very nice to hear that.

Day 7 – Monday 3rd May 2010

A 10.15a.m. swim today. Very nice to have a lie-in but I think I prefer an earlier start as there is less anticipation and less time to consider the madness of sea swimming. Coming to the beach later (it's a bank holiday today, so no work) gives me too much time to ponder what I'm doing and that makes me anxious, which gives me the butterflies, which makes me want to quit!

Fiona, Bob B and Midge and I swam around the pier. It was interesting as there were others there today who have been members of the sea swimming club for years who have never swum around the pier ever and here I am on Day 7 and I've done it more times than not.

The sea was very calm but it was raining (well, spitting really). Every now and then the sun came out and hit us, which was glorious, but basically it was typical bank holiday weather.

I realised today that as a swimmer I am really a non-swimmer: no technique to talk of and very slow. There is absolutely no way I can swim the Channel any time soon, I'm like a baby tsunami with the waves I create with each stroke. I somehow need to learn how to pick up speed. I swam as hard and fast as I possibly could but Fiona and Bob kept having to stop and wait for me. They should have brought a book to kill the time! Midge was not as quick as them, but she's a good swimmer and made me feel as if I was treading water. I am getting the feeling this is more about technique that strength.

Day 8 – 4th May 2010

7a.m. and here again. It's getting tough doing this every day. I'm not sure if I like it but I definitely don't hate it. I'm in the car, parked at the pier, listening to Heart FM but no Gaga thankfully this morning. The sea looks calm and the sky is blue, although the air is still fairly cold – about five degrees, my car seems to think. Time to force myself out of the car for the short walk to the Arch.

I should tell you about the Arch, I guess. It's down the slope to the right of the pier. A small place, just one room that is divided into three spaces.

As you come in you are faced head on with a noticeboard containing tidal information that may as well be written in Mandarin for all the sense it makes to me. To the right is a wall that seems to be held up by leaning bamboos that double as fishing rods to some quite eccentric swimmers here who somehow have the ability to fish while they swim - extraordinary!

To the left is an ill-fitting door that leads into a very small area that is the women's area. It's about a quarter the size of the men's area, which seems unfair to the lovely ladies, and is really just a large cupboard. Then back out and further left you walk into an open space that is the men's area, with a bench running all the way down the right hand wall with hooks for hanging your clothes. On the left, under some rotting windows, there is a smaller bench and a couple of chairs. Further down the room there is a slight return which houses one shower, then a shower curtain and another shower. In between this is a small urinal in the open with a hose next to it. The women shout (or sometimes don't), 'Coming through!' and the men then (or sometimes don't) hide their modesty. The ceiling is full of hanging stalactites, the air is a mix of steam from the showers and small flies and the floor is wet, raggedy and stone. And that is a very kind description! It does however serve as a place to hang your clothes, leave your bag and chat. The members of BSC seem to love it, so perhaps over time I will as well?

Time to go for it. I packed a jumper today as I'm rather bored of shivering for an hour afterwards.

Once again I went around the pier. Today it was just with 'Big' Bob Bicknell and we headed into a flat sea, which felt much colder than last week, if that is possible. Although it was very calm and the sun was shining all the way around I seemed to shiver as soon as I waded in. It only took us 28 minutes or so, which was really fast for me but probably slow for Bob! I, of course, am wearing flippers and he isn't; can you imagine me without flippers? I'd be going backwards I think!

Assuming the shivers die down and I have the energy after work I'm gonna grab a 10k run. I need to prove to myself I can be fast at something!

Day 9 – 5th May 2010

Day 9 – 5th May 2010

7a.m. It looks like yesterday: cold air but a calm sea. The sun isn't out today though. I can see three people going around the pier already, they must have started 6.30am, that's early. Me next!

It was really cold again, just Big Bob and me. I think this was our quickest. We didn't stop, not even for a second, and swam constantly from getting in to landing back on the beach. Boy, did my face hurt when I first went in the water. My body was fine but my face was like a pincushion, especially my forehead, which was seriously painful for about five minutes, it was like ice cream brain freeze. Then it went numb. Strangely, I warmed up very quickly afterwards with maybe only 20 minutes of shaking, so that's a good sign.

6th May 2010

No swimming today. I almost feel guilty about it. A company I consult for have their annual work conference today and I am an invited guest, which means staying over in sunny Watford. They are a financial services company and to be totally honest, I would actually prefer to swim in gale force waves amongst scores of jellyfish than attend a financial services conference. No slight on them, of course, as they are all decent people and a fantastic company but financial services as an industry is somewhat tedious these days. Thankfully I have to spend no more than perhaps one day a month on this part of my life and even that is something I am trying to cut down on.

As I couldn't swim today I checked into the hotel, found a park around the corner and ran around it eighteen times - a total of 13.6km in 1 hour and 11 minutes. My running is definitely coming on; can I see a marathon in the future once my swim is done? Afterwards I went to the hotel gym and did 40 minutes on weights. Looking in the mirror I can see a slight change to my physique already. Big Bob has a real swimmer's shape: broad shoulders and tailored in at the waist. It would be nice to see that happening to me in time; I've got to get something out of all this for me!.

Day 10 – 7th May 2010

After missing swimming yesterday I was almost looking forward to today's swim. Does that mean I'm hooked already? I almost didn't do it though because when I was walking to the Arch I got really painful Crohn's pains in my stomach. They lasted about 15 minutes and the spasms were breath-taking and energy-sapping. I eventually got myself together after sitting under the pier scrunched up in a ball for quarter of an hour. Luckily no one saw me apart from one drunk who thought I was someone else and offered me an open can of beer – almost funny that!

Once I was about a third of the way around the pier I was back on form. I think today was my quickest yet and also I did the whole swim without stopping, not even for a second. I think it took about 26 minutes. It's amazing how the sea took away the Crohn's pain, it's almost biblical!

Day 11 – 9th May 2010

I decided to swim on a Sunday as I had missed Thursday. I really must be hooked.

I met someone called Tony, Timmy or Tom today – everyone starts to look the same in trunks, hats and goggles – who swam the Channel two years ago. He was on course for a fast one but like Fiona he got a changing tide the other end and eventually completed it in about 17 hours. Amazing to think he could keep going that long. Fiona took 19 hours, 22 minutes and swam 36 miles – she is a goddess!

It was apparently 8.5 degrees in the sea today, so definitely warmer, although it felt the same to me. Calm sea again today. I keep getting calm seas, maybe Dad is up there keeping the tap turned low for me whilst I get my confidence. Thanks, mate.

Another first today, I did not use my swimming gloves. My hands were naturally cold at first but I definitely prefer no gloves. It made the swim easier but also meant I could take off my flippers easily at the end and walk out of the sea instead of clumsily falling and crawling, tearing at my gloves and yanking my flippers in annoyance. Definitely no more gloves for me ever again, I now enter the stage of gracefully leaving the sea James Bond style rather than Lee Evans style - yay!

Tomorrow after my morning swim, Mark Shepherd and Fiona are coming to Seico (my office) to start my training plan. That's a very exciting next step.

Day 12 - 10ᵗʰ May 2010

6.45a.m. and at the beach while the rest of the city sleeps. Lucky them. It's a calm sea though a little colder though than yesterday. About time it warmed up.

I swam fast today, I was actually quicker than Big Bob! Not true really, I suppose, but I got back before him which is quite major for me. Of course I had flippers on and he didn't, but still fair is fair, I am only on Day 12 and he is on Day Million something! He's a great support, I'm not sure I would be this far ahead if it were not for Bob and Fiona.

Mark came as agreed to talk training. We didn't plan much, which is a shame, because he only had a short time and seemed to spend most of it telling me all about his swimming teaching and what it will cost me. It was somewhat annoying if I'm honest as I was hoping to get a firm plan in place. Fiona couldn't make it as she was caught up somewhere. I get the feeling that while I have great people around me this is my challenge, and I will end up forcing my way through it like I do with most of my life.

Day 13 - 11ᵗʰ May 2010

My birthday today. I'm now the grand old age of forty-one and for my birthday treat I'm heading off to the beach for my swim. Who would have believed that a year ago? Certainly not me.

I'm fortunate at home to be able to see the sea and I am happy to report to myself that it looks nice from the bathroom window; a bright and sunny sky and it's only 6a.m.

6.50a.m: Air temp cold, only four degrees. That's nuts! The sea looks calm but you can see there is a drag on the water.

My right foot has been hurting for about four days now with my rheumatism and I'm using a walking stick, which really makes me feel stupid. Also my stomach is still rather Crohns-y but it's not stopping me swimming, no way. However I might speak to a homeopath about remedies, especially for my Crohn's disease, as I am getting quite a few painful moments and they are seriously enervating, which I simply can't afford in my new life as an Olympic swimmer (yeah right!). I'm hobbling off now to the Arch to start the day.

Wow that was a cold one! Colder than yesterday by some way – it's supposed to be getting warmer! Just Fiona and me this morning, which was a nice change. She timed me; 25.5 minutes around the pier, my quickest to date – yay me! She probably does it in 15. Walking back up the beach with my stick took longer than the swim!

Day 14 – 12ᵗʰ May 2010
Went in on my own (shouldn't, I know, but hey ho), swam for about a minute and came out. How rubbish is that? Feeling really annoyed with myself. I was only a few metres out and I swear I heard Jaws cleaning his teeth with the bone of his last victim. I might be going nuts.

Last night I had a late birthday dinner, which was a little rich for my stomach. Also I was already so tired as the twins were up for most of the night. I think we got to sleep about 3a.m! Walking down to the beach I ended up under the pier for about 15 minutes again with my Crohn's. I must have looked really bad this morning as even my drunk friend didn't say hello or offer me a drink.

But still only 1 minute in the sea is crap! All the above are just excuses that I simply can't afford. Now of course I feel guilty and my day is set up to be an unenjoyable one. At least my foot is better and the stick is back in the drawer.

Day 16 – 14ᵗʰ May 2010
Day 16 and still here (of course). Not exactly excited though. I have a slight pain in my right foot (my rheumatism playing up yet again) and my stomach

is tight. I had bad Crohn's which kept me awake pretty much the whole night but it is what it is.

The weather's OK, the sea a little wavy but not too bad. Tide looks out though, which is a pain as it means walking a distance. Water cold again, around 8 degrees. This morning Bob and I only - Fiona is going with others a bit later. I think she may be tiring of babysitting me and I have to say I am tired of being babysat. The waves and tide were rather strong. We swam to the buoy and then around the pier. Quite a tough swim today because of the waves and tide but we got around together. I am now very familiar with Big Bob's feet as I spend every morning chasing them around the pier. His feet are like a swimming Duncan Norvelle: 'Chase me, chase me'!

Day 17th - 15th May 2010

Reading back over the last seventeen days my life seems very up and down. I never realised the mix of emotions one can have on a daily basis. It's scary. For my birthday my mum paid for a much-needed night away for Sharon and me. Our three kiddies were divided between my sister Tracey and my mum - job done. We had a fantastic dinner and stayed over at South Lodge, a great hotel not too far from home. Sharon has now gone off to sing at a wedding, the kids are still with Mum and Tracey, so I decided to join the Saturday 10.30a.m.-ers for a dip in the sea.

It was a bit breezy but bright and warm. One of the weekend swimmers had a friend with him who swims every day in a pool rather than the sea, he had to come back in after a couple of hundred yards as he couldn't breathe because of the cold. Sounds like my first day a lifetime ago.

Fiona met me at 11a.m. and told me that Angus (her current Channel swimming protégé), herself and me are swimming pier to pier! That's Brighton Pier to the skeleton of West Pier and back. Oh shit. She didn't tell me that last night as she didn't want to worry me. It is a looonnng way.

Later - Back now and only just able to write with a steady hand. The sea was noticeably warmer at 10 degrees but it was very tidal and the waves were extremely busy!

This was the longest and hardest swim I have done to date. Getting to the West Pier was not too difficult but going home was really tough. When I got halfway back I felt stuck and didn't seem to be moving forward. I swum outwards to beat the tide and that did the job. It was hard on the mind a few times but I did it! What I do need to sort out now is my eating and drinking as I'm just not bothering with food. I think if I had eaten and drunk something before the swim it would have been a lot easier.

Another milestone, another experience, another memorable day.

Day 18 - 17th May 2010

Early morning interview on radio station Juice FM at 8a.m. today for the Starr Trust to announce an event we are holding at a local store, so I just did a quick buoy-to-beach swim at 7a.m. The sea was calm as glass and around ten degrees, shame I didn't have longer.

Mark Shepherd met with me today at my office. We have started the training plan at last, so I'm really excited. We have to put in some one-to-one pool times and some group pool times. Food still is a *major* problem for me as I just don't want to eat or drink and that is going to stop me! I need to take it seriously now.

Day 19 - 18th May 2010

The sea is looking *very* calm this morning and the air temp is about 10 degrees, so not uninviting it seems. In the car, 7a.m., just listened to Pixie Lott's cool New York song, feeling nice and calm - how pleasant!

Big Bob and I went around five buoys and the pier and then retraced our steps, it was over a 1½ miles and took around 36 minutes. Amazing how we are doing more and more and I can almost keep up. I'm really pleased.

Very salty water today (sounds weird but true) and very fishy, yuck! I need a strong-tasting coffee. I might even try to eat something at the office - how I am growing as a person!

Day 21 - 20th May 2010

Another clear day and the sea looking seriously calm. Tummy feeling a little uncomfortable again but not so bad I need to stop, and foot 100% fine. Swimming in the sea seems to help both conditions somehow. I'm not a religious man and have never read The Bible or any such book but I'm sure there's something in one of them about someone going into the sea and coming out cured of something. There may be hope for me yet!

Fiona, Bob and I did the same swim as yesterday and all is good.

Day 22 - 21st May 2010

I've got a 9.30a.m. London meeting today, so am doing a 6a.m. swim with the very early boys. Got a feeling I'm gonna be the Slow Joe again!

It was a very calm sea but very foggy. We couldn't see more than a few yards ahead and had to almost hug the pier to follow it around. Everyone at the Arch seems friendly, if a tad eccentric, which I like. The atmosphere in the fog made it feel like an episode of Scooby Doo, the mist rolling off the end of the pier. It took 13 minutes to get to the end and 11 minutes to get back. I wasn't massively far behind, which was quite surprising for me: 24 minutes, including a quick chat, that's the ticket.

Fiona and Angus are swimming to the Marina and back today. She reckons 2 hours. That's some swim, I can't believe I'll get that far this year.

I'm in the pool tonight with Mark at Falmer [a local sports centre], so two swims today, which is a first for me.

10p.m. - We did an hour at Falmer from 7.30p.m. - 8.30p.m. It was a group session of about 12 people. We went through lots of different swimming techniques and I swam well over 50 lengths. I did OK but wished I had eaten something! I got home after 9.30p.m., so ended up not eating anything today apart from an apple in London at about 11a.m. - not clever.

Day 23 - 22nd May 2010 (Saturday)

I've a 7.15a.m. meeting at Juice FM to talk about the Starr Trust. As there's no one at BSC who swims at 6a.m. it means I can't swim in the sea (I really am trying to stay safe if I can). Instead I'll use my endless pool at home. It's going to be weird going from under 10 degrees to more than 30 degrees. I'm not sure how useful it will be but it is swimming, so I figure it's worth getting up at 6a.m. for and it'll stop me feeling guilty.

I just did 30 minutes but didn't love it, I much prefer the sea. After yesterday I was really tired and feeling the ache, so that was plenty!

Having not eaten at all yesterday day or night I should have had breakfast, but here we go again, 11a.m. at work and only now am I about to have some fruit. I've got to stop this nonsense.

Day 24 - 24ᵗʰ May 2010

The twins were up and down until about midnight and then Asher came in our room from about 2a.m. so I'm very tired this morning and really can't be bothered. Hey ho, got to do it anyway as the Channel isn't getting any smaller. So in my car, parked at beach, yawning to the beat of the radio and contemplating my swim ahead. It helps that it's a beautiful day: 16 degrees in the air and was 24 yesterday, so the sea might be warmer this morning. Also swimming with Mark at 12.30 at Falmer today, double bubble.

I did my pier swim in good time. I lost Bob as he went one way and I the other. It was probably the calmest it's been, not even a ripple. I was surprised by how cold it was, though. Now at work drinking hot coffee and waiting for 12.30 and my next swim!

2.00p.m. – I had a solo lesson with Mark. It was actually really good, I learned so much in an hour. I breathed both sides for a change (not easy as I only ever breathe to my left) and went from thirty-three strokes per length to twenty-eight, that's five strokes less per length. Really incredible how a simply change to my stroke can save so much energy! Keep the wrist limp going over, stretch out with each arm in a Superman stance and then hard pull through the water. Need more one-to-one lessons urgently if I am ever going to be a swimmer.

Day 26 – 26th May 2010

The weather has changed. A very windy morning and the air a lot colder. The sea was definitely colder and was wavy, not big waves, but constant and slappy-in-the-face ones. As we swam to the pier it was splashy and pulling us back to the shore but as we swam around the pier it was very windy and at times felt like we were not moving. Going back under the pier was a real push as the waves seemed to be going both ways but when we came back out our side it became a bit easier.

Even though it was a hard swim it was enjoyable because of the conditions. Maybe having a bowl of cereal and a banana this morning helped a little.

Day 27 – 27th May 2010

Looks like it's not singing in the rain today, it's swimming in the rain, and fairly hard too. Another new one for me. The sea itself looks calm but that can be deceptive of course.

I went around the pier on my own. It may not be sensible but I've got to nail this and really have to take the risk. A lot of extremely cold patches were catching me out, which was weird. Also a very strong pull to the east towards the Marina, which made it very hard to keep a line and to head to shore. Good exercise, though.

It will be interesting to be in the sea when it's really got the hump!!

Day 28 – 28th May 2010

No rain today but the sea is very choppy indeed and pulling hard east again.

There is going to be a flotilla of boats heading to France at 8.30ish so the club members are going later so they can swim to see them. I have to be in London today at 10a.m., which is a pity as it meant I had to swim solo at 7a.m. – a shame, as that would have been nice.

Having had Jesse up until midnight, then joined by Mia for an hour and then Asher in our room at 3a.m. meant I was a tad tired (as usual) and as such I almost didn't swim, especially when trudging down the beach on my own with rough seas ahead. Pleased with myself that I went in, though. I didn't do the pier this morning, just a power swim around the three buoys. All alone but not a problem.

Really need to do a long swim soon. Also need to urgently start an eating plan and some core training. I did seven swims this week, so at the weekend I will do a gym and a run. Bring it on!

Day 29 – 1st June 2010

I seriously didn't want to get up this morning, I was just too tired! From 5.45a.m. until 6.30a.m. I wrestled with my conscience about not going. I went, of course.

Going around the pier, near the head just under the roller coaster, crazy Leo swam by and grabbed my leg, making me jump (if one can jump in the sea!). Then off he swam at incredible speed.

Coming back around the buoy I was almost level with Bob. For some reason we started an unofficial race back to shore and it was neck-and-neck most of the way. Usually I would let the person carry on and I would hold back as I know I can't compete, but this time I just kept fighting. I came in just in front of him. I was really pleased I kept going, it shows I can do it. Pretty soon I am going to lose the flippers on these swims and see what happens. Probably I'll be so far behind him I won't even see the balls of his feet but who knows... one day I might get to be level. You gotta have a dream.

I'm definitely ready for the day ahead now!

One new thing for me is that today I'm seeing a homeopath. Despite my scepticism I am going to do my very best to take it seriously. I certainly won't take any medication for my illnesses (pills only lead to more pills to more pills), but I really could do with finding a natural way of increasing my food intake and reducing the impact of my illnesses, especially my Crohn's disease. I used to take bucket loads of pills for my illnesses, varying colours, varying shapes and some of them so potent it scares me just to think about it. I'd take the green for the Crohn's, then the blue to stop the green side effects, then the yellow to counter the blue and the pink for the blah blah blah! But about six years ago I flushed them all away and decided I would be better handling the pain than handling the side effects of the pills. It might not work for everyone, but for me the power of the mind outweighs the power of the pills every single time.

Day 30 – 2nd June 2010

A whole month gone; that came about quickly. The sea this morning was calm with almost zero movement. It was about 11 degrees in the sea. I've almost forgotten what 6 degrees feels like. Big Bob and I went twice around the pier head and then onto four buoys, a big morning swim.

I then met Fiona for coffee and she gave me her own training plans and food sheets. I really want to follow these but it does strike me that each of us is so different that surely one plan can't fit all. She is 50+ and female, I am 40+ and male. She has been swimming 40+ years, I have been swimming under 40 days. She has swum the Channel; I have just about swum a bath. She seems physically very well and I have Crohn's disease. I do think it's great she is sharing her exercise and food plans with me but can she really expect me to follow them considering how different we are? Her food plan alone calls for more food in a day than I probably have in three days.

The homeopath I saw a couple of days ago listened and digested my story and ended up giving me a plethora of remedies, each one easy to take and all natural, each one designed for me personally and based upon my needs in this challenge. Two hours of her time, two hours of my time, £60 spent and all very positive. However, two days in and I have already stopped taking the stuff! Why? I have no idea. All I can say is that on the first day it sounded like a good plan Stan (as my Mia would say) but by the second I was already bored with taking the little pills - and that was that. My staying power on such things is pretty pathetic. I just hope my staying power on the swimming will hold. Thirty days in and so far so good, but this is just a drop in the 'ocean'.

Day 31 – 3rd June 2010

Another very calm day in the sea. Big Bob and I swam around the pier, got out on the beach Marina side, got back in and swam back around to the beach our side - two whole complete laps, beach to beach to beach. Not bad for Day 31! Took 45 minutes, temp about 12 degrees.

The swimming club can be very funny sometimes. A battle is going on in the Arch about decor. Some swimmers are putting up things that they find in the sea (fish skeletons, toy guns, shells etc) and other are taking it all down; battle lines seem to have been drawn between the morning swimmers and the weekend swimmers. No matter what the club, human nature is the same everywhere: conflict without communication is the norm in the world, even in our little Arch.

Day 32 - 4ᵗʰ June 2010

Builders start knocking down our house on Monday, yikes, so we are moving today to a rented house in Dyke Road, Brighton. It'll be a year before we can move back in. I hate moving house. We've been here three years and decided to basically knock it down and rebuild it with more floors and the way we want it to be. The mortgage almost trebles and the stress with it, another thing the Crohn's hates, oh well, I'm sure I'll cope!

I still wanted to have my swim, so I went a bit earlier. It meant swimming on my own, although others from the club were in the sea, so I was not totally on my own. I did twice around the Pier (same as yesterday), but as I was on my own I felt no speed pressure. Twice around the pier two days in a row - not bad going for a newbie!

Day 33 - Monday 7ᵗʰ June 2010

Sadly there was no swimming this weekend because of the move. No swimming or running but a ton of exercise, just the same! Why is it you hire movers to do everything and you end up lugging boxes yourself? Maybe it's just me not being able to sit and watch. Very tiring work and I am way too clumsy.

This morning sitting in the car at 6.15a.m., a little too early for most, yet the Chinese man runs past me again. I see him most mornings, dressed in long, formal trousers and a flowery shirt, doing a sort of cross-country ski movement. Fair go to him, though, as he looks to be in his hundreds and he runs every morning like he's late for a skiing convention.

My Crohn's kept me awake last night. Maybe I should have kept up with the homeopathic remedies, doh! So I'm a little tired today and really can't be bothered but I'm here so may as well swim. After an amazing weekend of weather it looks as though it's about to chuck it down. There is a swell moving towards the east, not rough but certainly not calm. My stomach is still hurting! I ate a kiddies' pancake before leaving home, one of those little syrup ones you get in a pack of six from the supermarket which I thought was better than nothing. I really could do with some water to drink (without salt and muck!).

7.45a.m. – It was very choppy out there, first impressions with the sea are generally wrong! I swam around the pier with Bob and Shoichi. We went to the buoy, then under the pier and around to go clockwise as the tide was pulling to the west. From the end of the pier to the helter skelter it seemed as if I wasn't moving. Shoichi is so smooth with his swimming it makes me feel really clumsy.

There I was thinking of it as a battle to end all battles, me against the sea, swimming like a demon possessed, when I spot Leo and David (who is in his seventies) swimming out past the pier carrying bamboo fishing rods and having a jolly time. David is certainly the oldest in the club and he is out in the sea every day around the pier, often with a fishing rod in tow. People are truly astonishing sometimes.

My tummy hurt throughout which was annoying and unusual and I think it drained me a little today. Tomorrow I aim to be a lot stronger.

Day 34 – 8th June 2010

Raining and fairly gloomy start today. The sea looks like it's moving around a bit, a lot like yesterday with rain added. I had a granola yogurt thing this morning. I really am starting to wish that I found eating (especially first thing) a lot easier. How do people start the day with a big breakfast? It just isn't natural.

I swam with Bob and Midge today and for a change we swam west towards the West Pier. The tides were against us coming back so it was a tough swim but I was really pleased I completed it.

I started reading *Channel Solo* by Marcia Cleveland today, a fantastic read, which opens one's eyes to hear how other people cope with this challenge.

After work I visited a training food shop in Hove and got my first supplements and an eating plan. These guys are really nice and seem to want to help me although I don't think they understand my relationship with food, or lack of it. It still feels as if I am just playing on the eating front rather than taking it as seriously as I need to.

Day 35 – 9ᵗʰ June 2010

This morning I started my sports supplements. At 5.30a.m. I took my first supplement shake, then at 6.30a.m. my second one. This was not particularly joyous but for me it is more do-able than eating food at 5.30a.m., which would simply not be possible. Ultimately it is the better of two evils.

I swam on my own today as I was a little early and didn't want to wait around, twice around the pier and then carried on and went to the three buoys as well. Afterwards I still felt energised. I guess it has to be the supplements I took. If they work then regardless of whether I like them or not I must keep taking them. Please, please don't let yourself down, Rob!

Day 36 – 10ᵗʰ June 2010

No sea today as I'm doing a two-hour swim at Falmer with Mark after work. Then it'll be off to Center Parcs with friends for a few days. We're really looking forward to the break and spending time with good friends and the kids.

10p.m. – I got to Falmer to the pool at 8p.m. to meet Mark but he didn't show. No call, no text, no letter, no nothing. I still went in, but after an hour I bailed out, it was so boring. How on earth does one do four, five or six hours like Fiona says I need to do?

Day 37 – 15th June 2010

Having had four days off from the sea, I am ready for a swim again. I really feel I need it. Back to the protein shakes as well although I really don't feel I need them. Had a fab time at Center Parcs; did a lot of activity with the three little Starrs and managed to squeeze in an hour's run on the last morning, but basically relaxed for a few days with good friends.

A nice swim today although my goggles kept leaking which stopped me doing a long one. The water was a fraction choppy and the air a fraction windy but it was dry, bright, warm and the sea around 14.5 degrees, which I found very warm. Apparently the Channel is around this temperature mid July-August, which is about two degrees less than Brighton. Just did once around the pier to break me back in.

Day 38 – 16th June 2010

Still not loving the power drinks, especially the 5.30a.m. and 6.30a.m. ones! However they seem to be working, so I will persevere as long as I am able to. But getting up at 5.30a.m. to have a drink breaks the little relaxing time I have, so I am sure that this whole power shake thing whilst good in one respect is bad in another. The kids keep me awake most of the night and now the power shakes the rest; I seem to be surviving on around two hours sleep. I don't need much sleep, I never have, but two hours really ain't a lot!

This morning I swam solo, a good strong swim. I'm still not a great swimmer, but each day I learn something and each day I must be getting stronger.

The wind chill was up so I was cold when I got back and had the shivers after my shower for about half an hour. It's ages since that happened.

Tomorrow Fiona wants me to do a long swim with her. Just thinking about swimming with her gives me butterflies, because I feel so inadequate in my swimming next to her. This is not something I am comfortable with.

Day 39 – 17th June 2010

We are going to the Marina and back (even Big Bob has never done that). I can't believe I am attempting this, it was only a few weeks ago I thought it impossible! We shall see.

I met Fiona at midday at the Arches. The weather was nice, warm and bright although the sea was colder than yesterday. In preparation for the swim I took my three drinks plus porridge and a banana but I was so full up that I felt like a sleep. Fiona told me I hadn't drunk enough water and encouraged me to drink some more but I just couldn't. I *so* should have listened to her.

We swam from the groyne under the pier (keeping close to the water's edge) and then all the way to the Marina. We touched the Marina wall, getting odd looks from the fisherman dangling their rods over the end and then we turned around and swam back, touching the groyne again, a full out and back. Total distance circa 4 miles and we did it in just over 3 hours; not bad at all considering my first time; in fact, flipping amazing!

Before we reached the Marina I developed bad cramp in both legs, mainly in the front calf areas. This lasted all the way back, and 2 hours later I am still hurting from the cramp. The rest of me was fine. I felt strong and focused for most of the whole swim, although at times coming back I found myself daydreaming and forgetting where I was.

When we got back and I told Fiona about the cramp she said she would not have guessed and that I did amazingly well to swim through it. However, she said that cramp was a direct result of me not drinking enough water and I should have told her, because it could have been very dangerous out there. I think it's time I started to learn those lessons. The cramp almost stopped me completing the swim and I do not want that to happen again.

I'm going to still go to Falmer tonight and do some gentle lengths to stretch out and practise my breathing, then a short time in the steam room. Tomorrow I'll go to the beach in the morning as usual, but just once round the pier in a sprint.

Day 40 – 18ᵗʰ June 2010
I'm tired and sore today after yesterday's exertions. But the kids all slept

through (for once), the Crohn's is not hurting and the foot is OK – life ain't so bad!

I did a simple, once-around-the-pier with Bob and Midge and went without flippers for the first time ever. It was weird, as they really speed me up and also act as comfort blankets. I felt not only slow but also a bit vulnerable. It was a decent swim all the same and whenever possible now no more flippers. It was funny thinking that whilst both Bob and Midge are much better swimmers than I, neither have every done the Marina and back and yet I have.

Day 41 – 21st June 2010

Monday morning once again. Taking the protein shakes is still tough, but I seem to have the energy when I get to the beach, so I guess I need to stick with it until I can replace them with real food.

Bob and I swam about one-and-a-half miles – all three buoys, then round the pier, then to the next two buoys and back. The sea was calm but around eleven degrees and there was a really strong current. A real battle to get to the buoys but a fly on the way back. Took about forty-six minutes.

Now at the office, still a bit cold and unusually tired. Asher was restless last night, plus my 5.30a.m. drink, that must be the reason. Also I strained my groin doing the Marina swim and it's still not 100%, which is an annoyance. I think a groin strain may be something that will stay with me on my swims unless I do something about it, so I need to either just grit my teeth and ignore it or else get treatment from a groin doctor. Do they exist?

Day 42 – 22nd June 2010

What a fabulous morning! Warm weather, sea around fourteen degrees and very calm. Bob and I swam for 56 minutes. It was gorgeous.

Tomorrow I have a 10a.m. swim with Fiona to the Marina and then the West Pier and back. Will be the longest so far and I am both up for it and nervous, very nervous. I so hate this babysitting feeling I get when Fiona needs to look after me. It must drive her nuts as well.

I finished the Channel Swimming book today – a fantastic read, really inspiring and interesting. Sharon's going to read it now, so will be interesting to see how she feels about the challenge once she's read the book.

Day 43 – 23rd June 2010

Today the plan is pier to Marina to West Pier and back. About 5 miles, maybe over 3 hours.

My feeds were pre-planned and I was up for it but Asher was up being sick at 4.30a.m., so that wasn't a good start. I took the fusion drink at 7a.m., which was fine. Having porridge at 8.30a.m. was really hard and I only got through half the bowl.

I've got to take the new Reflex banana shake in 10 minutes, which is really bothering me, then the Performance Matrix at 9.40a.m., when I leave to go to the beach. At least I'm then done with food for a while. You'd have thought at the age of forty-one I would be over this eating nonsense, I'm really annoyed with myself over it. But the swim is a big one so I need to chill and get positive. It has to be said, though, that a big part of my brain wonders if I could just get this done my way: no food, some water and a lot of determination. Surely my way is better than force-feeding on someone else's plan? The weather is beautiful, so at least that will help.

3p.m. – We swam, but it (I) was not great. I was sluggish and slow and my mind was everywhere except where I needed it to be. I never made it to the West Pier. We swam to the Marina and back but it took almost 4 hours. Sure the sea and tides were much tougher this time than last, but my mind and all that stupid eating took its toll. Fiona said my feeds were daft and I should not be turning up for a big swim feeling bloated but no-one told me that – I'm new to all this nonsense and was only following instructions. I know that completing a Marina swim is great but I'm pissed off at not including the West Pier and feel really down about it.

Fiona had agreed that she will personally take interest in my feeds now but that also bothers me. Do I need a babysitter on that as well? She wants to meet the food chaps and meanwhile I should stop taking the powders –

thank god! I really could not have done another morning of feeds like today, it was so counter-productive.

I'm gonna stop my swimming now until Monday as I need a rest. The kids are staying with my in-laws this weekend and we are off to Dublin on Friday to a spa hotel. I'll do some nice pool swims and light gyms whilst I'm there. Also will be having two glorious massages and doing lots of reading! That, plus no bloody protein shakes, should get me mentally back in shape for sure.

Day 44 - 28th June 2010

The spa hotel in Dublin was pure heaven. It was the business.

I went to the beach eagerly today and swam solo. Three buoys both sides of the pier plus around the pier each time. Water was warmer at last. No special feeds, just a bowl of cereal - so much better.

I saw Fiona afterwards and she said it was time to change the flippers as mine might be causing the groin strain, which seems to be getting worse not better. My current flippers, which I was planning on stopping using anyway, are actually surfboard ones rather than swimming ones (I didn't know!), so I'll get new ones like hers, but only for long swims. All short swims must be feet only, but for long ones I still need something for my confidence and speed.

Day 45 - 29th June 2010

I did an 8 kilometre run last night after work, almost sprinted the whole thing. It was good to be back out running. This morning the sea was warmer than it's been all week with a little choppy feel.

I swam solo and did two buoys to West Pier and then back to the buoy by Brighton pier - nice swim.

I met Fiona at 9.30a.m. and went to the food shop. That was good. I'm starting a new regime and only going to take supplements on long swims now (thankfully). Fiona is going to get me some Maxim for those really long swims when we feed in the sea. Apparently this is the thing all distance swimmers use. Meanwhile I will make a huge effort to eat well every night before a swim and to at least have some cereal and water before the swim.

New fins arrived today, which is good as we are doing a 7a.m. Marina and West Pier swim tomorrow morning.

Day 46 – 30th June 2010

Fiona and I were going to swim to the Marina, pier to pier and back, but she texted me at 6.18a.m. to say she had twisted her ankle. The anticipation of the swim had kept me restless most of the night, which is something I really need to work on – it's only a swim, for goodness sake!

I had porridge (proper oats this time) with a banana, at 6a.m. When I heard that Fiona couldn't make it I was disappointed but also relieved. It did annoy me that I was relieved we would not be doing the big swim, I should be so up for it by now!

Anyhow, without beating myself up further, I hit the sea at 6.40a.m., swam to the West Pier, then back to the Brighton Pier, twice around it and back to the beach. A decent swim all in all, in fact my longest as a solo swim and also without my flippers. I got back to the Arch about 7.55a.m., so it took me about an hour and a quarter. It was very choppy out there, real slap-in-the-face waves plus a lot of seaweed. Temperature was nice though, around 15C.

Day 47 – 1st July 2010

It's 6.40a.m. and I'm waiting at the Arch for Big Bob Bicknell. We agreed to swim together at 7a.m. but as usual I'm early. I'm not sure why but I feel a bit apprehensive today about swimming. It's not that I'm worried or anything, I just have butterflies. Annoying really. I seem to put every emotion at the moment down to swimming but it could just as easily be a work thing as I've got a lot going on with office moves, new staff, possible new partners (which scares me as I've been solo for over twenty years). Also the Starr Trust is very busy and there is a lot of pressure to keep pushing it forward. I may just let Bob decide where we're swimming today, it might be nice not to have to make a decision for once in my life.

I decided in the end, funny that! We did twice around the pier, beach to beach to beach. It was calmish and warmish, decent times and a nice swim. It cleared my head - the sea is like a counsellor sometimes (I'm guessing, as I've not been counselled to date, although the way my mind has been of late...).

Bob was naturally still faster than me, but only just. I am almost keeping up with him at last (no fins either). Hopefully in another month or ten he'll be keeping up with me. Fiona's my next target - some hope!

Day 48 - 2nd July 2010

Did a decent gym and swim session at Falmer last night; an hour in the gym and hour in the pool.

This morning, randomly and for no apparent reason, my foot is bad enough for me to need my walking stick. Hopefully it won't last long as it's very painful but also I look so stupid with a walking stick at my age. Hobbled down the beach like an old man and into the sea. The swim was pain free, which was great. Coming back Big Bob and I were basically neck-and-neck and I just pipped him. I pushed myself way harder than usual, as I was really angry about my leg. I'm pleased with that swim. Getting out of the sea and up the beach with my stick was almost like ice-skating - I was here, there and everywhere, but I made it all the same!

Day 49 - 5th June 2010

I woke up this morning with a blocked nose, rough throat, headache and left eye swollen shut! Where did that come from? At least my foot was totally fine. See, there is always good news in life. No way I could swim, so I stayed in bed and went straight to London for a meeting although I was hardly going to make a good pitch in that condition.

I am not a sick person, never have been, but recently I feel as if all I've done is complain about this and that. It has to stop now, I'm starting to bug myself about it, let alone everyone else. Is it the volume of training

I'm doing maybe?

Had a quick meeting in London, highly unsuccessful as expected (isn't life funny, that if you expect something it often comes true?) so back in Brighton by 2.30p.m.

I still felt bad and my eye was really puffy but hey ho, I headed for the beach and swam once around the pier. The water was warmish but the roughest it's been in a long while with waves breaking way out past the head of the pier and the tide pushing hard towards the Marina. I told the lifeguards I was doing a lap and they were cool about it, although I saw them checking my swollen eye out! It was a hard swim, about 35 minutes instead of the usual 24, but a great work-out for the body and a great release for the mind. I was fine until got back to the Arch, then suddenly I got really bad cramps in both legs at the front shin areas - lack of water again, I guess. Really, really painful but massively lucky it didn't happen out in the sea as I was totally on my own.

Eye etc no worse but no better so got some eye drops from the pharmacist. Tomorrow I've got a 7a.m. with Bob to do an hour and then a 3p.m. with Mark at the pool, oh dear.

6th June and 7th June 2010

Simply no way I can swim in the sea or the pool. It's conjunctivitis and is now in both eyes. I can't see much at all.

Day 50 – 8th July 2010

Eyes still swollen but not as bad, I can at least open them. I went to the beach but very nearly left it until Monday as the eyes are not great and the throat is very sore and my wife is not pleased I'm not staying in bed and resting. In trouble again! But a bigger part of me was feeling guilty about not swimming the last two days, even though I couldn't anyway! So I went down and did just once around the pier to get my confidence back. Very warm water today and a nice breezy, choppy sea, not dangerous at all.

A BBC camera crew was at the Arch this morning doing an advert for the

Royal Mail on the over fifties. I kept well away as nowhere near fifty yet, although with my puffy eyes I looked more like the grandfather of them all!

Day 51 - 9th July 2010

Eyes still not perfect but loads better. Feeling in good form and healthy, so ready to go. Had a bowl of porridge (yuck) and a banana - even had some water. Better breakfast effort at last.

Sun shining, and at 7a.m. already about 23 degrees. Gonna be a hot one. The sea temperature was about 16 degrees and felt really comfortable, calm with a slight drag to the east.

Bob and I swam from Brighton Pier to the red buoy at the far end of the West Pier (first time I have ever gone past the West Pier) then back to Brighton Pier, then through the pier to the buoy on the other side and back again. A really good distance that took 1 hour 16 minutes.

Bob was quick today! I think if we had kept swimming for maybe another half hour he may have tired and I probably would not have done but even at this distance he was super-fast. I was probably always 30 seconds behind him.

Good swim though and pleased with it after a few days off. Hopefully by Monday the eyes will be back to normal and I can do some big swims as planned.

Fiona said maybe next week we can go to Dover for a 4-hour swim. Apparently Dover is where the Channel swimmers train. Personally I don't see how much better than Brighton beach Dover can be, but she's the boss.

Day 53 - 13th July 2010

Raining again, but not too hard. Sea warm and calmish but a fairly strong pull towards the Marina. Bob and I went in at 7a.m. and did three (yes, three) laps of the pier, a first for both of us. Lap one we were together, lap two I was way ahead, lap three he overtook me and landed at the beach before me! It was good going and we pushed each other, which was very helpful. Fiona turned up for the final lap and as usual sailed past me. Afterwards Fiona and I grabbed a coffee and planned two 4-hour swims next week and then our trip to Dover on 1st August. That will be the big one for me.

Day 54 – 14th July 2010

Last night I went to gym, did 21 minutes on the bike, 21 minutes running and 21 lengths of the pool. There's a pattern forming here!

This morning the sea was messy. Waves were smallish but coming from each direction and tide very strong, so not easy to swim in. Bob and I went once around the pier to the buoys and back. Funny thing was the depth today - my goggles steamed up, so I stopped at the second buoy out and put my feet down and touched the bottom - very weird to be standing so far out.

Apparently tomorrow the forecast is for Force 6 winds and high waves. That'll be interesting.

I'm really trying to balance life at the moment. There's my home life: the three little beauties and Sharon my gorgeous wife, who I'm trying to make sure doesn't suffer with me being out a lot. Then there's work: I'm about to expand my company hugely and we already have thirty-plus staff and are about to hit twenty years trading). There's the Starr Trust, the charity we set up two years ago, which is growing by the day and helping children smile all over the world). There's the building of the new house; that's character building to say the very least. Finally, I am desperate to get writing again and have two books and two plays part started and desperate to be finished. All this on an average four hours sleep a night and not eating enough food - oh, and let's not forget a little Channel swim next year! The mind may not be as big as the ocean but boy, does it have waves of emotion and unpredictability!

Very fortunately I have amazing support with my family and friends - and I still get huge support from my dad, even though it's all sadly just in my head.

Day 55 – 15th July 2010

1) The Arch door lock was jammed and a locksmith is coming later, so eight

of us, not content with just looking at the sea, got changed outside and stored our bags in Fiona's car. No shower afterwards and a lot of exposed private pieces in the open air! Don't they have names for people like us?

2) The waves are here! It was very windy indeed and there was no way one could swim around the pier, so in we all went, Marina side of pier as it was safer (it's unfairly called the 'girlie' beach), and we basically stayed close to the shore and played. Through the waves, over the waves, around the waves, amazing. It was real rough and tumble stuff. You'd swim hard towards the pier but not move, like swimming in a huge endless pool. Body surfing and wave climbing at 7a.m. with friends in a rough sea is simply the best feeling. Why do people pay to go into wave machines when we have the sea? It was a privilege to be one of only eight people in a city of half a million to experience it - the rest are missing something outstanding. And best of all the temperature was around 20 degrees, a veritable bath.

Let's hope tomorrow is rougher but with the Arch open.

3) The first floor is now up on our new house and I have sea views from my balcony. What an amazing thing to know we have that to wake up to. I'm very excited!

4) The Starr Trust team are fab. The Swim4Smiles website is almost finished and we already have ten charities chosen out of the twenty-one we want to fundraise for with the swim. It's all coming together so quickly and I'm hugely proud.

Day 56 - 16th July 2010

Last night I went to the gym and did a 22 minute run, 20 minutes on weights and 25 lengths of pool. Spoke to Wendy (Sharon's personal trainer) and she's going to write me a gym programme; just something to start me off. I need to start following a plan now.

Swimming today at 6.30a.m. as I've got a meeting in London at 9.30a.m.

11.00a.m. and stuck in London traffic, so writing on the move. Another busy morning at sea. Not as crazy as yesterday but still very rough, loved it! Bob and I and a couple of others swam the waves to the buoy and back – it must have taken twenty minutes just to the first buoy! Leo, David and Shoichi swam around the pier in that. Utter madness! I was going to join them but didn't have the confidence as it really was rough and I didn't want to put them in danger for me. Sensible, I think.

Have loved the last two days, it's great to just play!

Day 57 – 19ᵗʰ July 2010

7.15a.m. – Did twice around the pier with Bob, he was speedy today!

Then I drove to Leicester and met with Dr Julie Bradshaw, secretary of the Channel Swimming Association and world record holder for butterfly across the Channel; yes that is butterfly across the channel; I can't even do the moth let alone the butterfly. We chatted for forty minutes about what she ate etc and came to the conclusion (once again) that the important thing is definitely carbs the night before a big swim and then finding what works for me during a swim and not just copying someone else. She has coffee or tea with glucose powder during one stop then tinned peaches (from a plastic bottle) the next and so on. It sounds nice, so I might try that.

We then did about 90 minutes in the pool at Loughborough University. Lots of lengths doing different techniques exercises: breathing, stroke, leg, body position etc. Very useful after a tiring, 3-hour drive. I might see her in September for another session. It's such a long way to go but I've got to take the help wherever it is.

Almost 5-hour drive home, traffic was a nightmare! Maybe I'll not go back too soon after all!

Tomorrow I've got a sea swim – 8a.m. for four hours – with Fiona. I'm going to do my first ever sea feed! Then 2.30p.m. at Falmer pool with Mark for an hour. I must get to the office some time as well, or they'll think I've left; lucky I have wonderful staff!

Day 58 – 20ᵗʰ July 2010

Oh my God! I swam from 8.20a.m. to 12.30p.m., that's 4 hours and 10 minutes! Fiona is a superhero. She stayed with me the whole way and when I tired she was still as strong as when she started.

We started at Brighton Pier and swam to the first buoy where we tied up a net containing a flask of Lucozade that had been warmed up. Then we did the same at the second buoy with a carbo drink. We swam onto West Pier, then turned around and came back to Brighton Pier, went through the pier and back to the West Pier buoy, where we stopped for about a minute and drank half a bottle of Lucozade. The rest of the swim was between Brighton Pier and the Marina, refuelling with Lucozade and the carbo shake at regular intervals. I reckon we swam about 6 miles in a fairly choppy sea.

When we went back to the buoy the final time before the last pier circle we met Angus, who was heading out to West Pier. He recently did two back-to-back, 7-hour swims in Dover and is now my hero, even though he doesn't realise I am alive (and it's very unusual for someone to totally ignore me, although that's all he ever does to me for some reason). Never mind, I still have a lot of admiration for him as I am sure he'll make it across to France. I know I have to do those swims as well and I appreciate that at some point I will be able to, but they seem a million miles away at the moment and totally not possible.

How do I feel now after all that? The food was OK. I started the day with a Fusion shake at 6.30a.m. and then had a large bowl of muesli with a banana at 7.15a.m. I couldn't finish the muesli as the banana made it a little sickly but I did eat 80% of it. I was extremely nervous before we went in. More than four hours felt so daunting but as soon as I got in I felt fine. The first part of the swim, up to the Marina wall (about 2 hours 40 minutes) I felt strong and fit and thought to myself that I could do Calais right there and then. My stroke was long and solid and my mind was on top form. I sang *Empire State of Mind* by Alicia Keys in my head for the whole swim and it was not a problem. But coming back from the Marina, when we hit about 3 hours, I felt sudden fatigue. My shoulders ached, my legs were heavy and my groin strain hurt. Fiona, keeping with me throughout, was an amazing comfort and that, along with knowing I had to call Big Bob to tell him how

I had done (so no way I was going to fail) meant I had to dig deep and keep going. Brighton Pier seemed so far away, but when I eventually swam under it again I got a real buzz that kept me going all the way to the next buoy. At this point I knew I had to go back and go around the pier again before heading home but as it was the final leg I knew it was in the bag. I upped my speed as much as I could, although my legs were fighting me, and headed home in good time.

After the swim and a shower at the Arch I went to the café on the seafront and had a jacket potato and tuna (I promised Fiona I would) as recovery is so important. I had most of the potato and some of the tuna but also had to have a jam doughnut that was staring at me from the shelf all covered in sticky sugar. The eating was actually really hard (apart from the doughnut) and I could so easily not have had anything. It seems I want to eat even less after a massive swim. How can that be normal? But I am a serious athlete now (not) and was not going to be beaten by a potato.

I am finally at work, just for a couple of hours, feeling elated and knackered. What a day!

Day 59 – 21st July 2010

My right arm is really bad after yesterday's big swim. It's hard to lift up or to use at all. I went to the beach this morning as I thought a short slow swim would stretch it out but after about 10 minutes in it told me I was wrong! When I came out Fiona told me off for swimming with this injury - sports people must rest an injury for a week. She told me to see her physio, Kim, who is trained in swimming injuries (apparently Fiona has had every injury going). I've booked in to see her tomorrow morning.

So no swimming until next week! It's a bummer, I'm really annoyed! But I must listen to the people who know and not try to be clever. Perhaps being over forty means you recover less quickly.

Day 60 – 26th July 2010

Five days off and now back to swimming this morning. I saw Kim the physio last week and she took down all my info and then spent about 90 minutes hurting me. She knew exactly which muscle was related to my groin strain (somewhere in my lower back) and then totally hit the spot on my shoulder - amazing. It was really good to meet a physio who is swimming trained.

After a few days off I went back to the sea today. We had a really nice weekend. On Saturday Sharon was working (in a concert somewhere), so I had the three little Starrs and took them to throw stones in the sea (I just can't keep away) and then Sunday we visited our great friends Nick and Karina Hall (Emily and Amelia as well) in Bristol for the day. It was a very relaxing weekend and fab to catch up with the lovely Halls, but I was ready to swim today, ready, willing and definitely able. I kept it fairly quick so as not to over-use the arm; just the three buoys, then round the pier and back. The arm and groin groaned a very little but I was fine. The sea was warm (cold patches around though) and a little choppy, but basically nice. Just me today, as Bob is away for a few days; he has abandoned me; he's probably sick of me by now!

After my swim I had another physio appointment with Kim - I think I should stop referring to her as a physiotherapist and rename her a physioterrorist. Boy, did she hurt me, but she is absolutely amazing and afterwards my shoulder and groin felt so much better. I'm seeing her again on Thursday for more of the same pain! I get a feeling she will now be a constant for the rest of my swim training.

Bad news for the day was for Angus! He is meant to be swimming the Channel in three weeks and has been training since 2007 and working so very hard but at the weekend he was knocked of his bicycle by a lorry and has broken his arm. Naturally, he is devastated and trying to see if somehow he can still do it, but god knows how! I really feel for him.

Other Channel news is that today a lady swam the channel in twenty-eight hours and forty-five minutes! She was fifty-two years old and only five years ago had a gastric band fitted as she was so overweight. That is the longest swim ever and not a record I want to break. It makes my 5 hours last week a little pathetic. Saying that, apparently she didn't swim with the

CSA so it wasn't ratified but it still sounds incredible to me.

After work I did a 12-mile run/walk. It was about 26 degrees and very hot. As usual I didn't eat or drink or take any water with me. I was OK for about 8 miles but then I was depleted. I can usually do more than that on empty but the swim this morning must have used up my reserves. When will I learn! I ended up doing 15 minutes of walking then 15 minutes running. When I eventually got home the house was empty and I had forgotten my keys, so I sat in the corner of the drive with my head under an old tap, drinking water from it to cool myself down. Maybe tomorrow I'll try again with some food and drink inside me. I did go past our 'house' and it's getting there brick by brick thankfully. If only the money wasn't rushing out as fast.

Day 61 - 27th July 2010

Not the best day today for me, annoyingly so. The sea was calm as calm, the temperature was cold at first but warmed up, and the tide so low I walked all the way to the first buoy. All in all, a perfect day for a long swim. Kim suggested 50 minutes max today to make sure my arm is fine, so out I went with the West Pier and back in mind and maybe then around Brighton Pier as well. I got about two-thirds of the way to the West Pier, then turned around and went back to the buoy by the Brighton Pier, put my feet down and walked in! What was that about? OK, so my stomach was not feeling great and I had a hard run last night and skipped breakfast this morning (obviously!), but all that is just excuse after excuse. I had no reason not to do it today and feel I have let myself down. Tomorrow I will put in much more effort and make up for it. I cannot let myself get days like this, especially for no good reason.

Sharon is going to a site meeting at Hill Drive (our house) today but I can't make it as I'm in meetings. Yesterday after my run I went to Hill Drive and climbed up to the first floor. The view from the balcony outside our bedroom is going to be amazing, right to the sea. This afternoon I am viewing new offices for Seico as well, which also have views over the Channel - love it!

Day 63 – 29th July 2010

It's not been a fantastic week for swimming generally. Although my arm and groin problems are definitely on the mend, I am still aware of them and not wanting to overdo it. This may of course just be an excuse I am using instead of admitting to some laziness creeping in!

This morning I decided to try to get some speed into my swim rather than go long distance. I swam twice around the pier, beach to beach to beach. It took me exactly twenty-one minutes on each lap, probably my quickest ever. Funny things though:

(1) The sea changed from very calm to choppy within a matter of minutes
(2) On my final lap I caught sight of the big helter-skelter at the end of Brighton Pier and it looked as though it was falling into the sea. It made me jump out of my skin and my heart missed a beat!
(3) I thought a large boat was coming towards me (it was a cloud), very disconcerting
(4) A seagull buzzed me as I was coming into shore

Perhaps there were magic mushrooms in my muesli this morning, all very weird!

Seeing physio Kim for another painful session on my shoulder and groin. As I've got my first Dover swim on Sunday I may need to take tomorrow off.

Next week I am going to step it up a few gears. I now have a gym plan in place for three times a week, plus my five sea swims and definitely at least one pool swim. I need to start getting back to some serious training, especially as I'm feeling I have let myself down since the big swim last week.

Day 64 – 2nd August 2010

Dover on Sunday was cancelled. I was both elated and disappointed at the same time. I saw physio Kim on Thursday and we decided I should not swim on Friday or Saturday in view of my Sunday, 6-hour Dover swim. My shoulder and groin were not 100% but not far off, so it felt sensible. However, on Saturday I had a call from Mark (who is in France on holiday) basically laying down the law. He said Kim had phoned him and was worried that a 6-hour sea swim at this time would damage my shoulder to the extent that I could be out of action for months, possibly permanently. He was very straight and to the point and said, 'In no way was this acceptable'. His call was followed by an email from Kim and also a text and then a phone call from Fiona, all saying the same thing. Apparently, my body is still new to the sport and is not used to the movement and punishment I'm putting it through, so my shoulder muscles are tearing and not repairing themselves quickly enough. They suggest I can still swim each morning in the sea but only short distances followed by 2- to 3-hour pool sessions. Being much warmer, the temperature of the pool plus the lack of movement (ie no waves) will allow my muscles to tear and heal in such a way that my body then gets used to being a swimmer, whereas the sea movement and temperature does not allow for this. I can also do two gym sessions and one run a week. I have to listen! Of course they are all just looking out for me and are 100% right but it's very frustrating as I have been really trying to get it together!

To get it out of my system, I then did a 10.4km run, which took one hour and one minute and averaged 5.46km per minute. This morning I just did a gentle swim, once around the pier. Darren, my brother-in-law and Starr Trust co-founder, came down and took some photos for the website; I'm sure photos of me in my Speedos on a Monday morning are not exactly going to aid our fundraising! Tonight I've got my first planned gym session at 6.30p.m. and hopefully Fiona and I will be at Falmer for a 2- to 3-hour pool swim this week. I may be cutting back on distance swimming in the sea for the moment but I've got to energise myself and up my game in the pool and the gym.

Day 65 – 3rd August 2010
Last night I did my first official gym session with the lovely Wendy Tyler, who really knows her stuff. She has planned a three-day-a-week routine for me which I can stick to for two weeks and then lower the repeats for week

three (my rest week) before I start again on week four. Wendy is going to personally train me for the first eight sessions and then I should be fine on my own; I'm not a total gym virgin so should be OK. It was a real all-over body job for around 90 minutes and I was pleased that neither injury bothered me.

This morning's swim, as instructed, was a gentle, easy one. Nice weather again today: air warm, water warm and sea calm, all very pleasant. I swam to the three buoys and then retraced back and that was that. In all about 30 minutes of gentleness. I know I have to take it easy but I can't wait for Big Bob Bicknell to come back from France so that I can at least up it a little. Come back Bob, all is forgiven; I need you!

Day 66 – 4ᵗʰ August 2010
Another short swim today as I am in the gym for 90 minutes this afternoon. Every muscle I have is now starting to ache and creak, oh dear! But it was still a great workout and lots of fun. I went at 6.45a.m. and the only other person there was David who was heading out to fish (he may be in his senior years but he remains hardcore!). The sea was back to being busy, with decent size waves and a real pull to the east. I swam to the end of the pier, which took about 10 minutes and then turned to head in. As I got to the helter skelter the skies opened and we had a burst of heavy rain. I couldn't even see in front of my face - huge fun. By the time I swam back, others were just about to go in and the sun was shining. Fiona told me Angus completed his back-to-back at Dover (7 hours on Saturday and 5 hours on Sunday) with his arm in a plastic cast and he is still planning on doing the Channel - amazing!

Day 68 – 9ᵗʰ August 2010
On Saturday I did a 90-minute gym session followed by a 40-minute run. This made five sea swims, one pool swim, three gym sessions and two runs in a week, and all aches are gone. Yay me!

Pool only today though. I must get those legs sorted if I am really going to be a swimmer. I'm not sure my legs do anything at the moment when I'm swimming!

Meeting Fiona for an hour, leg work only, at 8.30a.m. Falmer pool.

Sharon is away in Spain for four days so I'm gonna have to work my training around the three kids and work - somehow. This week might be a bit sparse on training as we also launch the Starr Trust website and the Swim4Smiles challenge to over fifty businesses this Thursday, so I have a tough but exciting few days ahead.

Fiona and I did an hour in the pool: 15 minutes of float work on my legs, 15 minutes of knee grip float and paddles, then 30 minutes normal. It was certainly challenging, and harder for me than a four-hour sea swim.

Day 69 - 10ᵗʰ August 2010
Went to Falmer pool this morning on my own as I've got to get the kids to school/nursery before I can do anything. I did 45 minutes on my legs, twelve lengths just floating and kicking, then the rest of the time with the knee float, paddles and normal lengths. Considering last Friday I could not do even one length just kicking with the float I have obviously come a long way already. The hard bit is getting the kicking in time with my arm stroke without a float. I feel like I'm having to learn to drive again but I have got to stick at it no matter how hard or boring it is.

I can't wait for Sharon to come home as I am missing my morning sea swim terribly and it's only the second morning she's been away.

Day 70 - 11ᵗʰ August 2010
Mark said he's not worried about my kick at the moment as he wants to concentrate on my arms. It would be nice if he did concentrate on my arms - or my legs or my toes or whatever is needed to get me swimming better - but I just can't seem to get him to turn up to meet me when we agree to it. I'm getting a bit frustrated by that and might very well end up thanking him for his time and going it alone.

Day 72 - 13th August 2010

Last night we had the launch of the new Starr Trust website (www.starrtrust.com) and the Swim4Smiles challenge. It was at the Grosvenor Casino in Hove and we had around sixty people there (mostly businesses), which was fantastic. Everyone seemed to really enjoy it and get behind us. Let's hope this turns into positive action. Of course now another sixty people expect me to swim the Channel. Oh dear!

On a personal note I need to get my brain back into gear. Having been about two or three weeks since a big swim I have felt lazy in my mind and have let negative feelings creep in for swimming, work, just about everything. It's rubbish feeing like this, especially after last night's fantastic evening. I am going to have a day of reflection at work today and put my mind in order - tomorrow the old me returns.

Swimming today was back in the sea, which was much needed. It felt really autumnal: the air was chilly and the sea, whilst warming up during the swim, felt cold when I first went in. Four of us swam together today to the buoys and around the pier, although I was the slowest again. Bob was holding back to stay with me (bless his heart), and the new chap (being about eighteen) was steady and quick. Even though I was the slowest, I do think that if distance was the target today I could have gone further and longer than all of them, so not all bad. Next week the old me will definitely be back with big swims, big gyms, big runnings and big dreams!

Day 73 - 16th August 2010

A good swim today and my head is definitely more positive, although not quite as it needs to be. My 'bible' is an incredible book called *The Secret*, by Rhonda Byrne and last night my sister Tracey gave me the follow up, *The Power*, which I will be starting tonight. Watch out world, here I come!

The sea today was very choppy, especially on our beach side, but the head of the pier held back the waves. Bob and I did twice around the pier and then went along to the groyne and back, exactly 59 minutes 55 seconds... we walked out slowly to make sure we'd done the full hour.

At the Trust launch party last week Fiona and Kim spoke to Bob and suggested we stay at my pace rather than his pace. Bob kindly obliged and we swam together the whole time. I feel a tad silly about this as it seems like I'm being given a handicap, but on the positive side it meant we swam at a more controlled pace rather than me chasing and thus swimming badly (hence the reason for this tactic, I guess). Tomorrow the plan is to do 1 hour 10 minutes, then 1 hour 20 minutes on Wednesday and so on until the end of the week.

After my swim I went to see Kim for my physio and as usual she beat me up, but not as badly as before, which must mean I'm getting better. She lectured me on my eating (apparently a topic of conversation at the Trust launch between her, Mark and Fiona) and all I can say is that she is 100% right and I wish I could deal with it. I am also at the gym for an hour after work today. This week I have planned five sea swims, two pool swims (with Mark if he turns up), three gyms and one run. I shall try to eat as well.

Day 74 - 17th August 2010
Last night I did a 6km run uphill, followed by a 45-minute gym session, so a good day's exercise.

This morning Bob and I swam towards (not all the way as he doesn't want to do that) the Marina and back, so a decent 70-minute swim. It was probably the choppiest it's been since I started (apart from the big wave day last month), so a really good work-out.

Off to the gym after work for another 45-minute session.

When we go back to the Arch I was face-to-face with a very annoyed looking Fiona (not for the first time - I'm not sure if it's me or if she gets uppity a lot). She was annoyed with me because I did not wait for her as agreed last night, because I would not agree to a two-hour pool swim today instead of the sea and because I was being stubborn and not listening to her. I had absolutely no idea what she was talking about, so she referred me to our text conversation last night. You should have seen her face when I told her it wasn't me she'd been texting and in fact I hadn't heard from her for a few days! She went white! On checking her phone it seems she was texting someone else and she had to dash to the pool and apologise to this man for being so rude. Even funnier is that the chap she'd been texting was on recovery from a serious illness and was just trying to be sensible and was probably really confused by her insisting on such a swim. Bless her though, she looked ever so shocked when she realised.

It's funny really, although I am getting a bit put-out by everyone feeling they can talk to me like a child. I know this is a tough challenge but I'm not a complete fool. I'm over forty, married, have three kids, run a business and a charity and plenty of other stuff so will you all please show me a little respect and understanding and stop treating me like a prat! Rant over.

Day 75 - 18th August 2010

The sea was gentler today than yesterday, yet still a strong current and rather chilly. Bob and I did about 80 minutes at my pace, but I think Bob picked up the speed a little to challenge me (good on him). During the first circuit of the pier I was already dreading the rest of the exercise for the day and wondering if I could cancel Wendy or Mark and trying to work out which one would be more angry with me.

After the swim I was running late for my first appointment, a Starr Trust meeting. We have selected the first fourteen out of the twenty-one charities we are supporting with the swim and now need to look at other applications we have had. After this meeting I made it to the next one only 10 minutes late and we agreed terms for our big office move. We have outgrown both our offices after eighteen years and though this is scary because it's a huge financial commitment for me, ultimately it must be done and it is all for the eventual growth of Seico, which in turn hugely benefits the Trust.

Left work at 2p.m. to meet Wendy at the gym (fitting in training and work is a battle in itself). We have started the next phase of training. Same cardio levels but a lot more on arm and shoulder stuff and core training. After my swim and dashing about at work I was pleased that I gave it 100%. Wendy was also pleased, which was good for me.

Then I met Mark in the pool for an hour. He swam with me for the first time (at long last) and we really got stuck in with training, which was simply fantastic. An hour with Mark seems to make so many changes (I just need to remember them all). Arms need to go around not straight, hands need to be shut, wrists need to be limp, legs to kick from thigh not feet, breathing needs to be quick gulps and looking forward, head up more not so deep in the water...I think that was all for today, but some really did stick and now it's a case or repeat, repeat, repeat! He is such a good teacher, I just wish he was reliable.

Tomorrow just a sea swim, as I've got a fantastic massage after work at the Treatment Rooms in Brighton, courtesy of my gorgeous wife. Friday is a repeat of today: sea, gym and pool.

Not sure where the energy is coming from (certainly not the food - oops as usual on that), but feeling positive, happy, strong and ready for more challenges.

Day 76 - 19th August 2010

Today should be named 'the day the seaweed came in'. It was extremely choppy. Bob and I swam around the buoys and around the pier once and were met with carpets of seaweed - layers of it. At times we were so tangled in it that we literally slid over it back into the sea. It was really challenging but a great workout and hugely enjoyable. I tried to use a lot of what Mark taught me last night but waves make it hard to concentrate. Is Mark teaching me to be a pool swimmer rather than a sea swimmer? Today made me realise how dangerous sea swimming can be, and even life threatening if you are not a strong swimmer or someone with a strong mind. The power of the sea is incredible and you must respect it while not being frightened of it or daunted by it. This is definitely a two-way street: you respect it, therefore you control it.

Day 77 - 20th August 2010

Another fine day in the ocean! Bob and I swam with Graham, who has just got back from Gothenburg having competed in the World Swimming Championships for the over sixty-fives. He came fourteenth out of around sixty. Amazing.

This afternoon I have another 1-hour gym session with Wendy and 1-hour pool session with Mark (if he turns up). Then it's the weekend, nothing tomorrow and just a small run on Sunday - yay, rest time!

Day 78 - Monday 23rd August 2010

What a morning it was! Without being dramatic one could say it was pretty much life and death stuff. Last night the heavens opened and the wind had a great night on the tiles. Getting to the beach at 6.45a.m., the sea was really rough, with waves breaking out as far as the end of the pier and white horses everywhere. The waves were easily topping 10 feet. It was a very daunting prospect. At the Arch there was just Bob, Leo (crazy man!) and myself. Bob wanted to stay close to shore and play around in the sea and practice strokes but Leo wanted a bigger challenge and suggested we walk to the West Pier, go in and swim back to Brighton Pier. Of course we went with that!

If you were near the seafront at 6.50a.m. you would have seen a funny sight - the three of us, in our swimming trunks, carrying our hats, goggles and swimming fins (you need them in this swell) doing the 10-minute jog along the seafront to the West Pier. Along the way we passed the British Military Fitness Club training on the grass. They looked at us with a mixture of horror and awe.

The three of us popped on our fins, hats and goggles and waded in. It must have taken a good 15 minutes just to get in as the waves were so strong and way above us; it was literally like swimming uphill and being shoved back just as you near the top. Leo and I completely lost Bob. It transpired that he stayed as close as he could to the shore and fought his way back to our beach. Afterwards he said that the sea kept pulling his hat and goggles off and he ended up in a bit of a panic. Leo and I swam out, trying to get past the breaking waves, but they were breaking out so far it was impossible. At the end of Brighton Pier, Leo decided to go around the pier and end up on the other beach, which is a much better beach to land on as it avoids the groyne and the steep slopes. He was right (of course), it would have been a safer option to swim around the pier, as it blocks the waves and you can then try to bodysurf back to shore.

However I did it my way, of course. I headed straight into shore, catching every huge wave behind me pushing me in, so I was back very quickly. However the sea had dragged me right up to the pier and I was heading into the end of the groyne at an alarming pace. I tried to swim away and back towards our beach to land safely but the sea and waves were too powerful. Interestingly, at no time did I panic or worry or even feel my heartbeat rise, which was a big help. I simply took a decision that the safest option would be to wait until the next three waves (they tend to come in threes) came in and then swim under the pier as fast as I could to avoid the fourth wave throwing me into the pier (that would be game over) and then emerge onto the beach the other side. It worked – I came rushing into the beach nice and safe.

At the Arches Bob was all showered and dressed and pleased to see me alive! Leo came in about 10 minutes later full of the experience (quite rightly).

Once again it shows you have to respect the sea, it is all-powerful! For me, the experience of total lack of fear and clarity of mind in those conditions was really satisfying. I just hope Sharon doesn't read this!

Day 80 – 25th August 2010

Day 80 at last. It feels like so much more than that. After a couple of very busy days the sea seems to have worn itself out a little. It was very flat this morning with minimal wave action. Bob and I swam all four buoys up to the pier, then under the pier to the next two buoys, then back round the pier, tracing around the four buoys and back again. The current made it hard coming back around the pier and we were swimming to stand still again, but apart from that a fairly decent and uneventful swim.

At midday I was back in the water, this time at Falmer, for a 90-minute session with Mark. It went really well and I managed to cut my stroke length down from 30 to 24, the lowest I have ever had it. A tough session, but very fruitful. I've got yet another one tomorrow, as well as a gym session and a sea session - ouch.

Day 81 - 26ᵗʰ August 2010

After a day of rest the sea once again asserted itself. Despite the waves, Leo took my underwater camera and took some pics and video of us all in the sea. The downside to the camera being there was the 'posing factor'. 'Rob, this way,' Leo called to me across the thrashing sea. Turning around, with my back to the waves, I elegantly trod water and got my greatest 'look at me in the water' smile ready. 'Watch out!' was the next cry I heard, too late, as the massive wave behind me pulled me down and over and around and eventually ran away with my goggles - the fifth pair I have now lost in eighty-one days.

So goggle-less and with eyes full of salt water, I swam (limped) back to the shore with another lesson learnt: even if someone has a camera and is going to make you a star, don't turn your back on the flipping waves!

Day 82 - 27ᵗʰ August 2010

7a.m., new goggles firmly glued to head, Bob and I head out to the buoy. Having forgotten all his swimming stuff, Bob was wearing someone's discarded swimming shorts, oversized goggles and my old hat.

We swam the three buoys on our beach side, then under the pier and to the next three buoys and around the pier and traced back. It took around 42 minutes and we were together throughout; a very decent speed at that distance. The sea was really cold but warmed up as we got going. The rain was quite strong, making me wonder which way was up a couple of times.

Swim completed and all showered, dried and aftershave on, it was only 3 hours later I was at Falmer with Mark in the outside pool doing another 90 minutes of vigorous swimming.

Recent news on Angus not great. He was meant to have done his Channel swim this week but the weather conditions stopped it. He now has two more slots available over the next two weeks. How frustrating for him, this is the second time it has happened and if he doesn't go this year it is not likely he will go at all. Have my fingers crossed for him. Determined it won't happen to me - have had long chats with Dad as he is way closer to the controls than I am and I am sure he can arrange fair weather for me.

A good day at work and the house build has really moved on apace. The roof is 90% finished, which means the scaffolding should come down next week. We have a nice long weekend as this Monday is a bank holiday and I plan on doing very little in the way of exercise.

Day 83 – Sunday 29th August 2010

Sunday today, which is usually my non-sea day. But today was different, today was race day, and I didn't know until this morning!

The BSC was holding its annual around the pier race, starting on the east side of the Brighton Pier on the beach, swimming all around and coming back on the beach on the west side between the groyne and the pier. This was my first-ever swimming race, and as a slow swimmer not one I was particularly looking forward to, but I felt I should take part just to prove to myself I can do it.

Sharon, the three little Starrs and Darren came with me for support. There were about twenty adults (aged sixteen to any age) doing the pier swim and about fifteen kids (under sixteen) doing the groyne-to-groyne race.

To avoid us all going in together it was done as a handicap, with the slowest ones first, with 30-second gaps between groups. Ridiculously I was not in the slowest first group!

The sea was really very choppy with big waves, strong winds and a very strong current pulling towards the Marina, which meant the whole swim was against a very strong tide. This made it very tough for everyone. Naturally the last person to go in, an eighteen-year-old, was the first back; super-super-fast! I was about the fifth to go in and came in (after Bob of course!) at about thirteenth, with a couple not making it around. As a new swimmer and a slow one I was pleased not to be last, although of course I wasn't pleased to be less than middle ground.

I definitely prefer distance to speed racing. The pressure of speed racing made go back to my old rubbish stroke and coupled with the tough conditions made it an uncomfortable swim for me. But it strengthened my resolve to get into the pool and crack on with my lessons.

Day 85 – 1st September 2010

The mind can be a very disturbing thing to have in your head sometimes. A 7a.m. start for a 2-hour swim with Fiona this morning. I was awake all night thinking and worrying about it, which was really frustrating. It's funny because I have done a number of long swims, so to be worrying about a 2-hour swim was nuts! Since my shoulder and groin injury I have not done any swims over an hour and whilst my swimming technique is way better and my fitness much improved, I have had doubts about my ability. Due to too little sleep and too much worry, my stomach played up this morning and that of course affected my Crohn's, giving me fairly bad pains and toilet issues (nice). So breakfast was a no-go, but I did manage half a banana (Fiona will not be happy). Also I was a little achy in my shoulders as last night I spent 90 minutes in the gym and then did an hour of pool swimming.

The sea was 95% calm and the tide not too strong. The air temperature was low at around 13 degrees and the water felt the coldest it had for some time, though my lack of food this morning and lack of sleep probably contributed. There were four of us to begin with, Fiona, Bob, Leo and me. Leo brought along the camera and took some fab photos along the way. We swam at a very decent pace from Brighton Pier to the West Pier, tying up the Maxim power gel and bottle of Lucozade to a buoy on the way. We reached the red buoy at the end of the West Pier in amazing time, stopped for a couple of photos and then we motored back to Brighton Pier, heading once around it and back to our buoy. At this point Bob and Leo headed in to the beach as they had had enough and I settled down to my gourmet Maxim whilst Fiona had her fill of Lucozade. I would happily have swum in with Bob, but Fiona would not allow that! She was angry with me for not eating breakfast, so no way she was going to let me off the hook now and she even threatened to tell Kim and Mark. So off we went back to the West Pier. My arm stroke was flagging a little for about 10 minutes, but then all of a sudden I was back to full speed. The Maxim, which was easy to take and tasted fine, must have kicked in. We motored back to the West Pier, then straight around the red buoy and back to Brighton Pier, taking in the furthest buoy by the pier and then back to my feeding buoy and then back in. Total swim around 2 hours 20 minutes, feeling cold but very pleased to have dealt with my demons again. I could have swum all day.

Day 86 – 2nd September 2010

After yesterday's epic journey I decided a small swim would be good today. Bob was feeling a little tired as well so he was happy to go along with that. I was feeling less cold – more sleep last night clearly helped. I still couldn't eat a bowl of cereal, which was annoying as I need to stay in that habit now, but I did manage a whole banana. We swam at 7a.m., and the stamina was certainly there as we motored the whole way around the four buoys. I felt particularly strong and quick and swam really well using the techniques Mark has been drumming into me. Even my legs seemed to be playing along.

Then a quick shower and dash home as it was Asher's first day at school and I wanted to take him with Sharon. Boy, was that hard! Sharon shed a tear and I had butterflies but Asher was beautifully calm and composed. He looked absolutely gorgeous in his new uniform. He is such a special little boy and just seeing him walk into his new classroom filled me with pride. I don't know what I've done to deserve such wonderful children, but I am grateful.

Day 87 – 3rd September 2010

Not a lot to say today as it's 7.35a.m. and I am at work and dry. I was planning on an early swim this morning as I have a very full work day but when the alarm went off at 5.30a.m. and I got up, I found that hitting the sea today was not going to happen! My neck is stiff, nothing bad, just a tad uncomfortable, but that was all the excuse I needed. Some days I still have to force myself to go (not every day thankfully) but today... well, today an excuse kindly presented itself. Of course within the next couple of hours I shall be attacked by guilt and will end up going to the gym and the pool for two hours and working even harder because of that but for now I shall enjoy salt-free skin for the day.

Fiona texted me last night to say that Angus had to cancel his swim this year. Apart from his broken arm, he now has a viral infection and is on antibiotics. He was still planning on swimming but his body is aching and his temperature is up and it is too dangerous in that state. He must have been absolutely gutted to cancel but it was the right this to do and a very brave decision to make. You have to feel bad for the guy as he has worked so hard and against so many challenges of late. However if it's meant to be then it will be, and he'll get his chance next year.

Despite my not swimming I am feeling positive and happy today. The sun is shining, the air feels warm, Asher absolutely loved his first day of school and was so excited about going back today, and tomorrow is the start of the weekend. What could be better than all that? xxx

Day 88 - 6th September 2010

Monday morning once again. Monday seems to come around at least once a week and always rather quickly. After a three-day break from exercise I was raring to go, although at 6a.m. on a Monday I guess raring is a bit strong. The sea was cold and for the first time in months I found my face complaining at the temperature but it soon warmed up once the waves started to batter me. Three of us this morning, birthday boy Bob (fifty-five today and not looking bad for it), young Mike (new boy to join the club) and me (no longer the new boy, hooray). Did the usual buoys and around the pier but it was like a washing machine out there! It wasn't so much breaking waves, just up and down. If one suffered from sea-sickness then today would have been the day. However it was a good swim, we didn't stop and when we got back to shore (basically all together) we felt as if we had really done some exercise.

Then 8.30a.m. saw me off to see Kim the physio. As usual her strong fingers made light work of my groin. Mmmm, that sounds a bit X-rated, but it was purely pain rather than pleasure, I can assure you!

Then off to Kent for my first business meeting at 11a.m., back to Falmer at 1.30p.m. for 90 minutes in the gym, then back to the office for a 3.30p.m. meeting.

Now on my way home to see the kiddies and help with dinner, bath, books and bed. The last job for today is a Trustees meeting for the Starr Trust to give out this quarter's donations, which is an 8p.m. meeting that usually goes on until 11p.m. We have raised nearly £25,000 to give out; a lot of Smiles will be created with that. Then hopefully to bed, ready for my 5.45a.m. alarm to get up and start again. When did life get so busy?

Day 90 – 8th September 2010

Today is my 'tide' story day. An interesting thing about the sea, which may just be Brighton, of course, is that when it is raining the sea tends to be calm. I'm not sure why, maybe it's a pressure thing. This morning it was grey and raining and not pleasant, but it was nicer in the sea than on the beach.

I got to the beach at about 6.30a.m. and spent 25 minutes on my own walking the pebbles and thinking about life. I always start my day, every day, thinking about all the amazing things in my world; my three beautiful children and all the things they do that make me laugh out loud, my wife Sharon who remains my rock, my mum, my sister, my two brother-in-laws, my in-laws, my friends, the house we're building, my company, the Starr Trust, my Channel swim and of course my dad, who I still miss every single day. It's really great to start and end the day thinking about people and things you love. It's not a religious thing – I'm not a religious person – it just sets up your day and ends your day so nicely to think about the people and things you love. It brings positivity to what could easily be a negative day if you let it.

Anyhow, the swimming! Bob turned up just before 7a.m. and we pretty much jumped straight in. Leo turned up soon after wearing his Captain Birdseye hat (a great look only he could carry off). The sea was coming in which meant that the tide was heading towards the Marina, so we set off against the tide and swam to West Pier, which took exactly 30 minutes. The swim back to Brighton Pier took exactly 15 minutes. We had less energy coming back as we had already worked hard on the first leg, so it is astonishing it took half the time to get back. This was not even a fierce tide but yet again it shows the power and strength of the sea. I need to learn more about the tides as I am about to do some long solo swims and that knowledge will be vital to stop me swimming to a standstill. And I have to start eating. This morning all I had before our swim was a glass of water. How rubbish is that for a long swim?

Day 91 – 9th September 2010

Yesterday I did the West Pier and back on a glass of water followed by a dash to work and spending four hours in the office in various meetings, drinking one cup of coffee and then getting in the pool at Falmer with Mark for a very intense, 60-minute swimming session (no idea how many lengths we did, but it was well into double numbers!). Then it was back to the office and more meetings until at 4p.m. I managed to eat a prawn sandwich. How rubbish is that? However on a good note, last night my shoulder was really aching and I was worrying that I had damaged it again. Why is that a good note? Well, it proved without a doubt that not eating before and after intense exercise causes my muscles to ache and ultimately will damage and tear them. So now I have had that confirmed, I would be a fool to not start taking that seriously. I sincerely hope I am not a fool, but time and my diary will tell.

Back to today and being more positive. It was a lovely calm sea and a clear, cool air with blue skies. It was very busy at the Arch. Mark decided to join us to see if my pool training has paid off in the sea and apparently it has. He was very pleased. Fiona was there with Angus and they were doing a three-hour swim in preparation for an unexpected last chance at the Channel next week, so all fingers crossed for him.

Day 93 – 11th September 2010

Five men in their Speedos and swimming caps driving along the seafront at 7a.m. on a Saturday morning - you have just entered the twilight zone.

This morning I joined Leo, Angus and two others for a swim from Hove Lagoon to Brighton Pier. We met at the Arch just before 7a.m., got changed and were driven to Millionaire's Row at the border of Hove and Shoreham, parked up and we ran down to the sea. It was very rough with lots of breaking waves way out, which meant we were constantly battered. In our favour was the biggest tide of the year pulling to the east (Marina) so it made it a quick swim although our constant battle with the waves meant it was far from easy. I felt quite frightened as I was in unfamiliar territory in a massive tide and really not strong enough to be there on my own. As soon as the others left me I thought 'Oh shit I might not make it back!' It sounds dramatic but it was scary out there.

All of a sudden I spotted Leo was still with me and he thankfully stayed for the whole swim, which made it more enjoyable as well as me feeling safer. He took some amazing footage on the camera, both photos and videos. A funny moment occurred about 20 minutes into the swim, just as we were near the King Alfred leisure centre. About three or four kite surfers came hurtling by, at incredible speed (luckily they saw us in time!) and as they flew by we all shouted out 'Good morning!' to each other. I bet that doesn't happen too often in rough seas about a mile out!

The swim took Angus and the others 1 hour 6 minutes and it took Leo and I about 1 hour 10 minutes, so we were not exactly slack. It was a very challenging, eventually enjoyable and worthwhile swim and one I am proud off. That aside, it was also perhaps foolish and life threatening and not to be repeated until I am stronger in the sea.

Day 96 – 15th September 2010

Last night I managed a 2-hour swim at Falmer without much difficulty, which was good. I was going for three but didn't get there until 3p.m., so time ran out. I took a Maxim gel after an hour and even though I didn't feel particularly stronger, I also didn't find it offensive.

This morning I woke up a little later than usual (after 6a.m.), which was annoying. I was really tired and my stomach hurt, which was definitely the Crohn's - after twenty-two years you get to recognise it. I almost rolled over, shut my eyes and went back to sleep, but the pain mixed with the guilt of not swimming made that thought last about 60 seconds!

The sea was really choppy, which made it a good workout. Fiona joined us, which was lovely as I don't get to swim with her much any more. We swam all the buoys, around the pier to the next buoy and traced back again. Going around the pier felt like we were in a washing machine, we seemed to spend an age going in circles without moving, but when we got past that nonsense the rest of the swim was great. The temperature has dropped but it's still comfortable. I'm not looking forward to the single digits though!

Crohn's disease is a funny thing, although I guess funny isn't the right word. My point is that whilst one can certainly take a lot of medication to try to control the pain, in reality the medication can end up causing so many other complications (in my case it gave me osteoporosis, eye problems, hand and feet problems, joint problems etc etc), which is why I flushed all my medication away about five years ago and now take nothing for any of my conditions. If only I had realised the effect that swimming, especially sea swimming, could have. When I went into the sea today I was in a fair bit of pain (probably 6/10 on my pain scale), however 10 minutes into the swim (and since finishing the swim) I was and still am pain-free. No pills, no tears, no whingeing, just a decent swim in the sea and all is well. Maybe others should try it.

Day 99 - 20th September 2010

I was rather achy this morning when I got up at 6a.m., the after-effects of a 14.5km run on Saturday afternoon. My running is going well at the moment - marathon some time soon maybe? Looking out the window at a very gloomy, wet and windy morning was enough to send me back to bed, but the thought of starting the week with a sea swim was too much of a pull. It was definitely a choppy one out there, but it was still a nice swim. Plodded around the pier, battling through the waves and then sailed into shore. The tide was so strong that we decided to land on the 'girlie' beach the other side rather than swim back to ours. I actually ended up two beaches down and had to walk all the way back across the pebbles to retrieve my flip-flops! I did enjoy it though, I'm definitely getting hooked on it.

Afterwards I headed down to Withdean Stadium for an hour with my physio-terrorist Kim. Having not seen her for two weeks and having been battered by a lot of swimming, running and gym work she decided to give me a full body beating! Absolutely no chance of me using the pool or gym tonight after that but god knows what state my body would be in if not for her.

Now back at work and guess what – the sun is out, the sky is blue and it's getting warmer by the minute! Funny old climate we live in!

Day 100 – 21ˢᵗ September 2010

A milestone – my 100th day and it's Official Peace Day (set up by my friend Jeremy Gilley from Peace One Day www.peaceoneday.org). It's kind of fitting... To recognise this day Leo, Big Bob, Fiona, Yvo and I jogged to the Peace Statue and swam back to the Arch.

The day started out very foggy and you could barely see more than 50 yards ahead. It must have been interesting to see six of us jogging through the fog in nothing but our swimming gear and goggles (I've some funny photos of this). When we got to the Peace Statue we took some more pictures and then headed into a very calm, quite warm ocean. It was a fantastic swim because as we swam back towards Brighton Pier the fog was lifting. A lovely way to celebrate a day of Peace. What did you do to celebrate Peace Day? Nothing? Well, next year why not give it a go?

Day 101 – 22ⁿᵈ September 2010

After yesterday's excitement I thought I would have an easy one today. So around the buoys and once around the pier in the lovely company of Bob.

A nice easy swim.

Tomorrow I'm not swimming as it's Sharon's birthday and we are heading for a whole day at Bluewater shopping mall with the credit card. I anticipate this being a harder training session than I am used to!

This Saturday I am off to Dorset with the swimming club for my first 'fun' swim around the coves, so I'm very excited about that. This week will be a bit of a rest week in terms of training; just five swims and one gym I think, then next week back to full steam again.

On an entirely different note, I started writing a new play last night. I need a release from work, children and training, and writing is the best tonic for me. Hopefully it'll be easy to write as my last two - it's a relaxing way of losing oneself. Naturally in my current mindset it should be a swimming story of sorts, but we shall see.

Day 102 - 24th September 2010

After a day of shopping yesterday it was so nice to be back to something less expensive and less dangerous like a dip in the sea.

Bob and I swam at 7a.m. to the West Pier and back and then onto the buoys and back, a decent, strong swim of 80 minutes without rest. It took a whopping 46 minutes of constant swimming to reach the West Pier (previous longest to the WP was 30 minutes) and then 12 minutes back, once again illustrating the power of the tides. Gotta hope that I have tides in my favour when I take on the Channel next year. We were warmish for about 40 minutes but then the cold set in and the hot shower at the Arch afterwards was most welcome. Tomorrow fourteen of us from Brighton Swimming Club are heading to Dorset for a day swimming in the lakes and coves, very exciting stuff.

Day 103 - Saturday 25th September 2010

We swam around Lulworth Cove to some amazing caves, then back to the beach and dressed for a pub lunch, then did a two-mile walk around the hillside to Durdle Door and had another fantastic swim. What an incredible place. The sun was shining, the sky was blue, the water was a decent temperature and the views were stunning. We could have been in the Mediterranean. The day was made even better by being with such a fun and happy crowd of people, all there just to enjoy the swimming and the scenery. It shows how beautiful England is. I am starting to appreciate what we have in our country and maybe I might even be tempted to go camping one day and to stop being so precious about home comforts.

Day 104 – 27ᵗʰ September 2010

Monday morning and so much to say! A little numbering may help me focus and stop this being a jumbled mess of thoughts:

Today would have been Dad's 65th birthday. Every day I think of Dad, so today is no different and needs to feel no different but I guess his birthday just focuses the mind a little more and makes me remember how lucky I was to have him as my dad .

Today's swim was once around the pier. Very cold when we first got in, it must be heading down to 10 degrees, and the air temperature was certainly under two digits. It was a real struggle getting out of bed but I simply had to go.

Walking was not easy as my rheumatism is playing up (why does this keep happening?), so it was a case of limping down the stones. However the sea does wonders for it and even though it hurt walking out of the sea, the actual swim was completely pain-free. Hopefully it'll be gone by tomorrow, usually it only lasts a couple of days at a time. The sea was so clear that you could see all the way to the ocean floor, even out at the end of the pier. Swimming back around the pier we went over an old shipwreck, which was fantastic as you could see every little nodule on it. Now, around an hour after we came out, I am still cold in the hands and feet. I guess from now on each morning is likely to get colder and darker - something to look forward to!

Where were the buoys? I didn't realise but at the end of September they remove the buoys from the sea. It's a safety thing as the sea can start to really rough up and they do not expect swimmers and boats to be stupid enough to be out there needing the buoys! Mmmm, will we be stupid enough to swim? Er, yes, I think we will! Shame though as the buoys give you the ability to spot distance and give you something to aim around.

This coming Friday we are planning a night swim around the pier. It's pitch black at 7.30p.m., so it will be exciting and somewhat spooky. I'm really looking forward to it but some of the others I am trying to tempt to come with me are not so sure!

Now it's 9a.m. and I think time for some proper work. I keep forgetting I have a company to run!

Day 105 – 28th September 2010

Last night I had about three hours sleep in total. It's been like that for about two weeks now, which is annoying. I only ever do around four to five hours a night anyway, which is all I've ever done, but three hours is a pain as it makes the night time so long and boring and it does make you a tad tired when you get up at 5.30ish.

The sea was amazingly clear again today, you could actually see every single stone at the bottom, even as far out as the end of the pier. The air temperature was slightly warmer today but the sea temperature continues to drop. As it's getting darker in the mornings now I decided to go at 7.15a.m. instead of 7a.m. and the Arch was busier; it was nice to see some faces again in the morning. Bob wasn't there today, so solo for me. I swam twice around the pier, beach to beach to beach. I did a fantastic pace the whole way around – a great swim and an amazing way to start the day. Oh god, am I dreading not being able to do this distance in the sea soon due to the temperature, which will mean the dreaded pool swims!

Day 106 – 29th September 2010

It's getting darker – even the pier was still lit up when I hit the seafront this morning. Did another beach to beach to beach today, so that's three in a row. It was still very clear in the sea, I saw literally thousands of tiny silver fish swimming all around me, which was really stunning. Bob and I were joined by Simon and on the way around we bumped into crazy Leo and others and then in the Arch afterwards there were the usual suspects I have come to know. I should mention LB especially (Little Bob Phipps – no reflection on his manhood!). A fantastic guy who is at the Arch every day and who does what we now call micro swims. LB is one of life's nice guys and welcomed me from day one and is a massive encouragement to me when I get to the Arch looking tired. Without support from LB and others this journey would be so much harder; thanks LB. Another jolly friendly start to the day. The swim itself was about 49 minutes, which in this temperature was good going, although I'm still trying to warm up now. Off to the gym after work for an hour and then that is another day ticked off.

30th September 2010

No swimming today but I still got soaking wet. Last night I took a call from Fiona to say that someone she knows, Jamie Goodhead, has been given his 24-hour call to swim the Channel, his last chance before the season ends today, and if he doesn't take it then he misses it for another year. He has already had one attempt, which was called off after 6 hours as his boat pilot had a suspected heart attack and had to be flown from the boat back to Dover. How unlucky is that? As it was such short notice and because it was about the third time he's been given notice, only one out of his seven crew were available and even his wife couldn't go as their children were unwell. So he called Fiona to see if she could be a crew member and if she had anyone she could bring... and there we were driving to Dover last night at 10p.m. with a bag packed full of warm clothes and waterproofs, ham and cheese sandwiches, penguin biscuits and flasks of sweet tea. It was rather unexpected as I was planning an early night!

We got to Dover after a ninety-minute drive through torrential rain and met them on the docks. Really nice chap, Jamie, being supported by his best friend and only crew member. The pilot boat (not a CSA registered boat) was just pulling in and needed to get going. Even though it was raining hard and the sea conditions were sounding tough, the decision to go was taken and we set off at 1.45a.m. The boat was a medium-sized fishing boat, manned by the pilot, his co-pilot and an unofficial official. They didn't even help us carry all his provisions to the boat! It was almost amusing when the official came to complete his paperwork and not only kept calling Fiona 'Jo' but didn't even check any bags in case there were drugs or something in there - really not encouraging.

We sailed out of the calmness of Dover Harbour and within seconds the boat was being thrown around like a rag doll in a washing machine. Boxes were literally sliding everywhere, Jamie's best friend was throwing up and Fiona and I were hanging onto the sides. After about half an hour Fiona applied the lanolin and grease to Jamie's body (I couldn't see in the dark if she was enjoying that or not) and then over the side he went and swam to shore. We couldn't really see how rough it was but he must have felt it. As soon as he reached shore the pilot honked the hooter and the game was on. Jamie ran back into the water - now it was about 2.45a.m., and it was him versus a very troubled sea. With his friend still throwing up it was down to Fiona and me to keep a watchful eye out on him, with Fiona shouting for the first 20 minutes at him to watch out for the boat! After about another 20 minutes, with the conditions now absolutely dreadful, the boat being thrown everywhere, his friend still chucking up and the pilot getting concerned for both his boat and the swimmer, the decision was made to call it off. So an hour into the swim Jamie was back on the boat feeling really upset and we were heading back to Dover with every other wave lifting us up and dropping us back down. I have to say, and I say this as someone without previous experience, that letting the swim go ahead in those conditions was perhaps not the correct thing to do, even if it was the last chance of the year. Fiona tried to talk the pilot out of going as she knew this was dangerous, but he seemed to just ignore her. I'm so pleased to be registered with the CSA as I really don't think that they would have done that.

The plus point to all this was that he came back safely. OK, so he never managed it due to the weather but in those conditions just getting back onto the boat safely was a miracle. I learned a lot: I experienced the highs and lows of a Channel swimmer (albeit secondhand), I got to see the process from Dover to boat and back again, and I got to see the Channel in complete darkness and in a storm. Oh and not forgetting, I got to understand the importance of swimming under the official CSA banner.

Having got home at around 5a.m., I grabbed about two hours sleep and then headed to work, where I currently am and on my third coffee already. An unusual but very interesting and unexpected evening!

Day 107 – 1st October 2010

I reckon I slept about six hours last night, which is the longest sleep I've had in years. The Dover trip tired me out. No actual swimming today but a day of play, trying to break into the sea! The waves were very high near the beach and only the foolhardy would attempt the pier. Part of me wanted to go in and around the pier because of the conditions but I am still not 100% recovered from my groin strain and I have to be sensible to a degree, especially as next week I am going to try two 4-hour back-to-back swims in the pool.

It's also not looking likely we will do the night swim as the winds are fierce and it is expected to be about 35mph tonight. Sometimes, despite one's best intentions, the weather retains control.

Day 108 – 4th October 2010

After a crazy dangerous weekend sea, today was strangely calm and silent. On Sunday, fourteen of the club did a Marina to pier swim. Only thirteen actually got in and only four made it back, the others getting washed ashore earlier. Even superwoman Fiona was washed ashore! In her own words: 'It felt like Poseidon had picked me up, slapped me several times and then thrown me onto the shore. That will teach me to have more respect for his territory.'

I was going to go as well but I had taken the kids to the pool instead, which I'm pleased about as I would have battled it out and potentially hurt myself.

Fundraising for the swim has started at last and is already over £5,000.

Got a long way to go, but a great start.

Off to gym this afternoon; first time since ten days off gym, looking forward to it. Before all that however a session right now with my physio-terrorist Kim. 8.30a.m. and an hour of being beaten up!

Day 110 – 6th October 2010

Now that was a serious swim!

6.30a.m.– 10.30a.m, 4 hours non-stop in the pool at Falmer. That was my longest pool swim to date and I'm really proud of myself. The first hour really seemed to drag - in fact the first 10 minutes felt like an hour but then the next three hours went by quickly enough. Fiona came along about 7ish and jumped in the lane next to me and then swam the rest of the time with me, which was great as it meant I had someone telling me when I needed to adjust my stroke or breath differently as well as letting me know when to feed. She's such a fantastic support to me, I really am amazingly lucky to have her.

As for the boredom factor, which is the real challenge of a long pool swim, it wasn't as bad as I had envisaged. Throughout the whole 4 hours I only had the lane to myself for maybe a combined half an hour. The rest of the time I had one or two people in the lane with me as well as people in the lane next to me. It was interesting to see so many people come and go and for me to still be there plodding along. There were the quick swimmers, the strong swimmers, the technically bad swimmers (all of a sudden I know the good from the bad!), the slow swimmers and swimmers of all sizes, some in for 5 minutes and some for 30 - but only me in for 4 hours! I think I enjoyed the last 15 minutes the most from the perspective of company as I was joined in my lane by two fit young ladies in their early twenties, wearing very tight swimming costumes. Of course at that point I may have sped up a little. Boys will be boys!

After the swim I came to the office to do a day's work, but my head was a little floaty and my breathing a bit uncomfortable, perhaps from the effects of the chlorine or the shallow breathing one does whilst swimming. Apart from that, at the moment I am feeling strong and - surprisingly - not too ache-y.

The food intake was a bowl of Rice Krispies at 6.10a.m., then a small bottle of water mixed with Maxim every hour during the swim, then a protein shake and a health bar after the swim and now I'm about to have a chicken salad sandwich (and maybe, only maybe, a cake of some kind).

With regards to distance today, I have brought this super cool watch that is motion-sensitive and counts your lengths, stroke rate, time etc. It told me I did 324 lengths of 25 metres each, which means I swam 8,100 metres, which is about 5.003 miles or 8.1 kilometres.

Tomorrow, if hopefully not too achy, I'll do a sea swim in the morning, but just a short one. Apparently today there were 10-foot waves in the sea and hardly anyone could get in. That would be a cool playground for the morning after today.

Day 111 - 7th October 2010

After yesterday's long pool swim it was really nice to get back into the only real swimming pool that deserves my love, the Brighton sea! It was very calm today, which after the last few days was a welcome surprise. Bob and I set off at 7a.m., just before anyone else got to the Arch, and did a once around the pier and then to the groyne and then in. The temperature is still dropping, albeit slowly. My face and legs hurt in the cold for about the first 10 minutes before I got used to it. Even though it was calm out there the tide was very strong and this meant that going around the head of the pier we flew but coming back around and under the pier meant we had to swim hard. It felt like a 'sticky' swim, meaning that even though I was swimming strongly I felt the sea was trying to hold us in place - not a bad thing as it does mean you have to work it. Funny thing was that at different times both Bob and I were hit in the body by a fish - not the same one, I assume, unless it was a fish who has the hump with us for disturbing its sleep.

The last time I did more than four hours swimming I was out of action for about three weeks but this time I had no problems at all and this morning I hardly ached and had no problem getting into the sea and on with the job at hand. Apparently Friday is going to be nice as well, so we are hopefully back on for our night swim tomorrow.

Day 112 – 8ᵗʰ October 2010

Morning 7.15a.m. – Bob, Bella and I swam once around the pier in a very calm sea. The tide was seriously low so we had to walk out about a quarter of the length of the pier; boy that was chilly! The tide was really strong and coming around the head of the pier felt like a real struggle. Even coming into shore, which is usually the easier bit, was a fight as well. A good morning's exercise.

Evening 7.45p.m. – Twelve of us went for an evening swim around the pier. It was great! The water was warmer than this morning but because you couldn't see the sea you didn't know if it was wavy or not. As it turned out it wasn't overly wavy but there were some waves that surprised us. We all wore light bands around our wrists and a couple had headlights as well. For safety we agreed to stay together but in the dark you really feel all alone, as you can't see anyone. We all met up at the head of the pier and trod water for about ten minutes to take photos and enjoy the amazing lights of the pier and the city far away from us. Then we did a big swim back around and under the pier and back to the beach. Because I couldn't see anyone I felt a few times that everyone else had already finished and I was the slowest struggling to get back, but of course every time I stopped and looked around I saw some in front, some with me and some way behind. The darkness really does throw you in the sense that you feel all alone even when you're surrounded. It was an amazing experience and one that so few get to ever experience, real Disney stuff! When we got back and changed, Fiona called the coastguard to report that we were all back and safe, which was a good result as losing someone would have been a bummer. Then off to the pub for a drink and a look at the pics Leo and I took. What a great night's experience as well as being another training exercise to boot.

Day 113 – 12th October 2010

How did you wake up this morning? Was it by putting your face straight into a bowl of ice and holding it there for ten minutes until all the colour and warmth was gone and the pain subsided enough to enable you to breathe again? No? Very sensible then. I, however, did pretty much just that! The sea was extremely calm with hardly any movement at all, which made for a fantastic swim in terms of effort. However getting in was coooold. It probably didn't help that I shaved at 6a.m. and so my face was already rather sensitive. It took almost ten minutes before it started to feel comfortable and I could relax into it. After I warmed up, the swim was nice and easy. The sun was coming up over the Marina and the sky was royal blue and the sea itself was so clear that coming back under the pier I could easily see a huge fishing net suspended across the pier. The fact that the net was empty makes me believe that the fish may have noticed it as well! Tomorrow no sea for me as I'll be in the pool for 4 hours; boring certainly, but a lot warmer.

Day 114 – 13th October 2010

I actually did a 5-hour swim, my longest swim ever, in fact my longest non-stop exercise ever in forty-plus years of being alive.

I got into the pool at 6.40a.m. and finished at exactly 11.40a.m. The only breaks were on the hour to have my Maxim from the bottle, which took maybe two minutes each time. The total number of lengths was 414, which equates to 10,350 metres, which equates to around 6.431 miles or 10.35 kilometres. Not bad going, especially considering the boredom factor.

I had planned a 4-hour swim, which I thought would be hard after my 18km run on Monday, but when I got to the 4-hour point I felt I could easily do another hour. It is a great achievement for me so early on. I am sure I will ache tomorrow but for now I am feeling OK and settling into a hot salt beef bagel and an apple Danish – gotta try to put back some of the 3,040 calories I apparently used up!

Tomorrow I shall do a nice gentle swim around the pier, no rushing, no real distance, just a nice, 30-minute swim in the sea. Very proud of myself, grinning like a Cheshire cat!

Day 115 – 14th October 2010

After yesterday's mammoth swim in the pool it was quite nice to wake up and realise I only need to a short slow swim today, albeit a cold one. The air temperature was about 10 degrees, which was lower than it's been recently, and the sea was probably down to around 13 degrees. Bob was on good form so he suggested we swim around to the beach on the other side and then back around again through the pier under the cafe and back. Basically one-and-a half-times around, which in this temperature was not far off the most I would want to do. The only pain for me was my inner thighs. Yesterday during my swim I used a pool buoy for the last two hours (this is basically a float that you grip between your thighs and which keeps your legs from kicking). It is a good aid for upper body work and helps me with my balance in the water. However can you imagine swimming in a pool for two hours with a float between your thighs? Basically my inner thighs are red raw, which last night in bed was really painful – but getting into a freezing salty sea this morning... ahhhhh! Boy, did that sting! After showering I smothered the area in Savlon, which also stung, but hopefully it'll calm down soon otherwise I'll be walking like a cowboy all day!

Day 117 – 18th October 2010

Another early Monday morning. I was at the beach at about 6.20a.m., earlier than last Monday, because today we are off to see Asher at school in his classroom and I needed to be home by 7.30a.m. I got to the Arch and was the first one there, wandered down the beach, straight into the water (naturally cold and very dark!), swam just passed the helter skelter, pretty much ran out of energy, swam back, trudged up the beach, slumped into the shower for a couple of minutes and now I'm at home feeling a little better and about to take Asher to school. The coldest part of today was actually the walk up the beach. I forgot my flip-flops and walking up the beach on

71

bare feet after my swim was really painful because of the extreme cold of the stones – I even had to stop a couple of times. As I was leaving the Arch at about 7a.m., Big Bob came in looking his usual cool and fit self. Gotta hope I look that good at fifty-five!

Those that live with Crohn's disease will understand when I say last night and this morning was a lot like taking Picolax. If you've ever had a colonoscopy (which I have once a year) then you will know about having to take Picolax the day before. Basically it cleans you out so that they can see clearly inside you but the effect is a massive lack of energy as your body is pretty much stripped of everything. If you've never had Picolax then count yourself lucky as it's bloomin' horrible. Living with Crohn's disease feels pretty much like having Picolax on a regular basis. As often as a few days every week your body gives up everything you are storing and leaves you sapped of energy. Last night was not a great night and this morning was pretty much a repeat of last night, so I ended up at the beach slightly anaemic-looking and without much energy. Having had this now for twenty years I am totally used to it so it really isn't a problem and I am not looking for sympathy, but I want my diary to reflect each day as it really is.

I remain hopeful that come my Channel swim day the weather is really good and my Crohn's is behaving. It would be rather annoying if the weather was good and my Crohn's was bad but each day is different and I remain absolutely positive that every day like today simply empowers me and prepares me even more for my swim day. Being able to get into the sea at 6.20a.m. on my own, in the dark and cold, really does show me I am strong enough to do this (if a little mad). Hopefully by the end of work my energy will return and I can get to the gym for an hour and have a decent workout with the weights, then tomorrow I'll get Bob to join me on a twice around the pier adventure. For now though it's off to Asher's school and then on to the office for what will have to be an easy day, as running around is quite out of the question

Day 118 - 19ᵗʰ October 2010
An early night did the trick and I'm feeling a lot better. I wanted to push

myself a bit more so I did twice around the pier, beach to beach to beach. Coming back around the second time I started to feel the cold, especially in my arms and feet. It's not going to be long before I can only do once around the pier; today took me around 40 minutes and soon it will only be a 20-minute swim. Tomorrow I'm back in the pool for 5 hours. Funnily enough I'm quite looking forward to it, how weird is that?

Day 119 – 20th October 2010

A mixed swimming day. On the one hand it was fantastic, on the other not so good.

I did my big, 5-hour pool swim today but rather than the 414 lengths I did last week, I did a whopping 444 lengths in the same time – that's 30 more lengths than last week, or 11,100 metres, or 11.1 kilometres or 6.87 miles. So physically it was really good and I could have done six hours without a problem.

However today was mentally very hard indeed, the exact opposite of last week. Last week I couldn't have physically done any more but mentally I could have kept going. This week I was physically very strong but mentally very tired. I did the silly thing of looking at the clock every 15 minutes, which made each hour go so slowly that I just wanted to stop and go to work! To say I'm annoyed with myself is an understatement. I know it's good that I still did my five hours but I am really beating myself up about it as mentally I should easily be able to do six hours and beyond. I do have a lot on at the moment and I have been a little drained with my Crohn's, but that is all excuses and I'm annoyed I made it so hard on myself.

I think next week I might skip my big Wednesday swim, just for one week, get myself refreshed and start anew the week after with a better head on me!

Day 120 – 25th October 2010

A different note from me today as only a small part written by me, the rest written by Fiona.

From me - After three days without swimming I was back in the sea today. Probably 10 to 11 degrees only, very calm and a beautiful sky. The moon was bright on one side and the sun on the other. Extraordinary. The coldness lasted for most of the swim although after about 15 minutes you do get used it. This afternoon I will do a 90-minute gym session.
From Fiona by email:

'Okay Mr!!! I've just read your blog!! Absolutely NO WAY do you miss your five hour this week unless you're paralysed or Kim tells you otherwise! Just because you had mind weakness! – an even BIGGER reason to get back in and do it. I'm just off to Falmer to knock out a two-hour swim before i see Kim. Yesterday i swam to the West Pier and back then round the pier twice on my own, in 11 degrees. Seriously we need to talk, tittering around the pier with Bob in the mornings is not going to get you across the Channel. I can understand that you love to have that time at the Arch in the mornings but it's a waste of time. Yes, if you then went off to the pool for a three-hour I would approve but you don't! Plus if you work already very strained muscles in cold water you will do damage beyond repair, you can certainly kiss goodbye to your dream. Speak to Kim! I've done it all!! But in the early part of my training, I had a further two years to get it right – you only have a few months. So........ Listen to me!!! xx'

My fault, I guess, for keeping such an honest blog!

Seriously though, how lucky am I to have someone who cares so much on my side? No way I can fail with that kind of support.

Day 121 – 26th October 2010
Another cold start. Air temp warmer at 10 degrees, sea probably the same. Very wavy out there, so much so that no one went around the pier. We stayed out for just over half an hour, by which time everything (and I mean everything) was numb! From a fun point of view it was great, cold but great wave playing. From a breakfast point of view it was just too much sea water for my liking! Every time my goggles steamed up I took them off to clean

them and was subsequently hit in the face by a cold wave and ended up swallowing half of it! This was the first time since I have been swimming that I have started to gag. In future the mouth will be saying firmly shut.

Finally, I know I shouldn't and I am sure Fiona will now be really angry with me, but I had to let you see the really funny email she sent me last night after the telling off she gave me in the morning!

From Fiona:

'Oh dear you've quoted me on your blog!!!!!!!!! bad grammar and all..........I've been kicking butt all day I'm ashamed to say. It started with poor Pete then you, onto Falmer where I verbally abused a poor little swimmer who clearly was in the wrong lane!! I spent the next 10 minutes apologising to her and reassuring her that I was a menopausal monster and that I would be better in the morning. I'm now safely locked behind doors at home!! which is where i will stay until the morning. It is now safe to go out!!!! Public enemy no 1 x'

Sorry, Fiona. It was just too good for me not to include!

Day 122 – 27ᵗʰ October 2010
Last night I had one of my no-sleep-at-all nights. I lay there from 11p.m. until 5.45a.m. planning how I was not going to go to the pool, then at 6a.m. I was up, dressed and heading for the car. As it is half term, the pool was much busier than last week. The early slot was still relatively quiet but after 9.30a.m. it picked up and at one point my lane was so busy I found myself having to walk for a bit, which forced me into the fast lane with Fiona and a speedy triathlete. It was great having Fiona back in the pool with me and she did around 4 hours, which was fantastic.

My aim was 5 hours again but I climbed out 15 minutes early. The middle lane ended up being very crowded with breast strokers (that's not a euphemism, by the way) and after finding myself being held back for about three lengths I decided I had to get into the fast lane. Soon after that Fiona left, but I was joined by a lady (although I am being generous calling her that) and a man, both in their later years. The lady swam like she probably drives, right across the middle of the lane, and as soon as she got level with me she stuck her hand in my face to stop me, basically slapping me in the chops. She'd then give me a look to say that I was crossing over the middle, yet I was so far to the left my arm was scratching the wall just to avoid her. It took all my restraint not to whack her back and tell her to stay in her half but I thought old lady bashing may not be appropriate. The man was very good at staying in his half of the lane but he was slower than a very slow thing on a slow day in Slowsville, doing a kind of half breast stroke/half doggy paddle/half walk. Usually I would have spoken to the lifeguards and asked them to move both these people out of the training lanes but it was already 11.20a.m. and I had been swimming for almost five hours and I thought it was time for me to move on. (I am not casting dispersions on elderly swimmers, in fact I probably saw about a dozen swimmers in their seventies today who were incredibly fast and quite beautiful to watch, but boy oh boy, another 10 minutes with those two and I may have been locked up by the gendarme!)

I was pleased with what I'd achieved and the fact I was getting my mind back where it should be. My shoulders were very tired though (they were tired after about two hours), so tomorrow I shall join Bob and the Arch team on the beach at 7a.m. for a very cold dip in what is likely to be a wavy, fun-filled sea. That should sort out any aches.

Day 124 - 29th October 2010

This morning was Fun with a very capital F. It was at least 25% rougher than it has been and although swimming around the pier was clearly do-able, it would have been a lot of work and possibly a worry. The best way of describing it is to picture a herd of white horses in groups of four or five, bearing down on you. From the moment we put our feet in the sea we were swamped by the waves. The wind and the tide were going from east to west, which meant the pull was away from Brighton Pier to the West Pier. Having got in and swum a couple of hundred metres out we were either climbing up huge swells and going over them or grabbing as much breath as possible and going under them. Because the water was so busy it raised the temperature by a good 2 degrees. After about 20 minutes, when it was just Bob and me, we came back to the beach ready to go in but couldn't resist going back in the sea for another ten minutes. It really was that much fun.

On a training note, a day like today is actually really important. First of all when you are swimming in these conditions you have to put on bursts of speed to fight through the waves and avoid them spinning you under or throwing you onto the beach or the groynes. This is fantastic for the shoulders and legs as sometimes you get three or four mountains of water hurtling at you in succession and you really have to run for it. Secondly, and probably more importantly, this is the best training ground for learning to cope in severe conditions and for getting yourself in a position where you respect the sea but are not frightened of it, or at least if you are frightened you are able to control the fear and keep your head calm and stay controlled. When I get into the Channel, even though the waves maybe a lot higher than today, I will feel completely able to deal with them because of days like today. It's certainly not for the faint hearted but when you get into it and realise your capabilities then you yearn for days like this.

No swimming today – 1st November 2010

I still don't seem to have shaken off this bad cold that took hold after my 5-hour swim last Wednesday. It's really unlike me – usually two days and a cold has gone – but I've never before gone into the sea day after day with a cold. Over the weekend I developed a bad chest that left me with an awful rasping cough that even sent the Hallowe'en ghouls into hiding. So after much guilt and asking the approval of Sharon, Fiona, Bob (any anyone else who would offer me solace) I have decided to take a few days off to get better. The intention is to take this week off from all training and then start fresh and anew next week, but we shall see. If I start to feel refreshed and better then I'll get back to it midweek. The key will be if the guilt of not training outweighs the guilt of training whilst unwell.

Swimming day 125 –Friday 5ᵗʰ November 2010

The last swim I had was exactly a week ago. I've done no exercise at all in this time but while I needed the time off to get better physically, I have found myself feeling mentally weak. Exercise for me seems to not only make me stronger physically but also mentally, which with everything I do is vital. Therefore even though my cold and sore throat persist, I just had to get up early and get in the sea. It was hard leaving the house though as Jesse is not very well and he was in bed with us and really wanted me to stay – whenever he's unwell he just wants me. The fact that I had to go to work anyway meant I had to leave sometime but it was still hard hearing him crying for me to stay. I'm sure it only would have lasted a few minutes but still pulls at your heart.

This week so far, as told to me by Big Bob every day by text, has been very rough, some days so rough that it's been dangerous and just not swim-mable. Typical that I've missed all the fun!

Anyhow, back to my swim today. I got to the Arch at 7a.m. and pretty quickly was joined by about nine others. Coming down the beach and seeing some very big waves meant that almost everyone went to the girly beach to have a play. Against Bob's advice I decided to join Leo and Simon for an around the pier swim.

Jumping straight in, we were faced with angry waves six-foot high. Swimming to the end of the pier through a very dangerous sea was not so bad, although it wasn't a walk in the park either. Getting around the pier added another level as we tried to avoid being thrown into the pier. I tried to follow Leo and Simon's line as they are way better at this than me. Having made it around the head safely I then saw mountains of water everywhere and could only just spot the shore what looked like miles away (only about half a mile in reality). It crossed my mind that maybe I had bitten off more than I could chew but there I was anyway, so it was a case of simply putting my head down and fighting through it. It wasn't long before the shore was almost in reach and safety seemed assured.

Of course in the sea one should take nothing for granted. A huge wave, and I really mean huge, literally swept me up, pulled me under, spun me around and then threw me face first onto the shingle. First time that's ever happened to me, and somewhat weird and shocking. Quickly getting myself on my feet I ran up the beach to avoid the following wave, just in time to see it grab Leo and Simon and treat them to a spin!

Walking back up the beach with them I was feeling tired and a little scratched up, but also quite full of life. At the Arch I emptied a bag of shingle out of my Speedos before showering.

Leo of course through all this still managed to take photos and movies – incredible bloke. Both Leo and Simon were real stars, staying near me the whole swim. I'm lucky to have such good friends so quickly in my time with BSC. All this and it was only just 8a.m. on a Friday. Funny old life!

In the afternoon I was at the gym, Esporta, and chatting to Ross Scrivener, one of their top trainers, and he said that he will get Esporta to support me as well as putting up a Swim4Smiles display. Ross is now taking over my gym training, which is fantastic as I can't seem to follow Wendy's plans on my own and really need someone there with me the whole time. Wendy has helped get me this far but she can't be with me each time as she doesn't work there. I am hopeful Ross can now take over that mantle and take me to the next level.

Also our Starr Trust's first-ever barn dance is almost sold out, Southern Water and Shoreham Port have agreed to support Swim4Smiles, and Darren, my brother-in-law, has just returned from the Middle East having visited two of our projects and is absolutely elated by what we are achieving there. Friday 5th November truly has been an explosive day of fireworks for the Starr Trust and for me personally. Fabulous!

Day 126 – Monday 8th November 2010

Anyone looking out of their window this morning would not have been surprised to see lashing rain hitting their windows and violent wind throwing leaves and rubbish all around. The clue was in the screaming wind that started at about midnight and was still screaming at 6a.m. Did that stop me from going for a nice dip in the sea? Did it 'eck!

Driving down to the seafront I did wonder about the sanity of it all and I really didn't expect many people to be at the Arch. On parking up by the pier, who did I see cycling past, almost flying up into the wind? My good friend and fellow crazy, Bob. There was me driving in thinking it was mad, yet he was on his bike! Gotta love that English 'can do' attitude.

Getting into the Arch, already soaked, we saw three sets of clothes for swimmers already in and we were then joined by about another seven. It seems that mad days really do bring out the madness in sea swimmers. By the time we were at the shore we were freezing cold from the 6 degree air temperature, crazy wind and lashing rain. Upon diving in and through the waves it was fantastic to warm up - the sea must have been a good 13 degrees, making it way warmer in the water than on the beach. Despite the conditions around us the waves were not mentally high, although they were constant, and the tide seemed to be having a rest, so it was a simply a case of swimming in, up and through wave after wave. Good fun and good exercise.

Onto the Starr Trust now; we have sold nearly 250 tickets for the barn dance! Amazing. The venue only holds 300 and that is without the entertainment we have going in; so 250 will completely fill the place up. A fantastic way to get the Trust message out there and get more people following Swim4Smiles and all the good work we are doing.

On the home front, Sharon and I took down the two cots and built the twins a bed each. Now all my babies are in proper beds. I guess that means that they are not babies anymore. Where did that time go?

Day 127 - 9th November 2010

Another day very similar to yesterday, although the wind was nowhere as strong. The sea was so wavy that Bob and I tried to swim around the pier but only got as far as the helter skelter because wave after wave pushed us back; We stayed out for around 30 minutes, which was extremely good as it was certainly a strong workout as well as staying acclimatised to the cold. Winter sea swimming is so different to summer sea swimming in so many ways - temperature, waves, tidal, rain, darkness, number of people, length of swim - but not all these are negative points as it is certainly much more challenging and a lot more fun.

On the home front, the twins are still not better and Jesse in particular is finding having a bed a bit odd. I found him this morning at about 1a.m. in the hallway near the stairs, scooped him up and brought him to bed with me for an hour and then took him back to his car bed, which luckily he was happy to go back to. I only had about three hours sleep but that's OK. Tomorrow is a pool day, which is a shame, but as I am doing two 3-hour pool swims this week rather than a single 5-hour I don't mind so much. Three hours sounds quite easy to me these days.

At 11a.m. I was heading to the Grand Hotel on Brighton seafront as they are presenting me with a fantastic auction prize that the Starr Trust can use as a fundraiser for Swim4Smiles. It is for next summer, a champagne lunch for eight people on the Grand's own yacht sailing around Brighton, followed by an evening meal for eight at Hotel du Vin. I want that prize myself! Hopefully it'll go for much more than I can afford...

Day 128 - 10th November 2010

The weather must have known I was in the pool today as it decided to stop raining, stop being windy and let the sea have a much needed rest - a perfect day for a sea swim.

I did a 3-hour swim today, which being a lot less than my usual 5 hours meant I was thinking it would be rather easy. I am pleased to say that it was rather easy. The first hour was quite tough but once I got through that, the next two went by in a flash. The pool was quiet, allowing me to have my lane to myself for most of the time. I also had Fiona in the lane next to me, always great company. For a change I decided to make each hour different. The first I swam as normal, the second I used a pool buoy and the last hour I used hand paddles (like solid paddle gloves that you use to pull you through the water and really work your shoulders). It made it a more interesting swim and by the end of the session I could really feel the workout.

Tomorrow I have another 3-hour swim followed by a 45-minute assessment by Ross at Esporta. My new trainer is going to help with muscle building and core strength. It'll be great having one person to do all this, leaving Fiona to help me in the sea.

I have decided to stop using Mark as my swimming teacher. Despite him being a decent swimming teacher, he never turns up, despite us agreeing the times and me agreeing his fees. I simply don't have the time to be messed around like this. It seems a silly way to behave but I guess he has his reasons and I am not going to judge him (or anyone) for how they choose to lead their lives. Equally, I cannot let someone else's problems stop me on my quest. Also I do not think swimming lessons are the way forward for me at the moment: swimming is. What I need is for someone to focus on my core strength and my muscle memory, so Ross now holds the baton and I get the feeling he is the man for the job.

Day 129 – 11th November 2010

Not having gone to the sea today I can only imagine how big it must have been. The weather this morning was appalling. I finished my second 3-hour pool swim as planned and then met Ross and we completed my assessment: body fat, muscle tone, water balance etc. At this stage none of it means much to me but he seemed to understand it all. He is now away for two weeks and on his return he will implement my new gym plan. He also wants to set up an eating plan for me but I told him not to waste his time, as I am sure I will ignore it. Silly attitude, I know, but I am what I am. I get the feeling that Ross will increase my physical week to yet another level, although I am not sure how that is possible as I seem to be constantly swimming, running and weight lifting. How my muscles aren't growing I'm not sure, but hopefully they'll get there in time for the swim.

Tomorrow I'm in the sea at 10a.m. because Richard Lindfield (local radio celebrity and a good friend of mine) is going to be filming me for the Argus blog. Hopefully the sea will be big and they can see the madness that sea swimming in November really is.

After tomorrow I may take a few days off from swimming as after two weeks I still am really badly stuffed-up with a cold, and I really need to shift it because I can hardly breathe through my nose. I am convinced it is the chemicals in the pool doing this, as they are madly potent! I probably shouldn't go tomorrow but I have committed to the filming and also I really want to finish this week off with a decent sea swim.

Yesterday afternoon Darren, Mel (my charity operations director) and I met with five of the charities that would like us to support them as part of Swim4Smiles. Oh my god, how emotional was that? It was so inspiring to meet such incredibly dedicated people but it was so draining to hear such sad stories about children who just need a chance in life. I so admire these people who make such a difference to these children around the world. I would swim the Channel twice over for any one of them, let alone all of them, if I were able. There really are some amazing people in the world.

Day 130 – 12th November 2010

So nice to be back in the sea today after two days in the pool. The sea really opens up my airways and lets me breathe again. I might need to take a week away from the pool and see if that helps. My thoughts that the pool chemicals are causing me to feel ill are confirmed by the sea clearing my nose. We were meant to be filmed today for the Argus but sickness their end meant it is postponed until next Friday - a shame, as the conditions today would have been a sight to behold.

The sea was really rough, so we went in on the girlie beach and played around. It was quite hard to actually swim as the tide was really strong and dragging towards the Marina and the waves were constant and dragging (literally like a clamp on your body) you out to sea. We swam a short distance out, but it felt a little scary as it wasn't an easy swim to get back in, so we stayed near the shore as much as we could. As for the temperature, it felt like 10 degrees today and my face actually hurt for a couple of minutes.

Whilst I do love these days, I really could do with a calm sea for a few days so I can do some sprints around the pier and work on my distance and speed. Another week over, another week of ups and downs (literally) and another week closer to my Channel swim! Fundraising still has a mountain of a way to go but we are almost at 10% of the fundraising challenge, which is £10,000 out of the £100,000 target. I personally think that is amazing in two months.

Day 131 – 15th November 2010

Boy, it felt cold today. The air temperature at 6.30a.m. was around 4 degrees and the sea temp was 10.9 degrees. I know that it is going to get down to half of that pretty soon but for now this is plenty cold enough, thank you.

After a few days craziness, the sea was very calm today. A once-around-the-pier swim with Bob probably took us about 25 minutes; the cold does slow you down but you want to keep moving because if you stop you will cool down even more. The pain for me is in my face, particularly around my temples – it really is quite agonising for a few minutes. After that you pretty much get used to it and then it's just a cold swim. The walk back up the beach is always hard on the feet and driving to work afterwards I was shivering a little. Hopefully we'll have a couple of clear days like today so that we can get some swimming in, but I think the waves are due to return later this week. As for the pool; if my cold goes then I'll do a 5-hour swim on Wednesday as usual, but if my cold persists I may just stick to the sea and the gym this week and return next week. I will definitely go to the gym after work for an hour as last week I only went once. My gym sessions need to start increasing but hopefully Ross will deal with that once he's back from his hols.

On Friday afternoon I met with Rodney Lunn, the CEO of Shoreham Port. It was a really good meeting as Rodney said that as well as making a financial donation to the Swim4Smiles challenge, he is keen for the port to support me in terms of PR and events as well and will let me swim in the harbour whenever I want (why would I want to do that too much? way too much diesel). Swimming in the harbour will be good for me to try as it will be yet another test in terms of swimming style and also good PR for both the port and the Starr Trust.

Day 132 - 16ᵗʰ November 2010

It really is incredible, the colours one sees when one is in the sea. The sun was red-gold, the pier was almost maroon, the sea was kind of milky, the clouds were virtually opaque, the sky was a mixture of light blue and dusk all swirled together. Seriously, a really poetic colourful morning... Never in my wildest dreams would I have thought sea swimming could evoke so many emotions and thoughts just through the colours.

It was so cold that 70 minutes after my swim I am at the office and my right foot (little toe particularly) is still a mixture of being numb and painful. I guess I should consider wearing swimming socks again but I really want to put that off as long as I can as I don't love the feeling of swimming in gloves or socks. There is talk about a wetsuit for the winter so we can stay in the sea longer; but I want to stay in just my trunks if I can.

Off to London for a day of meetings. I have got this ridiculous swimming cap line around my forehead - it looks weird to say the least! I desperately hope it fades for my first meeting; can you imagine walking into a high-powered London meeting with a dent around your head?

Day 132 - 17ᵗʰ November 2010

This was the first day we couldn't get into the sea due to the weather. After two very calm days, the wind made a triumphant return. Usually on a day like today we would go onto the girlie beach because the pier blocks a lot of the movement. Today the girlie beach was more like a lady with bad P.M.T, very angry and unforgiving. There was no way one would attempt to even step near the sea on that side. So there we were, eight to ten of us, standing on the edge of the sea trying to see where and how we could get in. The waves were so big and powerful that just looking at them made me wonder about the madness of going in. After attempts by a couple of people it was clear that going in would be very difficult, if not suicidal, but coming out would be potentially bone breaking. I am not exaggerating. I've been in some very rough seas of late but really haven't seen waves as powerful as this before. It was simply too dangerous.

You would have thought at that stage we would have all turned around and headed straight back to the warmth of the Arch and dry clothes, but oh no, this is the Brighton Swimming Club, common sense could never prevail. Instead, like a bunch of eccentric fools, led by Little Bob, we all lay down as close to the edge as we could get and let the waves crash over us! Just how crazy would that have looked from the seafront? We were like a line of adult pilchards along the seashore. It was huge fun but just lying there and letting the waves go over you was actually extremely hard from the strength of the pull. You had to literally dig your legs into the stones and push your palms as far down as you could, otherwise you were sent rolling down the beach, being scratched and turned on the Brighton pebbles as you went. But it was a lot of fun as it really made you forget you are an adult with responsibilities and let you feel like a kid again. But once was enough as we were there to swim, and swim was what we wanted to do. Hopefully tomorrow we can get in and out safely.

Day 134 – 18th November 2010

7a.m. and the first of two sea swims today. The second was at 10a.m. when Fiona, Bob and I went back to meet Richard Lindfield, the friend and local radio news reader who is going to make a film blog.

Swim number one made for a cold wake-up call. The sea was calm although the cold in the air and water made for what I can only describe as a 'character building' start to the day. We swam to the silver ball along the pier, then over to the doughnut on the groyne and then traversed back to where we'd left our flip-flops, all in about 20 minutes.

Swim number two felt rather strange, being back at the Arch in my Speedos at 10a.m. I had barely thawed out from the first swim and here I was again ready for another freezing! Saying all that, it was so sunny and gorgeous out by this time that it was a pleasure to be back down there. We met with Richard and two young lads he is training and they set up their camera and interviewed us individually, then filmed us in and out of the sea. It caused a slight stir on the promenade as people stopped to watch the three crazies in their swimming costumes and some Americans came over and asked if we were really going to go in the ocean - it was all very British to them! The interviews and swim lasted around half an hour and were good fun.

Aside from the two swims this morning, there was great debate in the Arch on my use of my word pilchards. This rowdy discussion was led by Little Bob and he was soon joined by all those who felt pilchards was not a kind word to describe my fellow BSC members. On the drive back from the Arch to work I gave this matter some thought but all I could see in my mind's eye were pilchards, although I could have referred to us all lying on the beach being washed by mountainous waves as sprats or plankton!

Day 135 - 22nd November 2010
Sea 9.8 degrees, air temp 6 degrees.

Not a fab start to the day. I woke up feeling sick and stayed in the bath-room for twenty minutes thinking I was going to be ill. I eventually got to the beach at 7a.m. The sea was very calm, hardly a ripple, although I swear it looked colder than usual. An amazing sight this morning though was the starlings, three pockets of them, maybe a hundred in each, doing these amazing dances around the pier. It looked like a spell cast by a great wizard - incredible.

My usual friends were in the Arch, all keen and ready to go. We headed to the sea and did our usual, some tiptoeing in, some staying close to the edge and some, Simon, Bob and I, just going for it. It was Cold with a capital C! After a few hundred metres my sickness came back on and I had to stop swimming and just float for a couple of minutes until it subsided. Somehow floating in 10 degree water for a few minutes seemed to do the job and I was able to slowly breaststroke back in to shore. Not my greatest swimming experience!

After warming up I headed to the office and had my first meeting of the day. Despite my feeling unwell and not performing to my usual standard,

I think the meeting went well enough. Then I headed home at full speed, just made the bathroom in time and spent the rest of the day and night in bed feeling not so good. This is the first time I've been sick for well over a year - I hate being sick.

Day 136 - 23rd November 2010

I was feeling much better this morning. Not 100%, but certainly a good 80%. This morning was Shoreham Port day. After picking up my brother-in-law Darren at 7.30a.m. we headed to Shoreham Port where we met up with CEO Rod Lunn plus his team, a number of our other charity partners, some local businesses that support us and also local press. The point of today was a PR exercise for the port and also a fantastic opportunity for us to put together a DVD for the Starr Trust for promoting our Swim4Smiles campaign. It was so amazing to see so many people turn up there at 7.30a.m. just to see me take a dip in the harbour in my Speedos - or maybe it was the free bacon sandwiches and coffee on offer?

After some chatting and filming I popped myself into my trunks and then we all headed off through the port to the harbour. It was surreal, to say the very least! With everyone standing on the dock in anticipation I climbed down the ladder from a tug boat and took the plunge. The temperature was certainly warmer than the sea, probably around 12 degrees, so that was pleasant, but the taste was somewhat diesel-y! I did a short swim from the dock to a waiting tug boat and back again, probably no more than 400 metres in all, and then climbed out to rapturous applause. I found it rather odd that people were clapping me for a 400-metre, relatively warm swim, but hey ho, one has to take the applause when one can. What was particularly nice was that at least four people, two from the port, told me they thought my swimming technique was 'fantastic' and that I simply glided through the water. Considering that I only started swimming properly in April that was super-nice to hear, although I would suggest a misplaced compliment. Another great PR day for the Trust and the Challenge. Every day seems to get more exciting.

Day 137 - 25th November 2010

Air temp 1 degree and light snow forecast, sea temp damn cold! I didn't sea swim yesterday as I had a big London meeting at 8a.m. about the growth of Seico Group. I talked for four hours non-stop and it was more tiring than swimming! I did manage a 90-minute pool swim and a 40-minute gym session after I got back though, so I still got some exercise endorphins in to keep that guilt at bay.

This morning the sea was extremely calm and there was a low tide, which meant a cold walk until it was deep enough to swim. Boy, could I feel the cold in my feet and my face. It was really painful by the end of the swim. My body seems to be fine, it's basically my feet when I come out and my face when I go in. I'll try to find a better swimming hat and maybe some swimming socks. Bob, Paul Smith and I did an around the pier swim, which in terms of calm water was easier but in terms of cold was a challenge. It took Bob and I about 22 minutes to get back. Paul was a few minutes after us but he was weighed down by swimming socks and gloves. He said they certainly provide warmth but if they slow you down it means you are in the sea longer and therefore get colder. It's an interesting point in terms of whether or not to use them.

After we were all dressed we decided to guess the sea temperature and I specifically said 9.2 degrees. Seconds later Fiona came in from her swim and proudly announced that her watch said the temperature in the sea today was 9.2 degrees! Boy, am I good! My feet were still hurting for a good hour after I got back to the office.

Tomorrow Sharon and I are heading to New York for the weekend (her birthday trip).

Day 138 - 1st December 2010

Back from my travels to New York, fab-est city in the world, and returned to blasted snow. Sorry to be a grump but snow and I just don't get on. It's disruptive to work, it's cold, it's disruptive to work, it's cold, it's disruptive to work...

A little about New York, not to rub it in but so I can look back one day and re-live the experience. Sharon and I became adults for a few days. No children meant no kiddie talk and no 'Daddy can we...?' or 'Mummy can we...?' Love them and certainly missed them, but getting to talk to Sharon without interruption was a 'neat experience' (NY talk). We shopped until we dropped, we ice-skated in Central Park, we saw Wicked (best musical ever) in Times Square and we saw Michael Bublé in concert at Madison Square Gardens, sitting just three rows back from the front of the stage. Oh yes and not forgetting, we did eat in between, including sarnies at Sardi's and cheesecake at Lindy's.

We got back at Tuesday midday after a decent nine-hour flight, all ready to get back to normal life. We were met head-on with a true English winter: snow everywhere and –1 degree. For the first time ever this had a brand new meaning and horror called Sea Swimming. Putting it out of my mind I went about the usual unpacking and time with kids and then bed, but the morning came around exceptionally fast, unfortunately.

Down at the Arch there were fewer people than usual but my good friends were there: LB, Big Bob, Mike, David, Dr Sean, Dr Mark, Martina, Charlotte and Flick. They all did a quick in and out but Big Bob and I went for a swim. The beach was completely white, the snow was still falling and the sea was very calm, luring us into its claws (claws being the operative word if you had seen our hands afterwards). We swam along the coast, then turned and swam back to the pier and then turned back to the doughnut. I bailed out half way back but Bob, being the big man, finished the swim. I think I did about 14 minutes before we trudged back up the beach. To say my feet and hands hurt was truly an understatement, I thought they would snap off. Just getting my flip-flops back on was so difficult that I ended up on the beach on my bottom as I couldn't stand to slip them on (Bob did exactly the same a minute later). Jumping into a very hot shower was clearly silly as I very quickly felt sick and had to squat down. It only lasted about 30 seconds but it wasn't very nice. I guess my blood pressure must have dropped in the sea very quickly and then the hot shower raised it too quickly. Need to be careful of that! Tomorrow I will go back again, although for the first time since I started this journey I really am not looking forward to it. I think I may just do 10 minutes max tomorrow as I don't want to overdo it and also I have to somehow get through the snow and to London by late morning.

The temperature was about 6 degrees in the water and minus one in the air, the coldest for me ever - so far - and utter madness!

Day 140 – 3rd December 2010

After yesterday's snow swim I stumbled out of bed at about 6.45a.m., looked at the clock and thought, 'Flipping 'eck', slowly got dressed without enthusiasm, climbed into my car with trepidation and slowly pulled out of the drive onto a very snowy icy road. After picking up Bob on the way (the mad fool was walking from Ovingdean to Brighton for his swim - he's way nuttier than me) we got to the Arch about 7.20a.m. and along with various others headed down the beach. Even though it was snowing on Monday when we went in, today was my first experience of walking down the beach in my Speedos with snow up past my ankles. The sea itself was very calm and it was a high tide, which meant no painful walking out and it was clear as glass, you could see straight through to the bottom. So in we all went, no hesitation because we are hardcore. I guess I was in for about 8 or 9 minutes, others a lot less and a couple a lot more. Fiona swam all the way to the silver ball and back but then she is Wonderwoman. In terms of pain, the sensation on my legs, arms and body was like thousands of little pinpricks, but that's OK for a short swim. My face was surprisingly all right, my feet were fine (I sensibly wore swimming socks), but my hands once again felt it the most. I might wear swimming gloves next week, as wearing both gloves and socks will allow me to stay in longer. Walking back up the beach with my socks on and having only stayed in for under 10 minutes I actually felt fine, unlike Monday's experience.

The air temperature was around -5 and the sea probably below 6 degrees, so the sea is clearly warmer than the air but being in the sea with just trunks on definitely feels colder than standing on the beach. I wonder when getting out if one considers the mixture of being in a cold sea and standing in the cold air is actually the calculation of both rather than just the chill of the lowest? Either way for me coming out of the sea all wet made the walk to the Arch a damn sight colder than the dry walk down! All in all it was a good swim and there was no reason at all for me to have felt nervous about it this morning.

Day 140 – 6th December 2010

Today it wasn't the weather that stopped me, it wasn't a bad cold, it wasn't even the pressures of work or home; no, today it was the Crohn's! To be truthful, it was the preventative side rather than the illness. Today was my annual check-up, which involved all day Sunday being really uncomfortable and exhausted having taken the dreaded Picolax, followed by a colonoscopy today under anaesthetic at the Nuffield Hospital. It also meant I had nothing to eat from 6p.m. Saturday night to 7p.m. Monday evening (basically right now) and with weight loss being a problem anyway this was not overly helpful. Normally two days not eating is not difficult for me but when you know you are not allowed to eat it makes you very hungry. I guess it's lucky Christmas is on the way as that will mean lots of food and chocolate, including my mum's cheesecake and trifle to fatten me up!

All went well with the tests, which is always a relief, and now I'm done and fit for another year. So tomorrow, assuming I can get some energy back, I'll have a sea dip, but I'm not gonna be able to get back to my 5-hour pool and gym sessions until next week as I need to get my energy levels back up. It's all part of life's little tapestry!

Day 142 – 8th December 2010

Another record today for me, 3.5 degrees in the sea, my coldest ever yet. Actually everyone down at the Arch said it was their coldest, and very unusual for this early in December. The air temperature was slightly up at one degree, so that certainly made a difference. Usual crowd in for a minute or two, with Bob and I doing a decent 11-minute swim from groyne to pier and back. My hands were frozen and painful, but my feet were not too bad as I had my swimming socks on. My body was ok. The stones on the beach felt the cold more than me as they were frozen solid in some places; almost as if they were laid as a road.

I'm going to finish this week just in the sea and then next week it will be back to the pool as well plus the gym. Tonight I'm meeting my new trainer Ross at Falmer to plan the diary for the next six months, which is well overdue.

Day 144 – 10ᵗʰ December 2010

I had a 7.30a.m. network meeting at the Brighton Chamber of Commerce and then a dash to the office as we are also moving offices today – the second and last day, I hope. I ventured into the sea at 6.45a.m. for my first ever freezing cold solo swim! The Arch was dark and uninviting this morning and after sitting there for about 10 minutes I gave up talking myself out of it and took the plunge. As it was both freezing cold and extremely dark I stayed very close to the water's edge and simply did the groyne to pier swim that Bob and I have been doing of late. The hardest thing was actually trying to unlock the Arch when I got back, my fingers simply didn't want to respond or my brain was frozen and forget to send the message down. After a very quick shower and change I was back in the car and heading over to the meeting to tell local businesses about the Starr Trust and to answer some rather odd questions, such as 'If my charity was an animal, what would it be?' I can't remember the answer I gave. Overall it went well and afterwards I met a number of interesting people before reluctantly heading back to work to get involved with the move.

Moving offices, especially two offices, is quite a daunting task, but the organisation my team brought to it was astounding and by the end of the day we were settled in and everything was working. A miracle indeed! It was quite emotional for me because the old offices held a lot of history. Who said there wasn't room for sentiment in business? How wrong they are.

Day 145 – 13ᵗʰ December 2010

A rather odd start to today. At 2a.m. Asher was up, having wet his bed, which meant Sharon and I had to find him a clean set of PJs and fresh bedding; of course by 2.30a.m. he was fast asleep and we were lying there wide awake! I eventually dropped off about 5a.m. and was woken by my alarm at 6a.m. Then followed a slow getting up and getting ready for my morning dip, only to find that Sharon's Chrysler had a flat tyre; joy, oh joy, on a Monday morning. Unfortunately as I failed my rocket science degree I couldn't change the tyre and had to wait for the AA. Even after twenty years' experience in tyre changing the AA man felt he also needed a science degree to do the job. Why car manufacturers make it so hard to change a tyre, I can't imagine. What if Sharon had been out with the kids and this had happened? Anyhow, my morning dip was clearly not destined, so here I am all nice and dry and warm at the new offices at 8a.m. and ready for the day ahead.

Tonight I am going to Falmer for my first pool swim in about three weeks. I'm just going to do an hour to get myself back into it, then later in the week I'm going to do two gym sessions with Ross and attempt a 3-hour and a 2-hour pool swim. I'm back in the game and it's exercise city all the way (allowing of course for some Christmas spirit in between.)

Day 146 – 14ᵗʰ December 2010

No flat tyres and no dramas, apart from Jesse getting me up at 1.55a.m. to kiss his finger better. I think he had a 'hurt my finger' dream! No reason, therefore, not to get down the Arch and take a dip in the sea. The air temperature was slightly warmer at around 3 degrees and the sea was still registering at below 4 degrees, so still crazy cold but slightly (only slightly) up on last week. Bob and I swam for 13 minutes, which in just your trunks (although I also had swimming socks on) is pretty good going. Having had a few days out and being at the hospital last week made it an extra challenge for me but Bob said I was full of 'grit'. At least I think he said 'grit'!

Day 148 – 16ᵗʰ December 2010

I had a boring night of number-crunching for work, which meant a lot of brain drain into the wee hours plus one or two rather large JD's on ice. A true athlete would have shrugged this off and headed straight to the beach for the daily ice bath, but being just a wannabe rather than a true athlete, I ended up skipping the ice and went for the warm pool instead! I did a 90-minute pool swim in what was probably 28-degree water (that alone was a shock to the system) and then got to work by 7.50a.m., all warm and with nothing hurting (except muscles, of course). My long distance swimming has suffered in recent weeks and I desperately need to get back to my 5 hours and beyond (I sound like Buzz Lightyear now). Tomorrow I'm in the pool again and also at the gym being trained, so that's a decent week's training at various levels. Diary permitting I am going to try a 4-hour pool swim next week and perhaps a 2-hour as well, but it will be diary permitting.

I just had a text from Big Bob to say that waves had returned this morning – waves and ice temperatures, blimey that must have hurt. Maybe the pool isn't so bad after all!

Today at work we have our CHOCS meeting with some of our charities, some of our business supporters, some of our schools and some new interested parties. (CHOCS stands for 'Children Helping Other Children Smile') and is a programme teaching social entrepreneurship to secondary school students.) Darren has basically put this together and has worked so hard. I am really proud of all he is achieving, because CHOCS is such a big part of the Starr Trust going forward. As its head of development Darren is putting so much time and thought into it that it is really starting to take amazing shape. I have no doubt that CHOCS will soon be on the lips of every school in Sussex. If you get a chance, log onto www.starrtrust.com and visit the CHOCS page; it's really very exciting and inspirational to see what is being developed here.

Day 149 – 17th December 2010

All four today: sea, gym, pool and unpopular!

Sea – Got to the Arch at 7a.m. The sky today was incredibly clear with loads of clouds on the horizon rather than in the sky, so looked like huge mountains at the end of the sea. Really amazing.

The air temp was a chilling minus three and the pebbles had frozen solid. The sea itself was bloomin' cold, probably around four degrees, and there were waves. It didn't help that a sloppy shave had left me with a huge cut under my chin that the salt water really took a liking to. Bob and I swam to the end of the groyne but I found myself heading out rather than along and very quickly was a few hundred metres out amongst the waves. Usually this would be normal but because I was freezing it made my heart skip a beat to see how far out I had gone. I got a little panicked as I knew I could only be out for so long before I simply couldn't move enough to swim in, so with head down I swam as hard as I could to shore. As it turns out it only took a minute or so to get back in so it was clearly not a problem, but it shows you just have to be so careful. Coming out and heading back to the Arch, which was only around eight minutes after I had gone in, I was very happy to be drying myself off and wearing my woolly Superman hat, although Superman I clearly am not! I guess every now and again a bit of the old fear is not a terrible thing as it grounds you and makes you recognise the safety factor of this sport and the importance of making sure you are not being overly gungho.

Gym – I had an hour with Ross at the gym. Once again he pushed me on lower body and core work. This element of training is completely new to me so it is rather painful afterwards. Hopefully after a few sessions it'll stop hurting and we can get down to increasing the reps [repeats] and the weights. Maybe one day soon I will even have nicely formed legs rather than Twiglets holding me up.

Pool - After my hour with Ross I did an hour in the pool, slow lengths back and forth, forth and back. It was very quiet, just one lady in the slow lane and me in the fast lane, so it was rather relaxing and easy. Next week I'll ramp up the hours, but it was nice after a hard gym session to unwind with an hour in a warm pool.

Unpopular - I must be unpopular at the Arch, even though I thought every-one loved me. Hey ho! I just heard they have the BSC Christmas meal tonight in Brighton, both the sea and the pool swimmers. Considering it is 4p.m. and I only found out because someone asked what time I was going, I guess my good sense of humour and striking good looks were just too much for people to have around the table!

Day 150 - 20th December 2010

I got sleeted this morning! It snowed all weekend, so once again we have icy roads, pretty roofs and a traditional Christmas feel just like we used to get when I was a kid. Unlike last year, however, the roads are totally useable, so as long as you go slow you can get about no problem, which meant no excuses this morning for not going swimming. Walking down the beach in my trunks it was odd to be hit from all sides with sleet, like thousands of ice-cold needles tapping at your skin, which oddly enough was not overly offensive, although I wouldn't say it was enjoyable. The water was 4.1 degrees, which in centigrade is below 40 and the air temperature registered −2, so a cold one. I swam for about 5 or 6 minutes and by the time I got back to the Arch my hands were seriously hurting. After a quick shower and warm-up I went with Bob, LB and Mike for a frothy cappuccino and chat and then over to the office to start the wind-down for Christmas.

Sometimes the morning swim can make me a little tired, but most days, like today, it readies me for the day ahead and makes me feel I could take on the world. For those willing to bear a little pain, I wholeheartedly recommend it!

Day 151 - 21ˢᵗ December 2010

This morning I swam out rather than along, going out beyond the Brighton Pier sign. There was a slightly weird feel in the air. Floating out in the sea it felt almost atmospheric, like something was about to happen - it's hard to describe. The sky was quite grey and what looked like snow clouds were on the horizon, although no snow is forecasted. It was very still, although there were large swells at the shore. Apparently there is some very large movement way out in the Channel, so perhaps some surfing waves are heading into shore for tomorrow?

They reckon at the Arch that this December is the coldest in the sea for many decades, perhaps on record. Typical that my first winter in the sea is like a scene from *The Day After Tomorrow*!

Day 153 - 23ʳᵈ December 2010

Coldest ever swim so far for me - a chilling 3.5 degrees in the sea and -1 in the air.

Being 23ʳᵈ December there were Christmas spirits at the Arch, with homemade flapjack and mince pies for everyone, both of which went down well after the swim. It was also great to see Fiona back with us as I haven't seen her for about a month.

The sea was once again very calm, although it was also a low tide, which meant a painful long walk out to get to swimming depth and by the time you reached it you were cold enough to go straight back in. I swam for about seven minutes, but that was enough. Today was so cold that my left wrist really ached - I broke this wrist about 15 years ago and it never mended (that was how I found out I had osteoporosis), and whilst it never gives me any real problems, the cold clearly got into it today. Apparently back in 1999 the temperature in the sea got as low as 1.9 degrees! I can't even imagine that.

Day 154 - 24ᵗʰ December 2010

My last swim before Christmas, although I expect to be swimming on Boxing Day. I have been humming and haa-ing about tomorrow, especially as my morning friends will be there at 8a.m. (before the once-a-year swimmers at 11a.m.), but Sharon feels it wouldn't be fair to our kiddies to drag them to the beach in the cold when all they will want to do is see what Santa has brought them. I guess considering they are still so young she is quite right, and there is no way I am going to leave them on Christmas morning.

The sea today was around 3.5 degrees or a little lower, with a chill wind blowing from the west, and this made it feel bone-chilling. As it was Christmas Eve I thought I'd make the extra effort and swam out past the middle of the pier, around the buoy (which is about two-thirds out) and then back in.

I guess we were out for about 14 minutes and by the time I got back my hands and feet were really hurting. I really should get some gloves like the others have, because they didn't look in anywhere as much pain as I was in. I know it all sounds a bit mad and begs the question why, but the feeling of accomplishment, along with the incredible scenery at that time of the morning and the comradeship at the Arch makes the whole thing more than worthwhile.

Now I'm nearing the end of this year it's really interesting to look back over my diary from that first day back in April to now and to see how far I've come and all the new friends I've made along the way. I truly believe some maybe friends for life. It won't be long before my Channel swim is upon me, which is quite daunting, but for now I'll sit back over Christmas, raise a large Scotch to my dad up there and just enjoy my accomplishments so far.

Day 155 – 27ᵗʰ December 2010

Christmas is over and the New Year blues are starting to set in already. I love Christmas, always have, but I've always disliked New Year. I find the whole looking back and planning resolutions to be most frustrating and time wasting. When Christmas Day is done I want to get on with life, get back to work and see what the next twelve months bring. I certainly don't want to be reflecting on the past or planning the future.

Having skipped swimming on Christmas Day I also ended up skipping it

Boxing Day, although I felt bad about that. The three kiddies jumped in our bed at about 6.30a.m. and cuddled up to us, with Jesse clinging to my neck and not letting go. Funny how missing swimming when I have it pre-planned brings on the guilts but snuggling with Jesse is a treat not to be missed.

This morning, however, which is a bank holiday, I was very ready to get back to the beach and into the sea. Even the pain of the cold isn't putting me off; in fact it may be that the feeling of extreme cold has become the drug and is making me miss it! This morning at 8a.m. I was at the Arch wondering if I was going to swim alone when the door swung open and in came Little Bob, soon followed by three others. Gotta love this place, nothing keeps us away. It was a tad easier than Christmas Eve in terms of coldness but the swim itself was a case of wave after wave hitting you plus a strong tidal pull to the west, so not really much swimming going on. I'm not sure how long we stayed out there, but I would hazard a guess at 5 to 6 minutes - certainly not long enough.

Having got home I found the kids up and running about and being extremely annoying. To say they received too many presents for Christmas is an understatement! Tomorrow I plan to stay in the water for longer - in fact, all day would be good! And bring on Wednesday and a return to work. Having got through Christmas with relative ease I am now finding myself becoming a New Year grump - not good! A long swim followed by a large whisky will do the job. I'll be nicer tomorrow, I promise.

Day 157 - 29th December 2010

Back to work at last, although isn't it funny how one is desperate to get back to work after a few days at home with the kids and now that day is here all I want to do is be at home with the kids again.

I was at the Arch at 7.30a.m., barely able to find the door due to the fog and misty rain, but there it was as solid and foreboding as ever. The air temperature had risen to a whopping 8 degrees but the sea itself felt colder to me today although the thermometer showed a slight increase. There was very little movement in the sea, either from the tide or the swimmers, and apart from a few waves at shore it was fairly still. Also, and at last, the tide was in, so a nice, quick entry instead of a painful walk out. I swam once again to the end of the pier sign and then headed back in. Part way back I heard a loud growl and gurgle, my heart skipped about four beats and I found myself swimming to shore at speed! I stood shivering on the pebbles with my heart racing like a Formula One car. Of course in reality I'd heard nothing and anyway in this temperature the only fish around would be the size of a half-eaten cocktail sausage, so it was clearly my mind playing tricks. Sometimes when you are out in the ocean on your own (and tired from too much festive feeding), your mind plays nasty tricks and takes you to the land of make-believe. You end up imagining all sorts of scary things are hovering under you in the darkness of the sea and before you know it you are hearing non-existent sounds and believing you are swimming over huge sea monsters and about to be dragged into some black hole. Then all of a sudden your hands hit the pebbles and sand and you realise you are all alone and the sea is nothing but a large cold bath. Your heart however takes a while to settle back down and as you are sitting at work typing this out you start to feel a tad foolish - believe me I do! I guess at least I got to start the day with an adrenalin boost!

Day 158 – 30ᵗʰ December 2010

Another 'weather' day much like yesterday: fog, mist, light rain, just as one loves and expects in the winter! I had a bit of a rush on this morning as it was a disturbed night and it made me oversleep, something I never ever do. Asher called us at about 1a.m. as he had wet the bed (something he has been doing on and off for a while now), so it was a change of sheets, change of PJs and then a short negotiation about him staying in his room or sleeping in ours. Of course, he won and we had the pleasure of Mr SnoreALot next to us for the rest of the night. Then at 3a.m. the door opens and in comes Jesse, straight over to me, jumping onto the bed and spending the next two hours wriggling and worming all over me until I am almost on the floor. I took him back to bed at 5a.m (luckily Mia slept through all this) and at last returned to mine with Asher still snoring like a gruffalo, so when I next awoke it was a very late 7.20a.m! This meant a mad dash, a quick dress, a jump into the car, a rush to the Arch and in the sea by 7.40a.m. Not bad, eh?

The sea itself was fairly calm with just a few large waves at the shore. One charmingly grabbed me and turned me over as I was coming back out. I only spent about six to seven minutes in the sea this morning but it was long enough to wake me up. Tomorrow is New Year's Eve, so soon it'll be back to the start of another year and the start of some very hard physical training for me. I am ready for it now, though.

As for the rest of today, it'll be a sad one. A very dear old friend lost his father over Christmas. He was a similar age to my father when I lost him four years ago, at the same time of year. Today is the funeral, which will be very sad for his family but also no doubt bring back some tough memories for me. I guess this is what life is all about: learning to deal with loss and being able to understand that life has to carry on regardless and we simply have to learn to remember and focus on all the good stuff that we shared and not focus on the sadness of our loss. All that aside I still miss Dad desperately today.

Day 159 - New Year's Eve 2010
New Year's Eve and my last swim of 2010. From my standing start as a non-swimmer back in April I have now swum on 159 days, have covered who knows how many miles, have swum in various conditions ranging from calm as a cucumber to raging torrents and from a scorching 20 degrees to a freezing 3.5 degrees. I have spent hours in the sea and probably a lot more hours in the pool, I have spent numerous hours running to the gym and numerous hours running away from food. I have made so many new friends and experienced so many new emotions. I have had what can only be described as a life-changing year! I wonder how next year will top this, but then I think about the actual swimming of the Channel and that certainly ups the game!

Today was a much nicer start as there was no fog, no wind and no rain; simply a cold but bright morning. I was at the Arch and in the water by

7.30a.m. and swam to my usual pier sign and back. The lovely Fiona turned up just as I was emerging James Bond like from the ocean (I wish). Being Fiona, she went out to the silver ball and back but I think even she found that tough because when she came back in she did look a little shaky. In these temperatures you really have to be so careful because you can jump in and get swimming, feeling all up-for-it and strong, but within a couple of minutes the cold can take over and you find your energy is sapped within seconds and your body is starting to slow right down. All of a sudden you can turn to shore and realise you are a few hundred metres out and completely wasted, but somehow you have got to get in even faster than usual as every second out there drains you further. That aside, the effects you feel after-wards when you are back in the Arch is incredible, like you've conquered the unconquerable. Today, despite the cold and the pain in my hands and feet, I absolutely loved every second of the swim. I came out of the sea all buzzed up and if my feet had allowed I would have skipped up the pebbles.

Tonight the Starr family are heading to Bristol to stay with our friends Nick and Karina for New Year, hence no New Year day swim for me, but on Sunday morning, 2nd January, I will be firmly back in the sea and it's full-on thereafter.

Day 160 - 3rd January 2011

My first sea swim of the New Year and very fine it was. Today is the last bank holiday of the holidays (at last), so it was an 8a.m. swim rather than the usual early 7a.m. start. The sky was clear, the sea was calm and the tide was just turning, so it was neither shallow or deep to get in, all very easy. The air temperature was 1 degree and the sea was 5.3 degrees - as confirmed by my fantastic Christmas watch from Sharon - loving my watch!

Yesterday my little Jesse was sick, so I spent the day looking after him whilst Sharon took Asher and Mia out. I find it tough staying in the house all day as I am a fresh air person by nature, so at 7p.m. after all the kids were in bed I popped on my running shoes and did a 10km run in exactly 48 minutes and 32 seconds. Considering it was dark, cold, at least 40% up hills and I hadn't run for about eight weeks, that was a decent time.

I am now officially back in training mode and the run up to my Channel swim has now officially started. I am no longer swimming the Channel next year, I am officially swimming it this year.

Day 160 – 5th January 2011

Back to the pool after too long a break. It was really daunting this morning getting up and heading to the pool rather than the beach. It's been so long since I did a long pool swim that I seriously doubted if I could do it.

I got up at 6a.m., having had a restless night. Jesse popped in to see me at about 1a.m. and I took him back to his room about two hours later, leaving me wide awake until 6a.m. when I got up. After I was dressed (10 minutes is all it takes me these days as I shower later) I hit the kitchen to make up my swimming feeds (water with Maxim and a banana), jumped into the car and headed to the pool. I ate a banana on the way, which I was rather proud of myself for doing (it's the little things that count). I got to Falmer dead on 6.30a.m., just as they were turning on the lights, and was in the pool and doing my first length at 6.40a.m. The first hour was really tough, I just couldn't get my rhythm right, but I plodded on. The second hour was a little better but I still swam like a crab rather than a fish, very annoying! The third hour saw the magic return and I swam really easily and smoothly. I had the lane to myself for virtually the whole three hours with just the occasional person joining me for the odd 10 minutes.

After my swim I headed straight up to London for a meeting and I can really feel the tiredness now setting in. It's been a good few weeks since I felt the exercise tiredness and it's quite a nice feeling. However as soon as I've done a few more pool swims that should settle back to normal. It's probably a combination of yesterday and today, which was a morning sea swim, 10km run, a 45-minute gym and then a 3-hour pool swim today. The other annoyance is that my breathing is a little painful again today, which I always get after a long pool swim, but the sea will sort that out in the morning I'm sure. Apart from that, all is good in the world.

Day 161 – 6th January 2011

One thing I forgot about pool swimming was the immediate cold, stuffed nose and bad throat I get. I have been sea swimming only for the last six weeks and even in 3.5 degrees and snow I have not had even the slightest of colds. I've done one 3-hour pool swim and here I am with a bad throat and a 100% blocked nose. I'll have to get a nose clip for next week as that might help but ultimately there must be some kind of supplement or homeopathic remedy that I can take that will lessen or stop the effects of the chemicals, otherwise I will be feeling like this all through the winter until the sea warms up enough for long swims.

Despite this problem, I hit the pool again this morning; silly I know, but silly I can be and a morning pool swim for an hour was better than a pitch black, solo, 10-minutes sea swim in the pouring rain.

This has certainly not helped my blocked nose but at least it was safer and did mean an actual swim took place. Tomorrow I am most definitely back in the sea. I need the cold, the waves and the darkness as it seems so much better for me than the warm, light and friendly pool – now that is odd.

Day 163 – 10th January 2011

An interesting and warmer sea this morning. I stayed out for about 12 minutes, which was a lot more than I have been able to, but because I stayed in longer it meant I took longer to warm up afterwards; I've got to remember that. Can't wait until it gets to 15 degrees again!

Sad news over the weekend. A 52-year-old man followed his dogs into the sea by the pier (on our beach) after they ran away from him. One of the dogs made it back fine, but the other dog and the man did not. The coastguard couldn't get to him in time and the cold temperature and strong tide were too much for him. You hear this all the time how someone tries to rescue their pet and ends up losing their own lives. The fact it was on our beach brings back to me how dangerous the sea can be. As I now have so many hours in the sea in varying conditions and temperatures I feel I have the experience to judge the safety levels and when we should and should not go in. Less experienced people don't have this and it can instantly become deadly. Incredibly sad for his family and for the whole city that this should happen.

Day 164 - 11th January 2011

For breakfast I tried something new, Beach Crunch. It consists of a mouthful of pebbles mixed lightly with sand and topped of with water that is heavily laden with salt plus a sprinkle of brown, god knows what over the top. Yummy, yummy, good for the tummy!

By the time I was at the Arch, 7.05a.m., it was still dark but the rain had stopped and the wind was blowing. Little Bob and Mike were heading back in just as Big Bob, Fiona, Martina and I were heading down. Lots and lots of waves in succession made actual swimming a challenge. It was more a case of constantly diving under the waves, riding high on them or being splattered by them. We stayed in for about 10 minutes and then headed to shore. Coming out the sea was the challenge today as the pull from the receding waves was very strong. You had to almost let it pull you backwards and then ride the subsequent wave back in as much as you could, kind of like two steps back and three forward, until you hit the beach. Fiona and I did hit the beach, literally face down. The fact that it was warmer today in the sea and the air made it much more pleasurable and the waves actually made it a lot of fun.

Tomorrow I'm in the pool for a three or four hour swim and then in the gym in the evening, so playing today was allowed!

The healing power of the sea is an amazing thing - not just physically but mentally... in fact, mentally more than anything.

Day 165- 12th January 2011

Yesterday I had a 6-hour meeting as part of a due diligence for a large deal I am doing at work. The only thing I can liken it to is the interview stages in *The Apprentice*, but about six times longer, five times more intense and four times more intrusive. I came out of the meeting feeling battered, bruised and tired, although I was told that the meeting went well; go figure! This morning I was planning on a long pool swim but after yesterday there was no way I could endure a mental test like that, I was simply too brain battered. Instead I headed to the beach for 7a.m. We all stood on the shore wondering about the sanity of getting in. The waves were very strong and had come from way out and were breaking onto the beach in all the wrong places. Big Bob and I ventured in up to our knees but with a huge wave coming I backed away quickly and saw Bob get taken down and washed past me back onto the beach. At this point we all decided 'I don't think so'. Instead, hardened as we are and desperate not to miss out on our morning swim, we headed over to the other beach on the east side of the pier where the waves were not as big and in we all went. It was still very rough and the waves were very tall but their strength was dampened by the pier, and we all felt it was safe enough. Bob and I stayed in for probably around ten minutes before heading back to the Arch and by that time I was feeling back to my old self. The healing power of the sea on the mind, in all its glory.

Day 166 – 13th January 2011

So what did the 13th January, 2011 bring? Well, for starters it brought back the pilchards! It was simply too dark and dangerous to solo swim, so a big group of us eventually headed to the beach. The waves were constant and full of water. I know that sounds silly but sometimes the waves are big but shallow in strength. Today they were big and very full, which meant huge walls of water crashing onto the beach. A few times we edged in and out, but ultimately we all wanted to come out alive, so it meant we stayed at the shore and just got pelted and pounded there instead.

Little Bob, being 'head pilchard' at the Arch, was the first to lie down and was soon followed by the others. Personally I didn't feel pilchard-y today, so I only joined them when the waves took my legs out. By the time we got back to the Arch we were carrying about three tons of stones in our shoes and swimming trunks, and were sporting a thousand little bruises where the stones had been pummelled into us. It was probably the best exfoliation any of us has experienced.

Last night at the gym I twisted oddly when I was doing some lunges and ended up with a strain in my hip flexor (who knew I even had one!). It's a muscle near the hip that is connected to a rather large band and it meant I could only walk on it after much stretching, and even then it was painful. Walking down the beach today it was really painful but the pounding waves and cold temperature (5.7 degrees, so getting better) seemed to help a lot. It still hurts, but a lot less. Once again the sea, in all its glory, is a good cure for pains and aches. I think a trip to Kim, my physioterrorist, is on the cards!

Day 167 – 14th January 2011

Another pilchard day, unfortunately. The sea was once again crazy and strong, but two of us swam and there was just the odd high-rise wave to climb over. Getting back in took some serious concentration and planning, as the waves hitting the shore were monstrous. Hopefully next week the sea will be a little gentler and let us have a swim as the temperature, whilst still cold, hit 6.1 degrees. At this temperature I reckon we could easily do a 15-minute swim.

After my swim (or non swim) yesterday I went to Varndean School along with my brother-in-law Darren to present certificates to our first full CHOCS children. CHOCS (Children Helping Other Children Smile) is our schools project and through it, Varndean schoolchildren have raised over £2,500 for CCHF All About Kids, which is one of our charities. I am so very, very proud of them all. The next CHOCS year has now started at Varndean with the new Year 10 children and we are proud to have the Grand Hotel Brighton partnering us with it, who are being absolute stars.

Last night we held our first Network Club 21 event for the Starr Trust, at the Lansdowne Place Hotel in Brighton. It was attended by more than forty people – a mix of the twenty-one charities we're supporting and some of our business supporters. It was exciting to see so many people getting to know each other and talking about their experiences. We officially launched the twenty-one charity list and played our promotional video. The total raised

towards our £100,000 target is just hitting £20,000, which is a great start
– but still a long way to go!

Day 168 – 17ᵗʰ January 2011
Bit of a busy day today; 7a.m. sea, 8a.m. physio, 9a.m. pool, 11a.m. office
for first meeting... Then office work until 7.30p.m., home to see the kids go
to bed, and then start packing up house for the move back to our almost
finished house in a couple of weeks. It's enough to make one feel tired just
writing it down!

The sea swim this morning was a little uncomfortable. As I had to see
Kim, I decided to go straight in on my own. It was very dark still and the
rain was teeming down. Getting in was fine, I swam out near the silver ball
and then headed back. The temperature was 6.4 degrees, and the waves,
whilst not massive, were still strong and were turning at the dip in the beach,
which means you have to time it right not to be dumped in the dip and then
sucked back out to sea. (This is exactly why the earlier boys, and then the
ones after me, all went to the girlie beach, as there is no dip there.) What
compounded the situation was that it was too dark and rainy to really see
the waves or the beach, and my flipping goggles kept steaming up. The only
way I could do it was to be brave and swim in, keeping a constant lookout
over my shoulder for the waves. I caught a wall of water as I was heading
in and went for it, but as expected I landed in the dip just as the wave
withdrew and another one appeared. Within seconds I was upside down
and being swooshed around on the bottom. Luckily I was close enough
to shore to push up from the bottom and then stand, albeit on shaky legs.
Then I quickly climbed out the dip and ran onto the beach. Walking up to
the Arch I was a little light-headed and also annoyed at myself for being so
silly and not taking notice of what the others did. Lessons, lessons, lessons!

After my swim I visited Kim for my physio, just half an hour on my hip
flexor. As usual she was a star and the pain is now completely gone. Then
I hit the pool at Falmer and did a quick hour of lengths. Now I'm at work,
coffee in hand, and ready to face the day of meetings that now await me!

Day 170 - 19th January 2011

Having exhausted itself from a week of storms the sea finally decided to give itself and us a break. The air temperature had plummeted overnight, which meant a thick frost on the ground and a temperature of around 2 degrees. The sea, whilst finally calm, had also dropped quite dramatically from a high at the beginning of the week of around 6.4 degrees to a much colder 4.9 degrees this morning. Despite this, and despite tough training sessions yesterday, I joined Big Bob for a 12-minute swim, the longest sea swim I've done in months. It did take a lot longer than usual to get my hands and feet pain free but a nice cappuccino in the Red Roaster after the swim certainly helped it along.

As for yesterday, apart from the gym session with Ross, which was about 50% harder than usual as he has really upped what I'm doing, I also went back to Falmer for an evening swim with Fiona and Big Bob. This was a first for us all and something we will now try to do regularly. We did just over an hour on speed training – freestyle, breaststroke, legs, butterfly – back and forth back and forth, 100 metres, 200 metres, three sets of 50 metres and repeat! It was a lot of hard work, especially after a long day but somehow getting back to exercise at that time of night really does wake you up and make you feel like the day earlier didn't even happen. After our session we headed to the outside pool and did a few lengths to cool down; being outside in the pool at 10.30p.m. was fantastic, absolutely loved it. Then it was a quick drink in the bar and home for 11.15p.m. and in bed for a couple of hours before Jesse did his usual 2a.m. visit! All that aside, getting up this morning for the sea was not a problem and really did the job.

Day 171 - 21st January 2011

Yesterday I had to stay overnight in London due to an early meeting, so no sea swim. I did manage to drop into Falmer on the way back and did a ninety-minute pool swim but the pool was full of very slow people wanting to win the 'how slow can I go' competition that must have been advertised somewhere!

This morning I was back to the Arch for my usual 7a.m. The air temperature was still low at around 2 degrees and the sea itself was startlingly low at just 4.8 degrees but there were hardly any waves in sight. Big Bob and I swam the same route as Wednesday, although we extended the swim further along the next beach, which resulted in us being out for just over 16 minutes. Considering the temperature, that is quite remarkable. I am not sure we couldn't have kept going and hit the 20-minute mark; maybe Monday?

Tomorrow I have a 6.30a.m. pick-up at the Arch for a trip to Tooting Bec Lido in London. There are about fourteen of us going from Brighton to compete in the Cold Water Swimming Championships – ouch! Apparently the water is only 1 degree – the coldest ever for me and almost freezing – and they have to break the ice to use the pool! I'm in just one relay race, whilst Big Bob, Fiona and some others are also doing personal endurance races; one relay is enough for me!

Day 172 – Saturday 22nd January 2011

UK International Cold Water Championships at Tooting Bec Lido, London.

Today was the day I had been both dreading and looking forward to. The temperature over the years has ranged from under freezing to over 5 degrees, so we had no idea what to expect. We arrived at around 7.30a.m. and collected our passes, instructions and swim hats. Between us we were competing in relays, solos and endurance races and we did OK. The London Swimming Club did extremely well on the day, maybe because there were thirteen of us and 130 of them! Next year we should hold it in the sea at Brighton and find out how well they fare when you can't put your feet down. The gauntlet is well and truly laid!

The day itself was very long as between races we were standing around outside and it was bloomin' cold. I felt warmer after my swim than I had all day. With competitors from around the world, some sporting very interesting head-dresses and bathing costumes, it made a tiring day a lot of fun and a great experience. I like the social side of BSC, such an eclectic bunch that it is always enjoyable.

Tooting Bec Lido today, the Channel next and the Olympics after that? Never say never!

Day 173 - Monday 24th January 2011

The day started dry, the sea was very calm and the tide was so low that it was a few metres before we could get under. Big Bob and I swam all the way out to the helter skelter, the farthest out we have swum since the summer faded away. The water temperature was still a shocking 4.5 degrees, so going out that far is not to be scoffed at. Coming back I did wonder how soon it would be before I could put my feet down. After about 10 minutes my arms were feeling heavy and my breathing was starting to labour and my chest starting to tighten but 4 minutes later we standing firmly on the sand and walking back in. A really decent swim in very cold water really does set me up for the day and doing it with my buddy Bob makes it all the more fun.

Back at the office at 8.05a.m., late for my meeting, I ended up sitting in my old jumper, woolly hat and gloves although luckily my brain was warm and firing on all cylinders. I guess it made my visitors think insurance broking is not such a dull thing after all!

One bit of great news on the fundraising front is that the Brighton Sea Life Centre is sponsoring me - as long as I swim in their pool with their sharks! Sounds like fun, as long as they've eaten first. The swim is on 11th May 2011, which happens to be my forty-second birthday, and people can pay whatever they want to secure a part of my body if the sharks pull me apart. With this in mind a good friend (and one of my biggest clients) has sponsored £5,000 although he has not yet chosen which part he wants! I'm not sure any part is big enough to warrant such an incredible donation but I guess that's a question only my wife is allowed to answer...

Day 174 - Monday 25th January 2011

Mia came into our room at about 1a.m., bringing with her a handful of dolls and an endless rasping cough. Asher followed, which meant Sharon ended up on the floor on Asher's mattress and I ended up in Mia's bed next to

Jesse. Basically only the kids got any sleep. A pattern is forming – I'm not quite sure how we break it.

Even so, I was at the beach and in the Arch by 7.10a.m., feeling somewhat subdued, then in the sea with Bob five minutes later. The air temp was around 5 degrees, but the sea had dropped to just 4.4 degrees. Despite this Bob and I stayed out for a whopping 19 minutes 22 seconds. Bob is pushing me now on my training and therefore decided that we would do speed training, so we swam 8 x 25 metre dashes from his towel on the beach to the groyne and back, with fifteen second rests in between. If this had been in the pool it would have been relatively easy, but at 4.4 degrees and first thing in the morning in a moving sea it was a decent challenge. Coming out I warmed up quickly enough apart from my hands, which really hurt for about half an hour. Despite the pain, hopefully we will do it again tomorrow; no pain no gain and all that!

Last night I did a fab gym session with Ross but that is all I can fit in this week. It's a busy week; yesterday was sea, work, gym and physio, today is sea, London meetings then packing tonight. Tomorrow is sea then meetings till 2p.m., then drive to Cardiff for a meeting and stay over. Thursday is more Cardiff meetings, then a 3-hour pool swim, then drive home for last-minute packing and then Friday we are moving from the rented house back to our beautiful, newly-built family home. How exciting – and buseeey.

Day 175 – 26ᵗʰ January 2011
Miracle of miracles we only had one child visitation last night! Jesse came in at 1a.m. and I took him back to his room at 1.20 and that was that. It was a real treat to wake up in my own bed with just Sharon. I felt refreshed and ready for my morning fix of a little BSC and saltwater.

There was no low tide so we had to swim from the shore and back to the shore knowing we couldn't pop our feet down if we needed to. This makes it a much harder physiological swim because once the cold starts to bite and your arms start to feel heavy and your breathing becomes laboured you look up and see that the shore is still way off and your head and heart start to react. I was back to the silver ball when my heart started to race and it took about a minute of slow, steady swimming and breathing to get my head back to a sensible place (basically understanding that I can get back in without a problem) until my heartbeat slowed to its normal rhythm and I could swim back to shore and start enjoying the experience. Sea swimming, particularly in cold water, is so much to do with mind control. This is what Fiona has said to me so many times and she is spot on. The sea temperature was 4.6 degrees, so still extremely cold, and apparently another cold front is on its way so we may see a dip in the temperature again.

When I was back in the Arch, David, our old warrior of the sea, remarked that someone had told him that I am still not eating before my swims and he was not pleased to hear this. He is absolutely right and again it highlights that despite my best intentions I am still not stepping up to the mark with my eating. He said they are counting on me making this Channel swim and I needed to start taking my eating seriously. I am still a new boy in the BSC and it was really nice to hear that they are rooting for me. It makes me feel I am becoming accepted as one of theirs at last. How nice to belong.

Day 176 & 177 - 31st January 2011

Last week I could only sea-swim Monday to Wednesday as I was so busy with work and our house move. My poor wife had to deal with the removal people all on her own, so the least I could do was get home late Friday morning and start unpacking. We farmed the kiddies off to our parents from Friday until Sunday night and then spent every second unpacking and getting the house in order. To say moving house is stressful is an understatement; what I would say though is that from an exercise point of view spending nearly three days and nights unpacking boxes over four floors is almost Olympian.

I certainly did not want to get up this morning as being in my new bed in my new room in my new house was just too comfortable. The fact that the three kids also slept all the way through was a fantastic bonus. But up I got and was down the beach by 7a.m. and ready (not) to swim. The air temperature had dropped to a silly 1 degree and the sea was stupid cold again. My watch said it was only 3.4 degrees. The swim, once I got into it, was fine but boy did it hurt. Once in the shower my hands really ached from the severe cold followed by the hot water - it's something I can't get used to no matter how many times I do it. Will it stop me tomorrow? Course not!

I also had a very hard gym session with Ross, once again stepping up the weights and reps on every exercise. My arms , shoulders, back, legs, in fact everything, feels like it's been given a bashing but aching from exercise is a great feeling - I challenge anyone to say otherwise!

On the fundraising front I have another piece of great news. One of my clients, a fantastic company called Execution, has pledged £10,000 in sponsorship for my swim. I feel blown away by their generosity, it's a whopping 10% of our total goal. We are really forging ahead now.

Day 178 – 1st February 2011

Today was a mad day in London with a 4-hour meeting followed by a dash across town to another meeting, hence no time for my morning sea swim. However, at 8.30p.m. I met Big Bob at Falmer and we did a really decent 60-minute power swim.

Afterwards we met Fiona in the coffee shop and yet another lecture began! As usual she was spot on with her points and there is no way I can possibly argue with a lady who not only is a fantastic swimmer, but also a successful Channel swimmer (and there are not many of those in the world). Her point was that I now have less than a whole season to train before my July swim and unless I start racking up the pool hours my body simply won't be able to deal with the endurance of the Channel. There are two issues with a swim of this nature: the mental endurance and the physical. While I get nervous and worried about the swim, ultimately I know that mentally I can do it but on the physical side, unless I can get my muscles used to long distance swimming I will end up tearing them in the first few hours and then it could be game over. Hence the importance of relentless pool swimming until such times as the sea temperature rises to at least 11 degrees (which will probably be May time). The other physical area is of course my eating, or lack of it. I need to eat within 20 minutes of finishing my swim, no matter the time of day or night, otherwise I am not feeding my muscles or putting back the calories I have used up, which can be as many as 1,000 an hour. It really is time for me to get a grip. I mean, how hard is it to eat a chicken sandwich and a tub of Ben & Jerry's ice cream? Most people would think they'd gone to heaven!

The other thing Fiona said was that the morning sea swimming at this stage is not helping me. The extreme cold is putting a strain on my muscles and I am far better having an hour in the pool than twenty minutes in the sea. The problem is that at heart I am now a sea swimmer and the thought of not doing this is upsetting in the extreme. So I think a balance is needed, where perhaps I limit my morning sea swims to just twice a week and have pool swims three to four times a week. Regarding eating, though, great intentions aside, my Crohn's may have other ideas as to what is and isn't acceptable.

Anyhow, I am now stepping up to the mark and tomorrow will be doing a 3-hour pool swim before work and two power swims and one distance swim every week, with just two sea swims to complement them and keep my head in order. The super-serious issue I need to address however is the chest pain I get after each pool swim. It is definitely to do with the chemicals used in the pool, which sit above the water and are breathed in. Whenever I do a pool swim I end up with a terrible cold in my nose but way worse is the pain in my chest; it feels as if the tops of my lungs have been burnt. This is the real reason I have been avoiding the pool. I have therefore decided that on Thursday I will use the outside pool only because being outside means the chemicals float away and are not breathed in. I am hoping this will enable me to swim without damage being caused (last night I was in pain all evening with it). Being outside it's only 20 metres rather than 25 metres and also it's a lot colder but I am a sea swimmer and it is nowhere near as cold as that. If that doesn't do the job I will have to find a different pool but that will be prohibitively expensive and a real nuisance!

Day 179 - 2nd February 2011

As I was in the pool last night and am in again tomorrow, I did a short sea swim this morning. My chest was hurting so much from yesterday that I needed the fresh sea air to clear it and make me feel better. Like the miracle it is, the sea air worked its magic and after a short swim my chest and nasal passages were clear. I even went in with bare feet today.

Day 180 - 3rd February 2011

A pool day. I changed routine; instead of getting up and dashing to the pool, I got up nice and slowly, helped get the kiddies get dressed, had some cereal (oh yes I did) and then pootled off to the office and was at my desk working by 7.45a.m., all nice and calm. Then at 11a.m. I headed to Falmer and did a four-hour swim in the outside pool, then had the biggest chicken sandwich and chips on the menu - it's all true, I have had two meals already today!

Swimming in the outside pool was certainly colder but I had a lane all to myself the whole time. So far I don't feel congested and my chest isn't hurting. Fingers crossed the pain stays away, then I know I can do long pool swims and stay healthy.

Tomorrow night, excitingly, the National Association of Estate Agents are having their annual ball at the Grand Hotel. Why is that exciting? They have chosen the Starr Trust as their charity of the year, which could mean thousands towards our fundraising efforts.

Day 181 - 4th February 2011

My 1-hour swim in the indoor pool on Tuesday left me with a stuffed-up nose and bad burning chest pains all night, yet a 4-hour swim yesterday in the outside pool left me with a clear nose and a pain-free chest. So outside pool it is and no reason now to be afraid of a long pool swim. That's my first bit of good news for the day. The second bit of good news was that for the second night running all three children slept in their own beds and didn't come into us until around 6.45a.m.

This morning I got to the Arch at 7a.m., blown all the way from the car to the sea by a strong gale. The sea was kicking up a huge storm with waves everywhere and it was a very low tide, which made it impossible to swim, so it was just a case of having a play. It was like running on a treadmill at full pace on the highest climb, brilliant cardio training! The sea was an incredible 6.4 degrees, a massive jump up from Wednesday.

Day 183 - Tuesday 7th February 2011
Usually Tuesday is a sea swim in the morning and then an evening swim, but today Bob joined me at 6.30a.m. for an early morning pool swim - and very nice it was, too.

The air temperature was 0 degrees and my windscreen was totally iced up when I left home. Bob and I were in the outside pool by 6.40am but even though the air temp was freezing, the pool was around 18 degrees and we did a very good, 90-minute non-stop swim. There were maybe six hardened swimmers in the pool at one point but Bob and I saw them all off! We got into the pool in the dark and were swimming as the sun rose and the sky went from black to blue - a seriously nice way to start the day. Coming out of the pool and holding onto the stepladder it was funny to feel thick ice coating it!

Excitingly I will be 'swimming' tonight, in the home gym I finished setting up on Saturday, on my Vasa Ergometer, which I bought four months ago. It is a very cool piece of equipment that you can only buy in the USA - basically, a swim bench built specifically for improving endurance and increasing power and speed. So tonight will be my first official Vasa training experiment. I'm quite excited!

Day 184 - Wednesday 9th February 2011
NEWSFLASH: we were stars for the morning! I got to the Arch at 7.15a.m. and found it busier than it has been for months with around ten chaps and five women present. The BBC were there, and they filmed us changing in the Arch and walking down the beach a couple of times, then in the sea we all went while one cameraman stayed on the edge and the other came in. Of course they had on full bodysuits whilst we were in our usual 'less is

more' outfits. By the time we headed back up the beach for the final time the cold had really settled in. My feet, which were completely numb, are still painfully uncomfortable.

I'm now sitting in my nice, comfortable office nursing a hot chocolate at 10a.m. and I am still not fully warmed up and my feet are only just starting to return to life. I ate nothing before the swim but as soon as I got to the office I scoffed down two hot crumpets with honey followed by a sugary jam doughnut left over from someone's birthday yesterday – clearly I needed sugar! I will definitely have lunch and dinner today as I am trying hard to up my food intake. Yesterday before my 90-minute pool swim I had two pieces of toast, after the swim I had two crumpets, then for lunch I had a chicken salad and at night, after my gym session, I had gammon, potatoes and cauliflower followed by two yogurts. I can't do much better than that!

No more swimming for me today, although I do intend to use my Vasa trainer again tonight. Last night I managed two, 5-minute sessions, which doesn't sound a lot but was jolly hard work and only my first time. I reckon once I've been using it for a few weeks, even if I just do a few minutes every day, I will soon be up to 30 to 40 minutes at a time. It's a really great resource to have at home!

Day 185 – Thursday 10th February 2011

Long pool swim, so no sea today. I'm at work nursing a cappuccino and contemplating staying here! Of course that won't happen as I am far too dedicated (hmmm)! I'm tired today, which is a mix of working hard, exercising hard and not sleeping enough. Last night I used the gym at home and did a 45-minute run on the treadmill, a 10-minute (split into two 5-minute slots) on the Vasa swimming machine, then some weights and some boxing. It was so fab to be able to do that at home rather than have to go to the gym, which I probably wouldn't have bothered to do last night. The VASA machine is aaaaamazing but bloomin' hard, although I guess after I get used to it I'll be able to do long sessions on it. I can really feel my shoulders working and afterwards I feel great.

Back to today though, the aim is to do a 4-hour swim in the outside pool. Currently it's bleak, dark and wet outside, which does not help my cause! Unfortunately next week I am so busy (London three days, Coventry one day and Windsor one day) that I can't do a long swim, just short morning and evening ones. It's good to take a week off from a long swim as the rest period is as important as the working period but it means that however I feel today there is no way I cannot do it because I can't miss two weeks in a row.

So here I am 4p.m., back in the office. I swam in the outside pool for 3½ hours but the constant heavy rain made it tougher than it needed to be and after all that time being hit on the head by falling waterfalls I decided to finish the swim with half an hour in the inside pool. Coming indoors was like entering a sauna and then getting into the inside pool I felt like pasta going into a boiling pot (of course, never having been a piece of pasta I am making a large assumption here). I truly don't think I could have done four hours in that heat, it was immense! The swim itself, now it's over, was OK and I'm really pleased to have done it but the first two hours were filled with thoughts of how soon I could get out. I wrestled with my brain about staying or going pretty much every 10 minutes, with 10 minutes feeling like an hour, but I stuck with it and by the middle of hour 3 I was determined to finish and with just 15 minutes to go I was ready to keep it up for another hour (but didn't as I had a meeting pending!). All in all, I was proud of myself for beating the mind and getting it done. Afterwards I headed straight for the cafe and had a huge chicken club sandwich and chips and a warming cappuccino. Gotta keep that weight loss at bay - must have used around 3,000 calories at the very least today! No gym tonight as I need to rest, but tomorrow morning a gentle sea swim will be nice.

Day 187 - Monday 14th February 2011
Valentine's Day and a day off from all exercise for me, though not because it's Valentine's. I have two 3-hour swims and one gym session planned for the end of the week and wanted a couple of days break from training for three reasons:

- It has been very constant and my mind needed a couple of days off
- I've had a couple of small twinges in my lower back and feel it is a little sign from my body telling me to take a break. Listening to your body is vital when you are doing extreme training, so I am learning.
- Work – need I say more!

Day 189 – Wednesday 16th February 2011

No swimming again, hugely missing it. I had to leave Brighton at 6a.m. to drive to Coventry for a meeting and then I didn't get home until after 7p.m., by which time I got straight into the kids, books and bed routine. I managed to grab an hour in the gym at home, which included my 10 minutes on the Vasa swimming machine, so all was not lost – in fact from a physical point of view it is tougher doing ten minutes on that than an hour in the pool.

This week was always going to be a tough one for endurance training as I have a frantic work week, this traditionally being one of my busiest months of the year. Although I had planned to rest my body, ready for a harder few weeks ahead, it doesn't stop the guilts setting in.

Day 191 – Friday 18th February 2011

The end of another week and another week nearer to my Channel swim. It's a funny thing because some days the thought of the swim is very scary indeed, almost impossible, then on other days it could be today and I would be up for it. Today is definitely an up-for-it day, for no reason as I can see it, I'm just up for a challenge. I had a 1-hour gym session with Ross and as usual he pushed me hard and used muscles that quite frankly haven't been used much for the last forty-one years. After that I was ready to go home and see the family but the pool called out to me, so I squeezed in an hour in the outside pool, all to myself as usual (hardly surprising at 5p.m. on a Friday). I pushed myself in terms of speed and made sure I used my legs as much as I could, which is not something I usually do. It was interesting actually, because when I thought about it I found my legs were quite happy to kick while my arms whirled. It may not sound that exciting to you, but this is the first time my legs and arms have worked together in the water.

The plan for next week is to do some swims and gyms in the early part of the week and then the back-to-back swim I couldn't fit in this week on Thursday and Friday. Fingers and toes crossed, because I really need to get these done!

Day 193 – Tuesday 22nd February 2011

A nice cold swim to start the day, then I want to tell you about yesterday's journey. Life is all about 'the journey', isn't it?

Yesterday after my morning swim I had two meetings in Brighton and then headed to Gatwick airport and jumped on the Gatwick Express for two afternoon London meetings. I was reading the paper when a very attractive girl in her mid twenties (I had noticed her when I sat down, of course!) got up from her seat further up the carriage, walked over to me and said, in a rather strong Russian accent, 'Do you mind if we talk?' She sat opposite me and waited for my reply. Of course I did what any English gentleman would do: put down my paper, looked up at her, thought about it for a few seconds and then said, 'Sure, what exactly would you like to talk about?'

'Oh,' she replied, 'you're English.'

'What did you expect?' I said.

'I thought you were European. I don't much like the English, to be honest.'

'That's a rather sweeping statement,' I replied. 'Have you met us all already'? I said this with a serious face (but hiding a smirk, because I thought she was pretty balls-y to not only sit with me but to then insult me as well).

'I find the English to be rather boring and never to be risk takers, never talking to anyone or ever doing anything interesting.'

I didn't at this point tell her that perhaps if she had been in the sea with me this morning that she may have seen another side to the 'boring English'. Instead I pointed out that perhaps what she considers boring others may consider exciting and vice versa, and that perhaps she should be more accepting. I suggested she learned to question first, listen and then decide. She thought about that for a few seconds, then threw me a sweet smile that seemed to suggest that perhaps she agreed.

After that the conversation flowed. She asked 'why?' so many times. Why read, why write, why do this or do that. Not in a negative way, just a questioning way. She was maybe 25, has a child, was starting her own shoe business, wanted to end up back in Latvia and was going to study economics in London. She said it's all about the end result and that one had to concentrate on what one wants and that is what life is about, getting to the end result. I disagreed and said it's about the journey, not the result. This took her by surprise. She said her friends all agree on this and what is life about if not the end result?

'Maybe when I was in my mid twenties I thought the same as you,' I said. 'It was all about the goal. Deciding where, what and how and then chasing it and eventually getting it; job done! But as you get older you start to realise that while it's very important to always have the goal in place to give you focus, it is actually the journey that is the important thing, as one never actually reaches the goal.'

'If no-one reaches the goal then why have one?' she said, interrupting me whilst I was in full teacher/student mode.

'Because having a goal gives you direction and that's important, not to everyone maybe but certainly to me - and I would suggest to you. As you get older you realise that the goal changes so many times, sometimes even daily. The important thing is what you learn along the way. Life is all about the journey we take. Sure, someone might reach what they consider to be their goal, their purpose in life, and that is great, but so few of us ever really do. But if it was handed to us on a plate with no journey involved then we have experienced nothing along the way and then perhaps we will realise that this was not the goal after all. That sometimes when we have a dream we can get lost on the way to it and end up finding a better one?'

At this point the train pulled into Victoria, she kissed me on both cheeks, thanked me for listening and said that perhaps she will tell her friends about the journey we have had and the journey of life. As I walked away from her I thought, give it another ten years and she may realise that her goal and the journey are one and the same thing! She liked the fact I listened and I liked the fact she seemed to question; in fact it was a shame the Gatwick Express is an express!

So what on earth has this to do with my Channel swim? It's all about the journey. Chatting to her made me remember what I have always known but so often forget. Sure, I'll swim the Channel, there's no doubt at all that I will start swimming in the UK and will end my swim in France, but that is just the end result, the goal. The important bit, the bit which has changed my life, is the stuff in-between. Since deciding to take this challenge on I have met so many people and made so many friends. I have swum in the sea in 18 degrees and in 3 degrees, I have swum in the sun, in the snow, in the rain, in the light, in the dark, I have seen the sun rise from the sea, seen it set. I have seen fish below me, even been bitten by some. I have been taken 12 feet in the air on large waves then thrown like a rag doll onto the beach and I have swum in the beauty of Durdle Door and the briskness of Tooting Bec Lido. I have met representatives of twenty-one charities who I will be swimming for and I have been interviewed for TV and radio. I have been invited to events to talk and I have gone to events to listen. I could write all day today about my experiences so far, and this is only since April last year. It's all about the journey!

So to my new Latvian friend whose name I never got, thank you for reminding me what life sometimes makes me forget: to enjoy the journey, for that is what life is truly about.

Day 194 - Wednesday 23rd February 2011

A rainy and somewhat gloomy start in terms of the weather, though starting the day in the sea is far from a gloomy start to the day.

Last night I had an hour in the gym with Ross and as ever he upped the game, so I was achy in my shoulders and legs and an easy swim and a lot of floating was in order. The rain was more of a spit and the wind was very low, so although there were waves, they were not a challenge. I swam out just beyond the silver ball and then swam back in and decided to do some floating. It's such a calming thing to do, floating in the sea, that if the temperature wasn't so biting you could stay there all day. It was still under 6 degrees, so staying in for 12 minutes was plenty.

Now I'm all suited and booted and ready to head off to the Gatwick Express. I am sure I will be bitterly disappointed when the train pulls into Victoria and I had been sitting all alone without the company of my Latvian friend. Maybe this time I'll go and talk to someone sitting on their own like she did to me. Then again maybe I'll just be English and read my paper in silence!

Day 195 – Thursday 24th February 2011

Last night I did a power swim with Bob, Fiona and another regular BSC member, Shoichi, at Falmer at 8.30p.m. The swim was very hard work as usual, with Fiona putting us through a rigorous training plan that included speed swimming, endurance swimming, leg work, shoulder work etc. What it does achieve, apart from the obvious physicality, is a regeneration of energy. Physical exercise is definitely the best tonic to regenerate energy levels. Children on the other hand are the best way to use them up again! Having got back home just after 11p.m. I was not best pleased to already see Mia waiting outside our bedroom. What followed through the night was a constant battle between Mia and Jesse and us, with them coming in and us taking them back from about 11p.m. – 5a.m. We need Supernanny, help!

At 7.01a.m. I woke with a sudden start, slung on old clothes and headed to the beach at breakneck speed. My swim instantly woke me up. The air temp was around 8 degrees, the sea was around 6 degrees and the wind almost nothing. If not for the cold it would have been pretty much perfect swimming conditions: a medium-low tide, a few interesting but not dangerous waves and only a very slight pull to the east.

Now back at work and once again tired – how did that happen! No more exercise today or tonight as I need to conserve energy for tomorrow. I am having a day off from work to just swim. The aim is a 6-hour swim, 8a.m.– 2p.m., followed by an hour with Ross in the gym doing stretching etc.

Day 196 – Friday 25th February 2011

Last night was a better night's sleep, which was hugely helpful. Mia came in twice but Sharon took her back both times and then she stayed in her own bed. Jesse didn't come in until 6.30a.m. (bless his heart, he came out of his room carrying his pillow and duvet at 10.30p.m. as we were coming up the stairs, but I took him right back – boy, did I feel like a meanie!). Asher came in about midnight bringing his bed stuff with him and slept on our floor. His snoring was too much for Sharon so she ended up in the spare room and I had our huge bed all to myself. All good for me as it gave me the energy I needed for today's swim.

I got to the pool before 7a.m. and was bitterly disappointed to see signs saying the outside pool was closed. I almost turned back as I didn't know how I would cope with the heat and chemicals in the inside pool but I was there with a plan, so I had to go for it. After about an hour of swimming a lifeguard removed the 'Closed' sign (apparently it was a mistake) and I leapt out and ran straight outdoors and grabbed my own lane outside. By midday (five hours in) I was very cold and getting tired, so I headed for the indoor pool for the final swim but as it is half term it was mobbed with screaming kids and over-active mothers, so I turned straight around and back into the outside pool. At 12.30 the fantastic Ross, my trainer, appeared with a well-needed protein shake, which energised me. When 1p.m. came and I had done my 6 hours, I thought to myself, 'Well, 7 ain't that far away' so in I stayed and 7 hours I did!

This time I broke the entire swim down into 30-minute slots; 30 minutes and then feed, 30 minutes and then feed. This helped enormously. I know it's all in the mind but breaking it down into manageable chunks as against full one hour slots was so much easier to deal with.

The hardest part of the swim was the air temperature as it was only around 5 degrees and that made me cold all the way through but despite that I kept going. As far the mind goes it was OK actually. Of course I thought most of the time, which was not wonderful, but each time my mind took me to negative thoughts (which it kept trying to do), I simply thought of my children, my wife, my mum, my sister, my nephews, my brother-in-laws, my house, my business, my wonderful father and all the things that make me smile, and I chased the negative away. It was the only way to stave off 7 hours of back and forth back and forth, but it worked a treat and it seemed less painful than the usual 4-hour swims I have done.

Afterwards, once dry and warmer, I went into the gym and Ross did 30 minutes of stretching with me, which hopefully will really help come the morning. He's a great guy, very supportive. A great club full of great people.

So there you go, the week is done and I have completed yet another milestone in my training. Now at home with a hot cup of tea and a digestive and ready for a little R&R.

Day 198 – 28th February 2011

The end of February already. Is it me or is life going very quickly?

After my long Friday swim I was pleased that all I had was aching shoulders. The mind took a few hours to switch back to normal but aside from that I was absolutely fine and there was no need to see my physio. On Friday night, rather than an early night and recovery mode, Sharon and I went to Hurstpierpoint for an Indian meal with friends. We ended up having a very relaxed evening and I ate some useful fatty foods. On the advice of Fiona I should then have had a few days off from exercise, but with Sharon out all day on Saturday I had three children to look after, so if one can consider that 'no exercise' then I guess I complied. Sunday I used my gym a little and did a 10-minute slot on my Vasa swimmer, so not a total relax but nothing I would consider 'planned exercise'.

This morning I was at the beach by 7.15 a.m., having had a basically decent sleep as the kiddies all behaved last night. The air temp was 5 degrees, the rain (which was quite heavy) was cold and the sea was a calm 4.9 degrees. Only nine morning sea swimmers in a city of half a million. Big Bob and I swam to the cafe half way along the pier, right up to the pier struts, then turned and swam back past the groyne the other side and back to our beach. It was about 13 minutes but that was plenty as the cold sea was setting into the bones by then.

The rest of this week, apart from my usual plethora of meetings in Brighton and London, will consist of two gym sessions, two home gym sessions, one x 12km run, three sea swims, one x power swim with Bob and Fiona and one x 4-hour pool swim on Friday. Next week I'll do another 7-hour swim, or if time allows a 4-hour swim one day followed by a 5-hour the next.

Day 199 – 1st March 2011

A swim this morning much like yesterday, with the exception that there was no rain, though the temperature in the sea has dropped to just 4.7 degrees. I am no longer able to remember what swimming in a warm sea feels like.

Our debut video promoting the Starr Trust Scholarship fund has been launched. We are raising money through the Swim4Smiles campaign for 21 children's projects, 20 being existing children's charities and the 21st being a scholarship fund for a local child. The video we have made will help us find a child who we are able to help smile. The song in the background, 'Every Child', was written by me and Rob Piatt, my writing partner. It's a cool song even if I do say so myself!

Day 201 – 3rd March 2011

This is how my day started before the swim, and this explains why getting in a freezing sea is actually easier than being a daddy!

I got home from London after a looonnng day at about 8.30p.m., by which time the twins were asleep but Asher was waiting for me to say good night, bless his heart. Within an hour Mia was up and coughing and crying. We settled her by 10p.m. but had no doubt the night would not end there. True to form, all three paid visits! Asher came in about midnight and put his mattress next to our bed and went straight to sleep. Mia turned up at 12.30, went back to bed 12.40, Jesse turned up 12.41, went back to bed 12.45, Mia turned up 12.46 and so on between then until about 2.30a.m., when Mia, poor love, sat in the middle of our bed coughing until she was sick, right in the middle of our bed! At this point Jesse came back in and started crying because his sister was sick and Mia started crying because Jesse was crying, and all the time Asher slept on, snoring his little head off.

The morning, however cold and early, was a welcome release for me.

I was at the Arch by 7a.m., having had to scrape thick ice off my wind-screen. The air temperature was 0 degrees but the wind wasn't too bad. Bob and I swam to the cafe along the pier and then having spotted the sun rising we swam towards it through the pier to the other side, like moths to a light bulb! If the sea has not been a staggering 4.9 degrees I swear we'd have kept swimming until we were right under it! After the swim we headed for the Red Roaster cafe for a welcome cappuccino before heading off to work for yet another day of big business. It took about 2 hours before I felt my toes returning to life – up to then I was walking like a penguin.

Day 203 – 8th March 2011

After work today I plan a gym session at home, then tomorrow I have a 3-hour morning pool swim, followed by a gym session followed by a 90-minute evening pool session with Fiona and Bob. How the weeks just fly by!

This morning I started the day in the pool rather than the sea, as I need to rack up the hours. I did 7a.m.-10a.m. in the outdoor pool at Falmer: 21 degrees in the water (nice!) and 1 degree in the air (bracing). Walking around the pool I slipped twice because the ground was so icy. With a true blue sky and no clouds it was actually a pleasure to be there, although having dashed from the house at speed I forgot to eat anything first; silly when doing a big swim. I did take my bottles of water with Maxim and also a flask of hot tea (first time of trying that), but not having any food inside me made it less comfortable than I would have liked. Even a piece of toast would have helped.

I swam fine for the first hour but after that I was thinking a lot about a nice hot bacon sandwich on brown bread with mustard, which is exactly what I bought myself when driving back to the office at 10.30a.m.

Having now spent the rest of the day beavering away at work I am now dashing off to a meeting, then at the gym at 4p.m. for an hour with Ross, then home to get the kids into bed for 7p.m., then back to Falmer for an hour in the pool with Fiona and Bob on speed trials. Then back home for 11p.m. and the first of the dozen or so visits in the night from the twins. I think two days lying by the pool with a book in the sun would do me the world of good but I can't see it happening any time soon.

Day 204 - 9th March 2011

After my full day of swimming, work and gym I ended up back at Falmer with Bob and Fiona for our power swim. It was particularly tough, especially having already done so much earlier in the day, and the really hard one was a set that included 1 length butterfly, 1 length backstroke, 1 length breaststroke and 1 length crawl, repeated four times in a row. Then it was 200 metres freestyle and then repeat the whole thing. We also did four x 50 metres just kicking with a float, plus a whole load of other speed stuff. I was pleased that I did it all especially the butterfly (or the moth, they way I do it), even if they were a lot faster than me. We used the indoor pool for the entire session as it was completely empty so we had a lane each, plus the temperature was slightly lower than the usual boiling and of course it's a full 25 metres as against the shorter outside pool. This morning, though, my chest was a bit tight and my nose blocked - chemicals once again, arrgggh.

After the session, when we were comfortably in the bar area having a drink, we saw ourselves on TV right after the ITV news. The weather came on and there we were, the three of us doing butterfly into the shore and then walking up the beach. It was only about five seconds long, but it was clearly us. National TV, get us!

This morning, following the usual broken night's sleep, I headed to the beach for what was going to be a very quick swim to unwind the muscles. It was windy and spitting and grey, giving the sea a moody, sensuous look. It was still low tide, which meant we were only ever up to our shoulders and the sea was smothered with waves. In warmer times we would have played for a good hour but it was still cold so we only stayed in for about

12 to 15 minutes. Great fun, though: Bob and I did some butterfly through the waves.

That is now most definitely it with regards exercise for today. I must rest my muscles for fear of tearing them. Tomorrow I'll do a sea swim and an hour at the gym at home and then Friday I'll grab a 3-hour pool swim.

Now, 9.37a.m. and another coffee in hand, it is head down and lots of work to catch up with.

Day 207 - 11th March 2011

This morning when I surfaced at 6a.m. (despite the kids doing their usual) I felt refreshed and looking forward to the day ahead. Just one day off from exercise was a good idea. Due to early meetings I couldn't do the pool today, but I was down the beach at 7a.m. and ready to swim. The sea was 90% calm with waves (some largish) near the shore and the temperature was up to 5.7, which whilst still extremely cold was more welcoming. Bob and I headed to the silver ball, went under the pier, around the other side, back to our side and back to shore. We pretty much stayed together the whole way - in fact, I was in front a lot of the way, with Bob only passing me coming back in. It was a nice change for me to be as quick as him, the Tuesday nights are clearly starting to pay off, but I do love the sea compared to the pool.

This morning I'm presenting Clickcover (my Affinity Insurance business) to two schools and this afternoon I'm in a meeting from midday until around 5ish. After that though I shall be heading home to an empty house (kids all staying at my in-laws tonight). I can't explain how good that feels and I shall have a swim in my endless pool, which is now fixed and working. It'll be great to swim in my pool as a swimmer, as I've never yet done that. I'm not sure from a training perspective how good it will be for me but I do know a number of swimming teachers who advocate them as well as a top Channel swimmer (a record holder) who trained throughout in hers.

Next week I'll make sure I do a 6-or 7-hour pool swim again as I still need to rack a few of those up.

Day 208 – 14ᵗʰ March 2011

After a lovely weekend it was nice to be back to the sea for my Monday morning wake-up.

We were in the sea by about 7.10a.m. and out after about 15 minutes. The temperature was around 5.6 degrees and the sea very calm. For some reason it felt warmer that usual when I got in but felt colder than usual when I got out, and 2 hours later I still have pins and needles in my fingers and am a little shivery.

This week I've got a busy diary at work and also a few training sessions booked in (pool and gym), so no doubt by the weekend I'll be tired again. The weekend just gone was great as we got some much-needed sleep on Friday night when the kids stayed out and we used the pool and steam room for the first time: fantastic! Also on Sunday we visited Chobham Rugby ground because they are supporting our Swim4Smiles campaign. I did a little talk to thank them and then they introduced a fundraiser they are having in April for us. Sharon and the kids came along and they presented the kids with rugby shirts. The boys put theirs in their bags but Mia put hers on straightaway and kept it on until she went to bed that night: gorgeous! They also gave us some fundraising tins they've had in the clubhouse the last few months and there was almost £400 in them. Astonishing! What great people they are to offer us such support. Every day more people surprise me with their generosity of spirit as well as their generosity of pocket. Despite all the bad and sad news in the world, such as the despicable action in Libya at the moment and the tragic conditions in Japan, there still remains an amazing-ness about the world that never fails to ignite both the passion and compassion in people.

Day 209 – 15ᵗʰ March 2011

Started this morning with a sea swim with Bob. The tide was pulling very strongly to the west but swimming against a strong tide is a pretty physical thing to do. We swam diagonally to the silver ball in the middle of the pier and then under the pier to the other side: a battle of man against tide. Once

I got through the pier and took a sharp right-hand turn to come back, it was like being shot from a gun. The tide literally picked us up and whooshed us through - 12 minutes out and 5 minutes back to the beach. I really enjoyed it!

After work it was back home to domesticity duties as usual and then just as exhaustion was setting in I was back up at Falmer for my 8.30p.m. pool start. Only Bob and me tonight but he pushed me hard. In the hour I think we did about 1.5 miles. He is most definitely a hard taskmaster but it was needed and almost enjoyable. What is happening to me? Am I actually starting to enjoy the pain?

Tomorrow, whilst I would love to be in the sea, Fiona the boss lady insists it's pool, pool, pool.

Day 210 - 16ᵗʰ March 2011

This morning I was back at the pool at 6.30a.m. for a 3-hour swim, which wasn't easy, considering I was swimming until 10p.m. last night. I swam in intervals of 15 minutes slow, 15 minutes fast for the whole time. It was interesting as at different times I was performing differently but this was not based on physical energy as much as mind set. It just goes to prove once again that endurance training in any sport is 90% mind and 10% body.

Day 211 - 17ᵗʰ March 2011

Two pools swims today; that was unexpected.

I did a 2-hour pool swim this morning before heading off to London for a meeting. After London I was back to Falmer for a gym session but Ross had forgotten I was coming and had gone home, so I went back to the pool. The plan was a 90-minute speed session. I started with 30 lengths slow warm-up, followed by twenty 50 metre sprints with 15-second rests, then three butterfly/back/breast/crawl combination, followed by ten 50 metre sprints with 10-second rests. It was at this point the pain set in. I got serious cramp in my front left shin area, which came on suddenly and was agony. Nothing I could do would stop it and it was impossible to carry on, so I limped inside and into the steam room.

Ten minutes later the cramp stopped but as I was about to go someone I know came in and started talking to me. I felt it was rude to just leave but 15 minutes later, when I was so hot and full of steam I thought I would collapse, I had to make excuses and go. The steam room is not a place to catch up with long lost friends - leave that to the bar area!

Day 212 - 19th March 2011

After yesterday's mammoth steam room session, I was probably two stone lighter! I was planning on going back to the pool again this morning but Bob and I got our messages all mixed up and after much texting and nonsense we ended up at 6.50a.m. at the Arch for a simple sea swim, which was much better as I have done three pool swims this week already. After my cramp yesterday I didn't fancy a big swim but I am clearly getting stronger. I found the swimming fairly easy which meant I was able to keep my speed up the whole time so instead of being the one at the back, we were actually in a direct line to each other - synchronised swimming but without the costumes.

Next week will be slightly different as I am in Gibraltar on work Monday and Tuesday. It means I'll have to cram the whole week into the last few days.

Emotionally it's been a hard week with swimming as I really haven't at any time felt like I wanted to swim either in the pool or the sea, but I guess that's simply how it is, one week you're hot to trot and another week you're not. The secret is to make sure that however you feel you still do it and that you always do your best. Your best of course can change from moment to moment depending on how you are at that time but your best is what you have to give each day.

Day 213 - 21st March 2011

Yesterday, Sunday, was a day of fitness for the Starrs. I'll tell you about mine first as it's quicker and far less impressive than Sharon's. As I knew I wouldn't be swimming today I did a decent training yesterday at home. Run on treadmill for 45 minutes, level 10/incline 6.5. Then cross-trainer level nine for 20 minutes. Then Vasa swim machine for 12 minutes/676 metres. Then 1 hour in the endless pool which was 35 degrees, so I slowly boiled! That was a decent all-round training session.

Sharon, however, topped that – she did her first ever triathlon! Swim, bike, run. Flipping incredible! My wife is now a triathlete – puts me to shame.

Today I flew to Gibraltar for meetings from midday until around 5p.m. I'm staying at the Rock Hotel, which is at the base of the famous Rock, which was just begging me to run up it. I did it a couple of years ago before I had my rheumatism; it's a tough run but a great challenge. Hopefully the last meeting will finish on time and I'll go for it. I've got to be back at the airport at 9.30a.m. tomorrow, so if I'm up in time I'll grab a swim or a run as well.

Finished meetings at 4p.m., all were very positive, so I ran from the bottom of the Rock all the way to the very top, getting some 'well dones' along the way from tourists and some curious looks from monkeys. Total time up and down, 47 minutes and 15 seconds, I'm very pleased with that. Now sipping coffee along main street and deciding which restaurant will have the pleasure of feeding me, eating all alone like Billy-no-mates with my head stuck in a book!

Day 214 – 22nd March 2011

Back to the UK at 2p.m., then was at Falmer by 3p.m. for training. Unfortunately the run yesterday up the Rock has brought on a bout of rheumatism in my left leg/foot. I was silly, really, to have done it. So there I was limping into the gym feeling annoyed that a run, however hard, could cause so much pain, but that's the illness and I knew deep down when I started the run that this was the likely result. Ross therefore worked on my upper body only, so after an hour of weights and pulleys I now have biceps like tree trunks (or at least saplings). After the gym I had a short swim in the outside pool, full pelt for 30 minutes.

After that I came home to find Mia and Jesse have been very unwell, Jesse sick with a fever and Mia breathing badly and having passed out, which at two years old is scary. Right now (9.30p.m.) I'm at home with

Asher and Jesse (both asleep, although Jesse is very restless) and Sharon is at Hospital A&E with Mia as she's got worse again. When your kids are ill it really tears you apart.

Dependent on how the night goes and how the twins are will dictate if I hobble to the beach for a morning swim or not. I get the feeling 'not' and also that this week may end up not as exercise planned as I had hoped. At least I've done a very hard run and gym and a speed swim already, so not all bad on that front. Right now the twins are the main and only focus I have.

Day 215 - 23rd March 2011

Kids - Asher fine, Jesse about 80% better and Mia now on a plethora of pills and a nebuliser but basically very much on the mend. Hopefully in a few days all will be healthy again in the Starr household and we can find out what caused Mia to pass out. The hospital thinks she overheated with a fever and it was just her body's way of dealing with it.

Training - This morning I had to help with the kids and then take Asher to school, so no sea for me - great shame as the sky was a royal blue and the air temperature is up to a massive 14 degrees. My foot is still bad and I am hobbling around on my stick, so it would be crazy to do a gym session again today, but when the kids are all in bed asleep (hopefully at a decent hour) I will use my endless pool for an hour. The way the pool works, with a very strong tide against you, means that an hour is physically very much like three hours in the pool. From a mental perspective it is easier than a long pool swim but still a major challenge, as you are always staring at the end of the pool and it never gets any closer (just like that lottery win).

Tomorrow I was going to head to the beach (I am now desperate for my sea swim), but it's my Asher's fifth birthday so I can't just run off. Assuming time allows I will do my meetings tomorrow and then head to Falmer for a 2 or 3-hour swim, and then Friday, no matter what happens (assuming the kids are OK) I will be down the beach at 7a.m. and literally drinking it in.

Day 216 – 24th March 2011

Asher was very excited with his presents, especially his Rapunzel tower – just what every five-year-old boy dreams off. He's such a great little boy, just the best in the world.

A good chance today that no exercise will happen, as I have a fairly full day of meetings and then need to be home by 4p.m. for his birthday party. If the kids do go to bed on time and if my energy levels increase, I will use my pool and gym tonight. If not then I won't beat myself up over it. Tomorrow I'm at the beach and then with Ross at the gym, so at least I'll end the week on a higher note. Next week I've left space in the diary to include two long pool swims; maybe a 4-hour and a 5-hour back-to-back.

Looking out of the window and seeing very bright skies and an air temperature topping 10 degrees, it does make one believe that long sea swims are not a million miles away at last. I desperately need them.

Day 217 – 25th March 2011

At last back in the sea, way-hay! 7.10a.m. with my boys and girls from the Arch, fantastic. We went out as far as the helter skelter and then back. Air temperature 10 degrees and a beautiful sky, temperature in the sea 6.1 degrees. My head felt really cold but that aside it did feel warmer generally and the coldness wore off really quickly afterwards. Early April 2010 was when I started my swimming and the temperatures allowed us to swim around the pier, therefore hopefully if the sea is kind it'll allow us to stay in longer. Twenty-five minutes is enough to get around the pier, which would be fantastic again. A couple of the Arch boys and of course Fiona (naturally) have already swum around the pier but all have suffered colds and physical pain. The worry of being caught out there makes me think that Bob and I are right to wait for it to get a bit warmer before we attempt it. I still feel I am too slow to risk getting hypothermia at the end of the pier and then trying to swim back. For once in my crazy life I feel I am doing the right thing.

After work I hit the gym with Ross and did a decent hour on weights, then went for a 20-minute hill run in the woods around Falmer. Now I'm back at the office finishing the week's work and all ready for a nice warm weekend.

Day 218 - 28th March 2011

April is only a couple of days away. The year is literally swimming by.

This morning the sea was very calm, although there was a lot of water in the swell at the beach edge, which does sometimes mean the next few days could have large swells coming in. The air temp down to around 7 degrees and the sea slightly up to 6.3 degrees; still too cold to go around the pier for me. I swam to the silver ball and back; could have done a bit more, but that was enough, especially with a lack of sleep again. The twins are at last on the mend but Asher was sick in the night and ended up in our room, joined by the twins at 3a.m., then again at 5a.m. Joy!

Back-to-back meetings today in London and not home until early evening, so will try to get an hour in the pool or gym at home, but I have the ironing to do; a husband's work is never done!

Day 219 - 29th March 2011

An exhausting swim today because of an exhausting night! Asher still not well and the twins visiting whenever the fancy took them gave us about an hour's sleep.

I was therefore pleased I managed to drag myself out of the house by 6.45a.m. I was so tired I swear I fell asleep twice during the swim! How one can fall asleep whilst swimming in 6.5 degrees in a fairly choppy sea I have no idea, but sleep I did.

The rest of the day is taken up with lots of meetings. I'll get back to Brighton around 7p.m. and head straight to the gym for an hour's training with Ross and then an hour in the pool. No doubt I shall be exhausted again tomorrow but I will be back at Falmer 6.30a.m. for a 4-hour pool swim, yipeeezzzzzz - oops, fell asleep again.

On a good note, Sharon and I went to a Ball at Hurstpierpoint College on Saturday night and a great night it was too. During dinner I was chatting to a really nice chap called Mark who was interested in my Channel swimming. I told him what and why I was doing it and the next morning when I logged into my website I saw a £500 donation from him! Unbelievable. People really can be so special. Mark, if you are reading this, I am so very grateful. Your money will go towards us Helping Children Smile – thanks, mate. x

Day 220 – 30th March 2011

I was still a bit achy in the arms this morning as last night Ross put me through a 45-minute upper body workout followed by an hour's speed swimming in the inside pool, but I figured that a good steady swim and some Maxim energy gel should soon sort that out.

I was at Falmer in the outside pool and had been swimming for about 30 minutes when it struck me that something was missing. Carrying on swimming I ticked off the following: swimming hat firmly on head, goggles snugly around eyes, swimming trunks (thank god) firmly in place. What could it be? So on I carried until I hit the hour and then pulled to the side for my first feed; water with Maxim that I made up before leaving home this morning. Arrggh, that what's missing! I'd made up 4 hours' worth of feeds in the kitchen at home and that is where I left them, along with the peeled banana I was going to eat for breakfast in the car. What to do at this point? I was ready for a 4-hour swim and had already completed the first hour, so I didn't really want to get out, but on the other hand not having any feeds at all, especially no Maxim, could cause me muscle damage and fatigue. Fiona clearly not going to be happy with me on this but on I swam. I figured I was here anyway so may as well go for it. So without any more stops at all, I swam, exceeding my 4-hour plan and doing a 5-hour swim with no stops and no feeds at all. As I expected, I was not hungry, not fatigued and my muscles felt tired but fine. Of course it's not clever, brave or sensible but it is satisfying to know I can do a 5-hour swim with nothing in me at all.

Afterwards I hit the steam room to warm up and almost dozed off. Soon after, all showered and dry, I had a very yummy chicken club sandwich and fries and a large cappuccino. Feeling full up, slightly tired but still pleased with my swim I headed to the office (where I am right now) to try to make sense of the 137 emails waiting patiently in my inbox.

Tomorrow it'll be a gentle sea swim to shake of the aches and then on Friday I'll go back to the pool for another long swim, this time with breakfast in my belly and Maxim at the side.

Day 221 – 31st March 2011

This morning the fog was thick enough to have to squint through the car windshield and the rain was annoying enough to get through my clothes and into my skin. The sea itself was rather busy, with a strong easterly pull and rather cumbersome waves; literally wave after wave trying to stop you getting past the shore. If my goggles hadn't kept steaming up I think I might have stayed in longer and played some more – the waves and thrashing sea raised the temperature to a scorching 7.6 degrees! Without the weather conditions, one could go around the pier safely again.

Tonight I have the kiddies on my own but tomorrow I'll either do a sea swim or a few hours in Falmer. Then it's to the office for meetings until midday, then to Gatwick for a meeting and then a drive all the way to Birmingham for a meeting early Saturday morning! Oh the joy of being me. I wonder why I have bags under my eyes?

Day 223 – 4th April 2011

With only about a hundred days until the Channel swim the mind is getting focused! Not that it hasn't been of course, but as soon as you start counting in days then the mind really starts to concentrate. The actual date is likely to be sometime between 7th and 14th July .

I started the day with a visit to Kim, my physio. It's been ages since I saw her so I thought some preventative treatment would be sensible. She said all seemed good and apart from the usual knots there were no problems. After work I did a 30-minute swim in my endless pool at home. It was toooo hot at 37 degrees (whirlpool temperature) and I couldn't breathe. Afterwards I was drained of all energy but instead of taking the opportunity to sit down in an empty house and recover I vacuumed the house, folded up the kids' clothes and did the big bucket of ironing. Somehow I have completely lost the skill of relaxing.

Day 224 – 5th April 2011

Some fantastic new charity fundraisers have hit my desk the last couple of days.

1) A lovely lady called Jill (sister of our friend Vinny Shepherd) is having a birthday party and is expecting about ninety people. She is asking for donations to the Starr Trust instead of presents. What a fantastic thing to do.

2) Mike at Chobham Rugby in Surrey has raised around £1,200 from a collection for the Trust from his members. Amazing. Even more amazing is that one of their supporters has agreed to match it pound for pound, making it an incredible £2,400.

3) More support from Chobham Rugby from two of their members who are organising a bike ride from Chobham to Brighton with all sponsorship to be given to the Trust.

4) An anonymous person of wonderful character has given us £500 online. I'm speechless again.

The £100,000 target we have set ourselves, which is a daunting figure to raise at the best of times, let alone in the middle of the world's biggest recession, is actually starting to look do-able. We've still a long way to go but these four amazing pledges of support will make such a huge difference.

Back to today and my training, which is of course four times more important now, thanks to the above pledges! I was going to do a 3-hour swim outside at Falmer but only managed 2 hours. The brain was not at its optimum today and coupled with that it was blowing a gale and raining. Two hours of rain and wind hitting you is plenty first thing in the morning! This afternoon I'm back at the gym for an hour with Ross on weights and then another hour in the pool (maybe the inside one if the rain persists), so that will be two swims and a gym today, which is enough for a grey-haired, forty-one-year-old father of three.

Day 225 – 6th April 2011

Finally the sea is warm enough to go around the pier. Yep, Big Bob and I are back in the room! I was first out the door and leading the Arch to the sea's edge. Even at 7.3 degrees the sea felt iceberg cold but in the two of us went. The air temperature was already around 9 degrees (apparently going up to 18 today), the sky was a beautiful light blue, the sun was halfway up its pole and there was a low tide. Within a minute of walking in we were swimming towards the helter skelter and heading under the pier, going through under the Danger Sign (interesting sign to read that far out) and around the pier clockwise. Going under and to the pier head was quick as the tide was easterly but coming back around was harder as we were swimming against it to the west. Bob and I stayed together the entire swim. It was a decent pace the whole way, neither of us going crazy but neither holding back and we reached the shore 23 minutes after setting off. Fantastic! To be able to do a decent swim in the sea rather than the pool is like the best Christmas present ever. I now need the sea temperature to keep rising and then the pool can be a once a week job and the sea a five times a week job.

Reading back over my diary I found 29th April 2010 was my fourth ever day in the sea and the day I first swam around the pier. It was under 7 degrees and an incredible milestone. To think that under a year later I can swim around the pier without it being a physical exertion and can almost keep up with Bob the whole way is astonishing. The next three months are going to be hard graft, but the end result will be fantastic. Life is good and a big thanks to my friend Big Bob, because without him I would not be where I am today with my swimming .

Day 226 – 7th April 2011

I was meant to be back in the pool this morning for a 2-hour swim but if you had seen what I had seen when looking out of my window this morning you would understand immediately why I ended up at the beach instead.

The sky was beautiful blue, the air temperature at 7a.m. was already in double figures and the sea was calmer than Mr Calm's very calm mind. We so rarely get these days that I simply could not allow myself to miss it. Big Bob and I headed out into the mill pond of an ocean. To keep with tradition we swam around the pier anti-clockwise. As I need to consider this part of my training, we pushed ourselves and swam at speed. If you consider the total length of the swim from beach, around the pier and back to the beach and add in a chilling 7.3 degrees, it's a good effort to keep up the maximum speed throughout. The total swim was just under 21 minutes, which in any temperature is a decent swim.

As I need to keep the pressure up I'll also use the gym tonight and will also grab a pool swim.

On the Trust side, I had another £1,000 pledge of sponsorship yesterday from a client. People's generosity brings us ever closer to our target. We are officially a third of the way there now, so lots still to do but an amazing job so far.

Day 228 – 11th April 2011

Not the best of starts today as I woke up with a bad headache – no reason than perhaps being overtired. Not able to get up at 6a.m., let alone go swimming, which was a bummer as the weather dictates a sea swimming day. I was still at the office by 7.20a.m. and feeling much better but annoyed that I didn't go swimming (that demon guilt again). I've only got one meeting at 3p.m., so if that finishes early enough I'll either head down to the beach for a half-hour swim or go to the gym. I really don't fancy the pool today. I will get a five-hour swim in the pool this week but I'll leave it until maybe Thursday, so I can get my head in the right place.

Aside from the ropey start this morning, the weekend was just glorious. The sun was out from early morning until late evening and we stayed at home the whole weekend. The kids were in the garden from 10a.m. until after 7p.m., we had various friends around, the new BBQ was up and running and life was good. The one downer for me, and boy did I feel so bad, was that Asher hurt his foot and as I lifted him up to check it out, his arm pressed the side of the BBQ. I'd stopped cooking about an hour before but it was still way too hot and that split second caused him two burns marks on his arm! He was brilliant and made hardly any fuss at all. The burns stopped hurting after plenty of aloe vera gel was applied but I felt (and still feel) awful about it. This morning he came running in to show me his burn marks and to put my mind at rest that they don't hurt at all, not even that much! Bless his heart, trying to make me feel better.

The rest of the week in terms of exercise will include three gym sessions (two with Ross and one at home), one pool speed swim and one five hour pool swim and hopefully five sea swims (if I can squeeze Saturday or Sunday in). I did manage a sea swim this Saturday at 7a.m., once around the pier in about 23 minutes. The sea was choppier than the few previous days, choppy enough to bash you around a bit.

On Sunday it was the Brighton Marathon and we had five people running for the Trust. My sister Tracey set up a Family Fun Day at Varndean School with a bouncy castle, car boot sale, cake sales etc., which was a great success. I had to pop to Falmer for a short while to help with a certificate giving for the young swimmers who had achieved their goals – apparently I was the guest of honour! How weird is that.

Day 229 – 12th April 2011

Still not feeling my best, which is most annoying. I can't work out if it's a physical thing or a mental thing as I am very bogged down at work and have some huge projects on the go and some major changes to put into place. Either way it is leaving me not at my best.

Last night I planned to use the gym and pool for an hour each. I ended up doing about 1½ hours in the gym and not using the pool.

I was down at the Arch before 7a.m. Rather than head around the pier because I wasn't feeling up to a deep swim, we headed against the tide under the pier towards the Marina. We swam fairly hard although I was lagging way behind everyone, and swam for around 32 minutes in total, the longest sea swim this year. I like to think that in a distance challenge I am the one who could keep going and going but on a day like today I felt like the one who was struggling to do just half an hour. Very frustrating. It took me two hours to warm up afterwards.

This afternoon I have a gym session with Ross and was not going to do anything other than that but it would do me more good to go to the pool first and do a fast hour's session, like the ones I've been sharing with Fiona and Bob. The thought of hitting the pool again is not exactly exciting me, especially as it would mean leaving the office earlier than I had planned, but I think it would be a good idea both physically and mentally. As for work, well I can do that tonight when I get home.

Day 230 – 13th April 2011

After yesterday's somewhat negative start I ended up on a better note. A pep talk and a more structured plan from Fiona certainly helped. After work I went to the gym with Ross and did a 50-minute core workout (those abs are burning today), then a 40-minute uphill run, then an hour's speed swimming. For the next three months I need to up my swimming time to include two x speed swims, which I can do in the sea, plus a 4-and 5-hour swim, which can be a mix of pool and sea dependent on temperature and sea conditions.

After yesterday's mammoth amounts, today is just a sea swim, total thirty-two minutes. It was a good power swim against a moving tide, which really challenges you to push through it. Tomorrow I'm in the pool for a 4-hour morning swim, then Friday a 5-hour swim. As Fiona keeps telling me, I must do two of these a week whether I want to or not, and while it's certainly a 'not' vote, I will do them nevertheless. Only three months to go, so I need to really knuckle down and get the pool hours in.

Day 231 - 14th April 2011

This morning was a pool swim as planned. The outside pool was busier this morning than usual, in fact I was swimming with two others for nearly an hour before I was able to get my usual private lane at the side. I really should put my watch back on and start counting the lengths to make sure I'm increasing the distance each time.

Tomorrow morning is pool again. I might see if I can fit in a sea swim on Saturday or Sunday as otherwise I'll have too many days away from the sea and that's not good for the mind.

Last night I didn't get home from London until after midnight, so I was a tad tired this morning. We saw Darren, my brother-in-law, in an opera in Covent Garden. He was the lead in a new piece by *Monty Python's* Terry Jones and played a GP's dog - don't ask, this is opera after all. As ever, Darren was fantastic and even though I'm not an opera person by nature, the piece was funny and easy to watch. My brother-in-law is seriously talented.

Day 232 - 15th April 2011

This morning my plan was a 4-hour swim but I only managed 3 hours. Last night was another one of those restless ones, with Mia being up five times and Jesse at least three times. To top that off some kids down the road decided to use their trampoline in their garden at 2.30a.m. Anyhow this morning I went to King Alfred instead of Falmer as I wanted to try a different pool to see how it felt, and had a meeting afterwards right next door. As they only have an indoor pool it mean I had to suffer the chemicals again and unfortunately whilst they are not as bad as Falmer, they still are not great. I could feel them affecting me within the hour and my nose is stuffed up and my chest is tight. Apart from that I felt physically fine with not an ache, and mentally I felt fine as well. The reason I stopped was that I was yawning a lot and taking down water and then by 10a.m. the pool started filling up with kids on half term and it was simply impossible to keep a steady pace. Tonight I'll do an hour in the gym with Ross on core work, so not a total disaster.

Next week I will be back at my beloved Falmer and will do my two long swims as instructed by Fiona. Swapping pools confirmed to me that I should stick to the one I know and Falmer has much nicer changing rooms and frothier cappuccino. I should buy the King Alfred and tidy it up, it's simply appalling. Oh my god, I could even build a theatre there as well! The mind is racing now, ideas, ideas, ideas jumping everywhere. Anyone got £100 million they could lend me?

Sunday - 17th April 2011

A glorious day, hot with blue skies, and it wasn't a work day. Not much sleep though last night. Sharon went for a 40-minute run while I did the breakfast and dressing duty and then when she returned I popped on my trainers and hit the road myself. I did a total of 7.8km in 40 minutes, an average of 5 minutes 18 seconds per kilometre. Considering I hadn't been doing much running of late and only had two hours sleep max, hadn't drunk even a glass of water or eaten a crumb and the sun was around 20 degrees I was pleased with the pace. I know it's not clever to do that without eating or drinking anything but it is good to know I can still do it in those conditions at my age.

The rest of the day ended up very physical as well. I ended up in the garden with mower ready to take on the ridiculous grass we had been cultivating! Since moving back home in February and having a new lawn laid we have not mowed once, so it was about a foot high and took a staggering 3½ hours just to mow it and another hour to pick up all the grass and edge it. Meanwhile Sharon and the kids, along with my sister and nephew, were creating more piles as they were weeding and pruning. So five hours after I started the mowing we were done and my back and shoulders were tanned. You would think that would be enough for the day, but oh no, this is the Starr household. So with the arrival of my mum, my in-laws and a family friend, we did an impromptu dinner for all, followed at 9p.m. with me tackling two weeks worth of ironing that had built up whilst Sharon was working in her studio. A tiring but fantastic Sunday. Will I have the energy for my planned 3-hour pool swim tomorrow?

147

Day 233 – 18ᵗʰ April 2011

Not a bad night's sleep, I think all the garden time wore the little mites down. By 6.10a.m. I was up, dressed and heading for the car, in the pool by 6.40a.m., swam past my 9.40a.m. target and kept going until 10.40a.m. Four hours, in the bag. I stopped on the half hours for a small slurp of Maxim gel followed by water, both of which made the swim do-able, but I really need to work out how I can eat something before my swims. Not wanting to be a food bore once again, I think it's time I dealt with this problem. I'm in the sea tomorrow morning for a 30-to 40-minute swim so don't need breakfast, but I'm back in the pool on Wednesday for another 4-hour swim and I think between then and now I need to work it out.

I've now got a longish day of meetings and paperwork, followed by an ECG at the doctor's at 5p.m. for my Channel swim medical assessment, followed by a meal tonight at my house for eighteen people! Yep, I did say eighteen...

Day 234 – 19ᵗʰ April 2011

Back in the sea today after too many days away from it. After our large dinner party last night we still managed to get to bed before midnight. The sea was very shallow today, so much so that I was still walking when I reached the silver ball half way down the pier. At 9.1 degrees it was cold rather than painful, and once the water was above my shoulders it was time to swim. I carried on heading out to the end of the pier, went around the big yellow buoy that has turned up 50 metres passed the end of the pier, swam around anti-clockwise against a weakish tide, back down the other side, through the pier under the silver buoy and was standing again in no time at all. By this time, 22 minutes from first walking in, I was surrounded by eight BSC members all enjoying the blue sky, shallow sea and rising temperatures. If only I'd not planned an 8a.m. meeting at the office I would have hung out a bit longer with them. On a day like today it really is a joy to be out there.

This afternoon after work I'll be popping on my running clothes and heading down to the seafront for a run on flat ground. I need to get back to running at least once a week now and being on the seafront at work really takes away any excuses not to. A run from the office to the Marina and back is probably about eight miles I would guess. Currently my shoulders, neck and upper back are aching from the Sunday workouts and the big swim yesterday but hopefully a long, flat run with deal with that. Then tomorrow it's back to Falmer for another pool swim; 3 hours, probably.

On 11th May, my forty-second birthday, I will be swimming with the sharks at the Brighton Sea Life Centre as a fundraiser. Hopefully the sharks will already have had their pilchards for breakfast and won't be interested in my skinny legs. It should be a fun event as a number of businesses and supporters of the Trust will be there, as well as local and national press. Also it should be a chance for not only more awareness of the Trust but also some actual fundraising. We are now already just over £35,000 towards our £100,000, fantastic so far but still a *huge* way to go .

Day 235 – 20th April 2011

I ran from my office to the Marina, through the Marina to the top road and then back to the office, total distance 16.6 kilometres in 21 degrees heat, no water (must stop that!) and total time taken 1 hour 5 minutes and 49 seconds. Considering I had swum the pier in the morning and then worked all day I was pleased with that time. I should be able to get under the hour and I think water and food would help, as I was getting tired at the end, which slowed me down. Luckily when I got back to the office I had the water machine waiting for me with ice-cold water and I managed to find an Easter egg in the Trust room and gulped it down in one. I did feel a bit bad afterwards as it was probably a donation, so I really must get to the shops today and replace it but I needed the sugar and it was sitting there just begging me to unwrap it!

Onto today! I wasn't completely sure I would make the pool as I was still achy from all the exercise from Sunday onwards, but by 6.20a.m. I was up and at it. The aim was 3 hours but like Monday when I got to that point I decided to keep going for 4 hours, which I did with little problem. The first 90 minutes flew by and I didn't even stop for a drink it went so quickly. The next 90 minutes wasn't as quick, but not actually a problem. The last hour did drag a little, so I broke it down into two 30-minute slots and had a banana in the first and water in the last. The thing about the pool swimming is that the thought of doing it is usually worse than the doing it and if you get your mind clear from the start and make sure you are in a very positive frame of mind it can actually be enjoyable to a point (I can't believe I am actually saying that!). So now with two, 4-hour swims, two sea swims, an 8km run and a 16km run since Sunday I've had a good training week. As for the rest of the week, I will do a 40-minute sea swim in the morning before heading to London and then will do a 1-hour speed pool swim in the evening. On Friday (bank holiday) I will just do a sea swim in the morning. As I haven't done a gym session yet this week I hope to get Ross to give me an hour on Saturday on my core, then I think that will be that.

In six days time it will be a whole year since my first dip in the big blue! The 26th is next Tuesday, first day back after the bank holidays, and I have a 7.30a.m. meeting, but no way I can miss a sea swim that day. That was a quick year .

Day 237 – 26th April 2011

What a beautiful Easter weekend it has been, a magnificent four days off work and the sun as bright as it could possibly have been. The whole weekend was a joy, with visits to Groombridge Park (what a fab place), BBQs at home and the kids outside from dawn till dusk – simply brilliant.

As I never swam on Good Friday I hit the beach on Saturday instead. Sharon and the kids came along to sit on the beach whilst I did a 25-minute leisurely swim around the pier. The water temperature was as high as 11.5 degrees around the pier and it averaged 11.2 degrees for the whole swim. I had forgotten how warm that feels on the skin.

Bank holiday Monday was another family day, so I didn't put any exercise in the diary but I did grab a 45-minute run in the gym at home plus 10 minutes on my swim machine, so not a totally exercise-free day.

Today, being Tuesday and a day back at work, started with a sea swim. I swam on my own avoiding deep water, as it's not a sensible thing to do alone (even though I've done it lots of times already, of course!). Total swim circa 40 minutes.

After my last work meeting I headed to Falmer and Ross put me through my paces in the gym. As it's getting close to my swim date he is concentrating on exercises that will strengthen my core as well as building up strength in my shoulders; boy, did he work me today!

Tomorrow I'll have another early morning swim as I am then heading off to the Sea Life Centre to meet the crew and the Argus reporter, in preparation for my swim with the sharks on 11th May. Then it's off to London as unfortunately today my mum's uncle has passed away, a fantastic chap who I loved dearly, and tomorrow afternoon is the funeral. Uncle Lou was a remarkable man and even though he reached the grand age of ninety-six it is still too soon for the world to lose such a wonderful, positive man. On the plus side it means he can be with Dad and share a large Scotch and listen to some fantastic jazz. Gonna miss you, mate. xxx

Day 239 – 28th April 2011

The funeral was a far-from-morbid affair. Uncle Lou was a grand old 96, although losing someone dear to you is sad no matter their age. He was one of the happiest people you could ever have met and even did an impromptu saxophone concert at the rest home for the other residents just last week. As amazing as that is, his older brother Ben was at the funeral to say goodbye to him. Ben is 102 and doesn't even use a walking stick. These family genes are amazing. My problem is I don't think I could afford financially to live that long! A very inspirational bunch, my family.

I was still very achy this morning from my tough gym session on Tuesday, plus a decent swim yesterday in the sea and a 15km run when I got back from London, so I had planned to just swim to the Brighton Centre and back. Being on my own I wanted to hug the coast again rather than go out into the void. But for some reason I felt really strong in the sea and ended up going all the way to the West Pier, then turned around and swam back again. I kept the speed the same the whole way there and back, a good strong stroke throughout, and at no time was I too cold or tired to do it. The temperature averaged 10.2 degrees, the sea was relatively flat, but the air temperature was down to around 7 degrees and the wind was quite brisk. The way I swam today, if the temperature had been maybe 12 degrees, I could easily have gone all the way to the Marina and back without a problem. Hopefully next week...

After my shower I suddenly got cold and was shivering for a good 20 minutes afterwards with very shaky hands. However, I had to get myself over to the Sea Life Centre because the photo shoot was moved from yesterday to today, ready for the shark swim in a couple of weeks. I have never been in the Sea Life Centre when it's completely empty and it's a fascinating place. I had to put on a wetsuit - my first ever time wearing one - and having now done that I really can't see why I've refused to use one all winter! It was easy to get on and easy to get off and was blooming warm. I really should invest in one in case the sea takes a long time to warm up, as I could stay out for hours in that. Silly me! Once I was all suited up it was off to the shark tank for some photos, which took about 20 minutes, and then back into my civvies and back to work. An interesting start to the day, and a good strong swim.

Funny how your state of mind can really effect your mood and your training; a bad mindset and you get negative and feel you can't swim and a good mindset and you're positive and could swim every sea in the world. Gotta keep the mind focused and relaxed; that will be the key to my success.

Day 240 - 28th April 2011
Today is the special bank holiday Friday for the Royal Wedding. The forecast was for rain and mist all around London but the sun shines on the righteous and it was pleasing to see a bright blue sky and around 20 degrees. Luckily the same could be said for Brighton and a glorious day was had.

I was in the water by 7a.m. Like yesterday I swam on my own keeping my pace the same throughout and went to the West Pier and back again. The tide was going to the east, so I was swimming against it going and with it coming back. The odd thing was though it took me 17 minutes to get there and 23 minutes to get back when it should have been the exact opposite but there you have it, the sea does what it wants. It is so great not being in a pool with others all around you, swallowing cupfuls of chemicals. The sea may not always seem the cleanest of places and certainly it has its fair share of salt but one thing it doesn't have is chlorine. The temperature was an average of 10.1 degrees, which was fine to swim in but meant I was shaking like Shakin' Stevens when I was driving home to have a hot shower. Sharon commented that it was because I was only wearing a T-shirt; it is possible she was right.

After my shower I helped Sharon get the kids dressed and while she headed up the road to our neighbours for a Royal Wedding garden party, I headed to Falmer for an hour of shoulders, chest and abs with Ross, which after my sea swim made it a really good challenge.

An hour later, feeling all worked out and healthy I headed home, got changed, downed a protein shake and was up at the neighbours just in time to see the royal couple say 'I Do'. Whilst I was not that bothered about the whole royal wedding business to start with, actually it was beautiful and they seem a great couple. How refreshing to have the TV on and be witnessing something good, positive and happy.

That should have been my day done and dusted but oh no. Mr 'I don't like heights' here ended up having to climb a 30-foot ladder at a tight angle and shimmy off the end into my bathroom window (which thank goodness was open). All I had was my brother-in-law at the bottom with his foot on the ladder to try to keep it steady whilst I climbed as fast as I could and focused on the wall in front. All that had happened was that Sharon's dressing gown had got stuck in the door but it was enough for it to not be able to open from the inside so I had no choice but to go in through the window. All I was thinking as I was climbing up was that if I slipped I wouldn't be able to do the Channel swim. What a stupid worry to have; surely dying would have been more worrying!

Days 241 – 3rd May 2011

Weekend/entertainment: 9.9/10. Spent the weekend at Warwick with friends and had the whole of Sunday at Warwick Castle. No doubt whatsoever that it is the best castle in the country. If you haven't been there then you need to, simple as that.

Weather: 7/10. Blue skies, air temp circa 18, no rain and a slight wind. What more can you want for the start of May?

Family: 10/10. Kids just wonderful all weekend. Sure the odd strop, but they are kids, aren't they!

Exercise: 8/10. I score this based on what I wanted to do, what I did and how I felt. Apart from Saturday and Sunday I have swum to the West Pier and back each day for the last five days, have used the gym every day and also run twice. So feeling strong, fit and up for it at the moment.

Health: 5/10. Not so good on that! Friday night I woke up 4a.m. and was throwing up from 5a.m. until 10a.m.; weird, as I was fine when I went to bed. Sharon drove us to our friends on the way to Warwick and as I was still suffering from a headache, stomach ache and general lethargy she carried on driving all the way there. I grabbed about an hour's sleep in the car and by the time we got there I was 70% better. An early night in the hotel and by morning I was 90% better and ready for a good day ahead. Three days on I still am not 100% but probably 85% better. The other thing, which literally is a pain, is that I have a flare-up of my rheumatism and my right foot is swollen again and painful to walk on. Hopefully it won't last much longer as it is quite debilitating. It did not, however, ruin a great bank holiday weekend.

Back to today and at the Arch by 7a.m. Big Bob back from his hols so we headed out to the West Pier. The tide was pulling hard east towards the Marina, so the swim to West Pier was very tough. It was heads down and swim as fast as we could all the way. We seemed to be at the Brighton Centre for a lifetime! I hate swimming past that building, you never seem to go past it even in a still sea, so against the tide it really is mind-bending and stressful. Anyhow, of course we got as close to the pier as the sea would allow and then turned and swam back with the tide. Total swim to the pier was 26 minutes there, 17 minutes back. Considering I'm not 100%, that was a good swim. This afternoon after work I am with Ross at the gym for an hour; hopefully the health will hold up, although no chance of any leg work as my foot won't allow it.

The Argus business page shows a nice photo of me at the Sea Life Centre in my wetsuit by the shark pool, accompanied by a great article.

Day 242 – 4th May 2011

Health: 7/10. Feeling much better, only foot still hurting. Walking up the beach today after my 55-minute swim I found someone had taken my sandals from where I had left them so by the time I got back to the Arch I was in a lot of pain. By the time I reached my car for the drive to work I was very glad to use my disabled badge and park very close by.

Swim: 7/10. Sea back down to under 10 degrees (9.8 by my watch), wind chill very high, air temperature only 8 degrees; however, sky very blue and sun out, so not all bad.

Sitting at work now, and apart from my aching rheumatism my shoulders and arms are very heavy. Because we couldn't do any leg work at the gym last night it was an hour on the upper body and abs, so I was already seriously achy when I started this morning.

Day 243 – 5th May 2011

The toughest swim this year by far, not helped by my rheumatism still hurting (albeit so much better than yesterday), my Crohn's causing severe stomach cramps (oddly this does usually happen after a rheumatism flare-up) plus only about 3 hours sleep as both twins very restless and in and out of our room constantly until about 3a.m. when we gave up and let them stay.

I met Bob at the Arch and we were in the sea by 7a.m. We swam to the West Pier (now my daily routine), then to the large red buoy, around the buoy and back to Brighton Pier. The wind was really cold and strong and was pushing the sea to the west whilst the tide was strong to the east, causing a washing machine effect, pulling and pushing the whole time whilst being hit from all directions by very bumpy waves. Imagine driving down a road at 10m.p.h. in an old Mini with no suspension to talk of and with large speed bumps so close that they are almost touching. Do this for 55 minutes and it may give you some indication of the bumpy feeling the waves give. If you imagine the speed bumps spitting in your face at the same time then you are almost there. When we eventually hit dry land both Bob and I were relieved, yet incredibly satisfied with our achievement. It really was what I would consider to be the preserve of an athlete in terms of endurance, speed of swim and mental resolve. So a year on I am now starting to feel like a decent swimmer at last. I have to say, though, that if Bob hadn't been there today I would not have gone. I guess he'd say the same about me (hope I'm not being too conceited when I say that). Not only did it mean I had to keep going but because we were literally side-by-side during the entire swim it gave us both a level of security.

Day 244 - 6ᵗʰ May 2011

A day in my diary that I will reflect on a lot, as it is the first day I failed to complete a swim. I'm not sure how I feel about it at the moment as it was only an hour ago but currently I am not so much annoyed at myself as concerned that I didn't have the resolve to finish it. I met Fiona and Angus at the Arch at 9.30a.m. with the aim of swimming to the Marina and back. I was already tense and nervous when I got there because they are both so much faster than me. Once again this is me worrying about the speed of others rather than concentrating on my own swimming ability and the fact that a Channel swim is about endurance. Even the fastest swimmers and incredible athletes fail the Channel, whereas others with less obvious physical ability have completed it due to their mental resolve. So why do I worry about others being faster than me? Who knows why, but I just do, and it isn't healthy as it puts me in a bad place at the wrong time.

Anyhow back to the swim... we headed straight off, hugging the coast and swam against the tide, although it didn't seem like a massive tide to me. I lost sight of Angus fairly soon on but Fiona was easy to spot as she is

Above: Just two Bobs; Little Bob on the left and me on the right; my second day ever at the beach, 27th April 2010.

Below: Alone in the sea having swum around Brighton Pier and heading back under the pier to my beach; not for the faint-hearted!

Left: My first and only marathon; Brighton 2012.

Below: Fiona, Big Bob and me at the Red Buoy end of the West Pier, Brighton. My first ever pier to pier to pier swim.

Above: Already down to under 9 stone, doing a fund raising publicity swim at Shoreham Harbour. The taste of diesel still lingers on!

Left: Leo and Shoichi at our 'delightful arch' ready for their regular 6.30am morning swim.

Below: Oh dear, never turn your back on a wave whilst out at sea; my goggles and hat snatched and never found.

Above: Leo, Big Bob, Midge, Fiona and Bella before our night swim around Brighton Pier.

Below: The BSC boys (me far right) heading to the girly beach for a safer morning swim

Above: BSC girls Martina Watts (thehealthbank.co.uk) and Charlotte Savins enjoying a 7am 'pilchard' on the girly beach by Brighton Pier.

Below: Brighton Pier before the rest of the city wakes up.

Above: At the Brighton Sealife Centre before my birthday swim with sharks.

Left: My first ever snow swim; photo taken by Big Bob who was also braving the cold; we went in men and came out women!

Above: Leo and Fiona greasing me up in the middle of the channel ready for my big swim; we all seem to be enjoying it a little too much for my liking.

Below: Starr to Starrfish; my training journey ends and my channel swim begins.

currently wearing a wet suit, which is most sensible and something I *must* do right away. I got to the Marina in what I considered a decent time and then headed back but found myself not swimming anywhere near as smoothly as I first was, even though we were heading back with the tide. It seemed no matter where I tried to put my mind I just couldn't stop thinking about the swimming and it made every stroke seem clumsy. I kept going as fast and as quick as I could but by the time I reached the second beach before the pier, just near the Sea Life Centre, I was so disorientated and unconfident that I headed straight into shore and walked back the last two beaches. Certainly there are a number of things that should make me not beat myself up too much. The Marina swim is notoriously hard as there are many rip tides and lots of freezing cold spots, my frame of mind wasn't great and the temperature was under 11 degrees and even in Dover where the Channel swimmers are training they only do an hour in this temperature whilst I did one hour forty minutes and was really feeling it coming back. Ultimately I set out for the Marina and back and only did 4/5ths of the swim instead of the whole thing and that worries me and bugs me .

So what now? Well, I think Fiona is right and if I am to skip the pool and just sea swim then I need to invest in a wetsuit so that I can do 3 to 4 hours at a time, otherwise I simply have to go back to the pool. So this weekend I will go and find a wetsuit and next week I will hit the Marina and back and restore my confidence. Interestingly Angus, who did complete the swim in about 1½ hours, was saying that he is starting to put back on weight in preparation for the swim in July and whilst he is by no means fat he is certainly packing way more than I am. He said he is eating every piece of chocolate and every doughnut he can find as well as having massive meals every night. Having experienced the cold today it is a concern that I have lost even more weight: I am currently about 9 stone 10 pounds. I will certainly make a concerted effort at weight gain, aiming for at least a stone more, but I am constantly fighting my Crohn's disease, which of course does the exact opposite for me.

Whilst writing this I took a call from Marlene, the lovely 'medium' that

Dad comes through on. I know that sentence sounds mad but how else can I describe it? Marlene is a world-renowned 'medium' and she came into our lives randomly soon after we lost Dad and since then has told Mum the most amazing things that there is simply no way anyone could have known. One thing was that Dad had met the twins and they are one of what we have already and one of what we don't have. At this point no one was pregnant, no one was trying and there were certainly no twins in the family. About eight months later Sharon fell pregnant with twins and we had one of each: a boy (of which we have one already) and a girl (which we didn't have already).

Anyhow she rang to say that Dad tapped her on the shoulder and said I am getting more like Mum each day and I need to stop being stubborn and to use the right equipment when I do something! Also he said he will be with me every stroke. Clearly I now have my dad beating me up as well as Fiona and of course both are right. The choice is yours as to whether you believe this sort of thing, but because I can't prove it either way I prefer to go with the comforting option that Dad is still there and has still got my back for me. I love him and miss him so much but how nice to know I still have him.

This week I've done the most sea swimming I've ever done: Brighton Pier to West Pier and back every single day and then Brighton Pier to the Marina and mostly back today. Next week I need to up it again and make sure I never bail out early again. I simply cannot and will not do that!

Day 245 & 246 – 9th & 10th May 2011

I have been a bad boy! No swimming or exercising yesterday or today. I had intended both days to swim to West Pier but circumstances of the mind were pitted against me. I had a lot of decisions to make at work, some rather tough, and these were at the forefront of my mind. With any business one sometimes has to make tough decisions to ensure it not only survives but continues to grow and mine is no different. Having been trading now for twenty years I need to ensure all its components are working as they should be so we can see in the next period of growth. All that sounds very serious and very sensible but the anomaly is that people are always involved and when one is considering people one has to juggle head and heart; not an easy thing to do. As such, my heart was really not in swimming, exercising or anything other than 6a.m. - 6p.m. at the office.

Now that is behind me I can get back on track. Tomorrow I will be swimming to the West Pier and back then at the Sea Life Centre straight afterwards. Tomorrow, being my 42nd birthday, also heralds the Swim with Sharks event, which sees me getting into the big tank at Brighton Sea Life Centre in front of about fifty local businesses, The Argus newspaper, the BBC and ITV. No pressure there then! After the swim we are holding a networking event to introduce Swim4Smiles and the Starr Trust generally to everyone there. The key is to ensure people understand what we are trying to achieve with the fundraising and really get behind us to support our twenty-one children's charities.

One thing I have learned about myself through this whole Channel swim experience is that I really am not one for the limelight. Of course it is really important to get our message out there and that naturally involves me being in the spotlight at certain times, but while I have no problem speaking in public, I am not happy being the centre of attention. Some people love it, some people need it, but I for one am much more of a private person and am much more comfortable directing from the dark corner. So once the Channel swim is finished I shall not only look forward too much less training but also to much less exposure (in every sense of the word!).

Day 247 - 11th May 2011

My 42nd birthday today and actually feeling most of those years, unfortunately.

A very interesting and one off day today. At 6.30a.m. I was in the sea in my wetsuit for the first ever time. Big Bob was with me and we headed out around the pier anticlockwise into the tide, then headed out past the pier to the first buoy and then the second buoy and then back to the pier, under it and to our beach (the buoys are at last back in town - the yellow round variety of course). The swim was very odd to start with as the wetsuit not only shields you from the cold but also lifts you way into the air - I felt like I was floating on the top of the water. The wind and the tides were blowing to the west and we were swimming to the east but to start with I felt I was being skimmed across the water to the west and bit by bit away from Bob and the pier. When I looked up I was way over to the west; it was a weird feeling. As soon as I realised where I was I put my foot down and swam hard to the pier and very quickly was back on track and heading around. The other thing about the wetsuit is the extra speed you have by being so buoyant. I was always at least 25 metres ahead of Bob and at each buoy was waiting for him. He remarked that it must be good for my confidence to be so fast now but the truth is that I cannot kid myself that it's me and not the suit and to think anything otherwise would be false economy. I am doubtful my wetsuit will be invited out to swim with me ever again to be totally honest, it just felt false. Is that a bit odd?

By 8.45a.m. I was at Juice Radio station for my live on-air interview about the pending swim with sharks and the general story about the Starr Trust and the Channel swim. Apparently the interview went really well (I've no idea what I said of course) and by 9a.m., along with the cameras, we were heading back to the Sea Life Centre for my next interview with Sussex Radio and then my swim. I know it's great for publicity for the fundraising but it does all seem a bit over the top as it's only a swim!

Arriving at the Sea Life Centre I was astonished to see more than seventy people - friends, businesses and media - all waiting to see if I lose a limb. The atmosphere was tremendous and everyone seemed to be enjoying getting the chance to look around without hordes of school kids and holiday makers. After my interview I was whisked away to the offices, passed yet another wetsuit and invited to the tank. Funny thing was that when I left the beach this morning I put all my swimming stuff in the boot of my car and left it there - it didn't occur to me to bring swimming shorts or a towel! As such I ended up having to go commando in the wetsuit (for which I apologise to whoever's wetsuit it was) and afterwards I ended up having to dry off using toilet paper.

Anyhow back to the swim... with everyone either sitting up top in the seats or down in the tunnel I was ready to face my public! The Sea Life Centre lady stood at the side in her wetsuit having advised me not to put my hands near the shark's mouths or the turtle's beaks and instructed me to get in by the tunnel and swim around it, making sure to breaststroke to avoid splashing - apparently that spooks the sharks! So in I went to loud applause from above and thumbs-up from the tunnel. Within seconds a rather large shark came heading straight at my face. At this point my pulse raced, my heart raced and I started to wonder about the madness of it all: do I swim to the side, do I put out my hand or do I go for the penalty kick right on its nose? At the very last second the shark looked at me, seemed to shrug indifference and then swam around me. I realised he had no interest in me and that was perfect; it seems we were going to have a wonderful relationship. The rest of the swim was calm and I swam with about ten sharks of various sizes, two of the most wondrous and huge turtles (they were about eighty-five years old) who followed me everywhere, a massive stingray that was twice my size and numerous other fish I couldn't even name. I swam for about half an hour in total and apart from faces peering at me through the tunnel and camera flashlights going off every couple of minutes, it was really peaceful and quite magical. Although I would have loved to have stayed in, I figured it wasn't fair to everyone watching so I headed back to the side and pulled myself out, to be faced head-on with a TV camera from Meridian and a reporter firing questions at me. Actually the guy was super nice and the publicity for the Trust was so appreciated by us that it was a pleasure to talk to him. The interview was shown on TV twice already.

After the swim we headed to The Terraces restaurant above the Centre and had a lovely meeting with everyone. The Terraces put on a fantastic cooked breakfast, coffee and cakes and apart from me thanking everyone, local councillor Vanessa Brown also gave a lovely speech. The feeling in the restaurant was really amazing with everyone seemingly wanting to hear more about the swim and the charities we are supporting and showing me great support. I truly can't think of a better way to start my birthday.

Afterwards, when everyone had gone back to their day, my lovely wife took me out for a birthday lunch and then we picked up Asher from school and took him to Falmer for his swimming lesson – it seems all us Starrs are swimming at the moment. The day then ended with dinner and presents at my sister's. I feel utterly spoiled by everyone.

Day 248 – 12th May 2011
Back into my wetsuit (I really can't believe I put it on again) I headed off on my own to the Marina against a very strong tide, total swimming time about 1 hour 45 minutes. It was a decent swim to start the day and I was pleased that in the wetsuit I could do that time without feeling the slightest bit cold – perhaps I really should have invested in this a while ago. The only thing I didn't realise was that in a wetsuit one really must apply Vaseline quite liberally because swimming for over an hour has left me with uncomfortable burns on my neck.

Day 250 – Saturday 14th May 2011
As I didn't swim on Monday I made up for it with a decent swim today. I wanted to be alone – I seem to be enjoying swimming on my own at the moment, so with Angus going west I went east. It was a bumpy ride but my wetsuit kept the cold at bay and kept me high enough in the water to limit the waves. I got to the Marina in 1 hour and 5 minutes, against the tide the whole way, and I got back to my beach, via around the pier head and the buoys in 35 minutes.

I headed straight for Burger King and got a breakfast muffin and hash browns; very not like me, but I have been told to put on a stone and by George, I shall try!

Day 251 – 16th May 2011
A very mixed swim today, enjoyable, frightening and good exercise.

a) *The Enjoyable Bit.*
Was at the Arch by 6.20a.m. and on my own; clearly I'm reverting back to my introvert days. This is in no way a reflection on those I swim with regularly, it is just somehow good for me mentally to swim on my own for at least half of the week. The sea was bumpy today, the temperature was 11.5 degrees exactly and I swam for 45 minutes (skin only), the air temp around 12 degrees and windy. The wind was pulling to the west as was the tide, so it was a battle not to be blown into the pier or to the other beach. When I walked in I was very much at peace in my mind so even though the sea was rough I was very calm. I swam out and around the two buoys, then headed for the pier...

b) *The Frightening Bit.*
It wasn't so very terrible, just a mind issue. I got to the helter skelter near the end of the pier and found myself swimming on the spot for a good five minutes, but in a rough sea so far out on your own every minute of not moving feels like 20 minutes. The waves and tide were so strong that they were trying to keep me back and it had the effect of swimming on the spot. My mind then decided to tell me that I was in a rip tide, which is basically something that holds you still or pushes you out and is very hard to get out of. It was nonsense of course as I know there is no rip at that point, but when you're out there alone your mind tries to take control and throw negatives at you. It took quite a lot of resolve to stop swimming, float for a minute to take control of my mind and then continue my swim further out around the pier...

c) *Good Exercise.*
I had to go around or back and around was safer as it was with the tide. Battling around the head of the pier against the waves and trying to avoid being pushed into the struts was a fantastic physical adventure and great exercise. When I got around the head and headed back down the pier the tide really sped me up but it was also doing a fine job of dragging me to the west rather than back to the east. It took a strong swim to get back to the pier and under it to my beach and then a stronger effort to land on the beach without hitting the groyne by the pier.

Hopefully the rest of the week will be as challenging because I could do with a decent week's swim in terms of mental ability and strong currents, although at least two days of calm would also be useful as I want to add in a couple of Marina swims - impossible in conditions like today.

Tonight after work I'm going to use my home gym as I need to start building up time on my Vasa indoor swimming trainer; it really builds up strength on the pull through which I desperately need now for speed.

Day 253 - 18th May 2011

I felt like having company today so I waited for my friend Big Bob and together we swam around the pier clockwise. It was a seriously good swim, very physical indeed. The tide was really strong and wanted to stop us going forward whilst the waves were constant and choppy and wanted to keep us smothered. But supermen as we are, we battled on and got around and back safely and in one piece.

Tomorrow Leo has suggested a jog to the Peace Statue and then swimming back with the tide to our beach. If the tide is as strong as today it will probably only take about 30 minutes at most, but should be a good swim as it's a fair distance and the waves, even if they are heading with us, will make the swim a challenge. Tonight after work I'm at the gym with Ross doing an hour on core exercises; hopefully we'll leave the arms alone as they are still aching from the swimming machine earlier this week.

Day 254 - 19th May 2011

As planned we met at the Arch at 7a.m. and walked to the Peace Statue. It was such a low tide that we walked straight down our beach to the sand and then had a lovely twenty-minute walk all the way along past the West Pier to the Peace Statue. The walk was so nice and relaxing that I was very tempted to forget the swim and just turn around and walk back, and I think others may have felt the same. However, we are swimmers and swimmers swim! So in we went and headed around the buoys and straight over to the red buoy at the end of the West Pier. The conditions were completely different to the last few days with hardly any waves, very flat and a light tide pull to the West (the direction we were heading). The swim took about 25 minutes and I would guess it was about a mile in total, maybe a little more. A really lovely start to the day and a good swim as well.

Day 256 – Saturday 21st May 2011

Saturday morning and an early start. I was up just before 5a.m., my bag was already packed by the front door with my clothes for after my swim and my wetsuit was waiting patiently to assume its position as my fake skin. I drove to the Arch, dumped my bag on the bench for later and then drove to my in-laws house, right by Hove Lagoon, but I was sure I had forgotten something! It wasn't food as I had eaten some fruit, it wasn't the wetsuit as that was firmly wrapped around me and it wasn't my Arch key as that was secured tightly in the wetsuit. Then it struck me like a thunderbolt: I'd forgotten my bloomin' swimming cap and goggles, a serious error as I had intended to try to swim around 8km and there was no way I could do that without goggles and hat. The only option was to walk the 10 minutes back to the car, then drive back to the Arch, grab them from my bag and head back to the lagoon, but deep down I knew that as soon as I got back in my car I would end up going home. Also I knew that the others were planning on a lagoon to pier swim at 7a.m. and I wanted to be done and finished before they got there as I really needed to do this solo and not be pressured into the whole 'I've got to keep up' thing I do to myself. So nothing else I could do but head out to sea...

Luckily it was fairly calm, although each time I put my head into the water the sea slapped coldness into me, proving how much warmth one gets from a swimming cap. Then there is the salt; I ended up with eyes getting redder by the minute and my neck aching from having to swim with my head so high. All that aside, there was a positive to this. To be able to look at the coastline, the birds, the sky and the clouds without goggles was really amazing. They definitely dull your senses.

I kept really close to the shore for the whole swim as it was a long way and I was on my own. Being under no pressure to do the swim in a certain time or to catch someone up or even to complete the swim actually made me really relaxed. I just plodded along (probably not going too slow truth be told) and apart from the sore eyes and cold head I really enjoyed it. I got to the West Pier in about 1 hour 30 minutes, I got to the Brighton Pier in another 25 minutes and to the Marina wall in another 45 minutes, so around 3 hours for the whole swim. When I got to the Marina I actually felt mentally and physically strong enough to turn around and swim back against the tide but my eyes were too sore to swim back so I swam to the adjacent beach and jogged all the way back along the shore (which was mostly sand) to the Arch, where I showered, dressed and then power walked the 5km back to my car. This week I have swum on six days and used the gym three times, so a very decent effort that deserves the rest of the day off.

Some hope! The rest of the day was spent with the kids being a right royal pain in the a*** and Sharon and I digging up a million weeds in the garden. No rest for the wicked. Tomorrow however the wicked will not swim or gym; Sunday is the day of rest, is it not?

Day 257 - Monday 23rd May 2011

It seems the chemicals in the pools around Brighton are driving more people towards the sea. Quite right too if you ask me; pools are too boring, too warm, too crowded and full of chemicals whilst the sea is just full of life and inspiring. The wind this morning was really making a fuss and it meant there were proper waves again; been a while since we've seen that. Big Bob stayed out for a good half an hour, but I did just a short ten minutes. After Saturday's swim my neck was still a little bruised so I didn't want to overdo it, and I fancied some fun.

Asher had a swimming gala at school today and it was amazing to see him so proud of himself swimming around the school pool. No doubt he will be a far stronger and quicker swimmer than his old man!

Clairvoyant evening on Friday raised over £1,000 for the Trust as well as bringing in new supporters. Heatwave expected in UK for June and July, which will bring the sea temp right up!

Day 259 – Tuesday 24th May 2011

Another bumpy ride this morning in the sea; it feels as if we are building up to a stormy one before it calms down again. Listen to me, the expert after a year!

I arranged yesterday to do a two-hour swim with Leo and Shoichi who are taking part in a 12km river swim at the weekend, which should take about three hours. As usual I doubted my abilities to keep up and unusually I was the only one in a wetsuit, but I did this not for warmth but for speed, as it certainly increases my pace wearing it. This is borne out by the fact that we all swam in a line the whole way out and then on the way back I was already at the beach having taken off my wetsuit before they surfaced. I think without the wetsuit I would have come in well after them.

Leo had got leg cramps and Shoichi had begun to really feel the cold (it was circa 13 degrees in the sea and cold in the air) and had turned back, which was sensible as it would have been dangerous for both of them to go on. For me this swim proved two things; first, how much warmth a wetsuit provides as I was actually overheating slightly, and also that because I am used to doing hours in the pool and also to a great degree in the sea, I am well placed to just keep going where others start to struggle.

Day 260 – Wednesday 26th May 2011

Last Brighton swim of the week for me as tomorrow it's off to Sorrento in Italy for a three-day break for our 10th wedding anniversary, leaving the kiddies with my in-laws at my house. We desperately need some time together away from work and kids as the last year has been a rollercoaster. I will be taking my swimming and training stuff as I still expect to do both, but hopefully in warmer climates!

Getting to the beach at around 6.30a.m. today it was odd to see four different groups of teenagers sitting around as if it were midday on a summer

Saturday. One group, Mohicans amongst them, were sitting around a fire, another two groups were huddling near to each other as if planning a council of war and the final group, made up of just three boys in grungy clothes, were leaning back to back fast asleep like praying monks. I wish I'd had my camera with me, Brighton certainly is eclectic!

The sea was so flat with zero wind but the tide was pulling hard to the west, I had to work really hard. Watching from the beach you would have thought it was effortless but those of us in the sea would challenge that fiercely. Total swim about 46 minutes, so a decent one again.

Off to London now for five meetings, feeling physically good at the moment, apart from a small ache in my collar bone, a remnant of the goggle-less swim on Saturday.

Day 261 – Tuesday 31st May 2011
We had a fabulous time in Italy, just Sharon and me and a good book each around the pool for three days. The batteries are now sufficiently charged to take me through the final weeks of training.

This morning I was at the Arch, all alone as usual, at 6.15a.m. Jeez, it was cold! The temperature in the air was around seven degrees and the sea had dropped down to just 12.5. I think that being in the sun meant I had lost some temperature tolerance but I swam for 80 minutes and my hands were too cold to turn the key in the Arch door when I got back.

After a hot, 10-minute shower I was certainly a bit better but it still took my heated car seat and the air con set to high before I truly started to feel warm again.

Tomorrow I'll do another session but in my wetsuit. The sea really does need to warm up now as I've got to be knocking out some long swims and I want to do them without the wetsuit on. I'll aim to do at least 90-to 120-minute swims everyday in the sea this week, apart from Saturday when I'll do a 12km again, perhaps longer if I'm able to. Tonight I'll head into the gym once the kiddies are asleep and work super-hard.

By the way if you are looking for a book to read then please try *Three Cups of Tea* and then *Stones into Schools* (I read the first three years ago and the new one in Italy). These books, both by an amazing American called Greg Mortenson, are exactly why I set up the Starr Trust. Incredible is an understatement.

Day 262 – Wednesday 1st June 2011

A beautiful start to the day, although a little warmer would not go amiss. The sky is very blue today and the air temp well into double figures; the sea as usual is slow to catch up, although it did creep up a bit from yesterday to an almost enjoyable 13 degrees. Apparently we have a heatwave about to start, which will last through June and July; if it does then I will be a happy boy.

I hadn't planned a long swim particularly as last night at 8p.m. Sharon and I used the gym and I really did work hard, arms, legs, core and my Vasa swim trainer (which has to be the hardest machine I've ever used). Afterwards we used the steam room at home (second time we have managed to use it) and I stayed in for 20minutes sweating out the day's issues and jolly nice it was too. Last night we only had two visits, both from Jesse, so I got a decent four hours of sleep, which really does make a huge difference to energy levels. So while I hadn't planned a long swim I ended up going to the Marina and back, around 3 miles, in 1 hour 20 minutes, which was the fastest I've ever done it. The current was so strong going that I felt like a bullet.

Afterwards, I saw Fiona in the Arch and she drummed into me once again that for the next six weeks I *must* do 3-to 6-hour swims every week, preferably twice a week. As she said, I don't want to end up taking on the Channel and wishing I had trained more and with six weeks to go I need to up my game once more. We are going to get together next week, plan my feeds and put in a structured final training plan, which will pretty much be 90% swimming and 10% everything else. Whilst I remain nervous and scared, I remain optimistic that on the day the weather and tides will be with me (courtesy of my dad) and then I will rise to the challenge.

Fundraising has now hit over £40,000, so almost halfway there.

Again I remain optimistic that with everyone's generosity we will make the £100,000!

Day 264 – Friday 3rd June 2011

Happy anniversary to me. Ten years ago today I married the most amazing girl in the world and 10 years later I have managed to keep her. She must be a saint.

Last night was more fun and games in the Starr fiefdom. Jesse and Mia with us at 11.50p.m. and after taking them back at midnight they had both returned by 12.30. We took them back again straight away and Mia stayed put in her bed for the rest of the night. Jesse, however, wouldn't stay put so the battle lines were drawn. Every 10 to 15 minutes from 12.30 until about 2.30a.m. I met him at his bedroom door and took him straight back to his bed. He screamed at me throughout and woke Asher, Mia, Sharon and every sleeping entity within a 2-mile radius, I expect. At this point Sharon took over and did the same until about 3.30a.m., when she eventually won the battle and he stayed in his bed until 6a.m. when he bounced onto my stomach once again.

Despite the lack of sleep I couldn't miss swimming again, so I was at the Arch and in the sea on my own by 6.20a.m. The sea was wet and cold (as expected), but it was relatively calm. It was also a low tide, which meant a long walk out, which today I didn't mind as it gave me a chance to wake up. I managed a decent swim, especially given the sleeping conditions of the last two nights.

Day 265 – Saturday 4th June 2011

The plan today was 3-to 4-hour sea swim, but the best laid plans...

Jesse had a high temperature last night (this is getting boring, isn't it!), which meant yet another night of no sleep with him up and down all night. My plan was to be at the beach by 10.30a.m. (Sharon was at the hairdressers at 9a.m. getting prettied up for our anniversary party tonight), but by the time she got back Jesse was still not at his best so I couldn't just run off. I ended up at the beach by midday but as I needed to be home by 2.30p.m. to set up the house for tonight it didn't give me much swimming time. Also the wind today was really strong, which meant that the sea conditions were not conducive for a long swim. Anyhow, in I went at midday and swam to the West Pier and back; total swim time 43 minutes, which was a decent speed considering the conditions. I have to just take each day as it comes and do my best on that day based on the conditions around me.

The party was one of the best we've had. Eighty people, a fantastic band, an amazing catering company and lots of fun until 3.30a.m.

Day 267 – Tuesday 7th June 2011

A full-on morning. I dropped my car into the garage last night for its MOT, so this morning I cycled to the beach. It was a great way to start the day, especially as it's 95% downhill all the way. Knowing I was doing a Marina swim I thought it best to eat something first, so at 5.30a.m. I had a bowl (well, half a bowl) of muesli with chopped banana; each mouthful convincing myself I was just taking down energy rather than food. It worked for the first half a bowl, then I realised it was food and gave up - still gotta work hard on that mindset.

The sea was really starting to cut up rough and was choppy as Big Bob and I swam to the Marina against the tide the whole way; this was Bob's first time ever swimming to the Marina. It took exactly an hour for us to touch the Marina wall and for once I got there first by a whole metre. As usual it was a rather unpleasant place to be, with large bouldering walls reaching up high into the sky, covered in slime and barnacles and a grimy looking sea sploshing against it. We immediately turned and headed home (the Arch, despite its rather sad look still feels like home when you are that far out at sea). The return journey saw Bob racing ahead and I couldn't seem to catch up with him. All was going well until I got to around three beaches from the pier and whilst in a daydream about things to do later in the day, I didn't see a large wave bearing down on me and I turned to breathe just as it hit. I must have swallowed a pint of seawater in one go and within seconds I was throwing up both the sea and also what was left of my cereal and banana; most unpleasant! I had no choice but to turn straight to shore as each time I tried to right myself another wave would hit me.

I was on the shore very quickly as luckily I had stayed close all along, although perhaps being that close was the reason the waves were so big. Having beached myself I walked a few yards to clear my head and out of nowhere came a fellow swimmer called Yvo. She must have seen me from the beach swimming in and, bless her heart, she ran straight over and offered me her coat; so lovely to have fellow sea swimmers keeping an eye on you. I declined, however, then left it a couple of minutes - by which time a chap with a camera saw fit to take a dozen or so shots of me standing in my wet trunks and wiping sick off my body - and then I waded back into the sea for the final few hundred metres. Coming under the pier a few minutes later I was surprised to see Bob just ahead of me; I really thought I was way behind at this point. I guess I must have been faster than I thought I had been because Bob certainly looked like he was still going at a decent pace.

Having landed pretty much together we walked slowly up the beach and grabbed a hot shower each. Bob, this being his longest-ever swim in probably twenty-five years, was a star. What a massive swim for him to do. I truly believe if I had not been with him I would not have gone at the speed we did. The total swim was one hour to the Marina against the tide and 1 hour 20 minutes back with the tide. It should have been the other way around!

I cycled to work, stopping on the way at the cake shop for a sausage roll (now eaten) and an apple Danish (waiting to be eaten). Some two hours later I am still a little heady and keep getting sea water run from my nose onto my desk; charming!

It was a good swim in a tough sea and I should be pleased with that, but a big part of me really expected it to be so much easier by now that it was. Whether it was my mind not being 100% focused, or my body being tired or just me not being as strong a swimmer as I need to be, I simply don't know. Either way I will forge ahead with my training, making sure I knock out another decent swim at the weekend.

Day 269 - Thursday 8th June 2011

It's over. I can't believe it, 269 days wasted. The devastation started last
night. Fiona and Bob came over to my house, to talk - so I thought - about
the crew and what we need to have prepared for the swim in four weeks.
The conversation did not go that way and in my heart of hearts I knew it
wouldn't, even before they turned up. In essence Fiona said she would not
personally sign me off for the swim, as I have not put on the weight I need
and that has meant I have been unable to do more than 3 hours in the sea
without feeling the cold. At this point, I should be doing 6-to 8-hour swims
in the sea at least once if not twice a week; they are doing that in Dover
already. She is correct, because after three hours the cold really gets to me
and I have felt so hypothermic that I have lost my mental ability to direct
myself. If the sea was the same temperature as the outside pool (20 degrees)
I could keep going for hours but it is never reaching more than maybe 14-15
degrees in the Channel. And that is impossible with my weight; down to 9
stone and staying there. I should be at least 11 stone by now - I was always
between 10½ - 11 stone before I started the long swims.

The problem I have is that I just can't put on the weight they need me
to put on. In the last four weeks I have eaten probably twice my normal
intake and yet I have _lost_ another 3 pounds from last week and am exactly
2 pounds less than I was a month ago! It seems that the more I eat on top
of my usual intake then the worse my Crohn's gets, I end up in pain and my
body simply removes everything I've put in (sorry about the description).
When I am swimming my Crohn's pains stop almost instantly, but when I
am pushing myself to eat the pain starts and nothing is absorbed. But if I
don't put on 2 stone I won't be fat enough to take a 15-to 20-hour swim in
the cold waters, as I will lose about 2 stone during the swim and will end
up at about 7 stone - which is not only ridiculous to think about but physically dangerous. Both Fiona and my GP, as well as Sharon, of course, worry
that even at that weight in that temperature I will refuse to come out and
ultimately I could suffer a cardiac arrest and die. Apparently a couple of
years ago a twenty-five-year-old did just that and died during the swim, one

of more than thirty people who have died in recent years in the Channel from their body not coping.

I know I am physically strong now and my mind is up for the challenge but my body is letting me down to the extent that the powers that be simply won't let me go. I am sitting here agreeing with them and understanding this is not my choice on the one hand, yet on the other feeling I am letting myself and everyone else down. My mind is saying I cannot control the Crohn's to the extent that I can put on the weight but then it is telling me I am a quitter, which is something I have never been in my life. Total devastation is a slight understatement. I actually cried tonight for the first time since my babies were born.

However all may not be lost. Either way, whatever happens, I will complete a Channel swim. If it is possible to change my solo swim into a relay then that will solve the problem, as I would be swimming as a team and I can easily knock out 2-to 3-hour swims at this weight. I'm not sure about the rules on relay swims or even if I'm eligible, but I've got to have some hope.

Either way I will not let my Crohn's stop me - not now, not ever. We have already raised nearly £50,000 for our twenty-one charities and we need to raise another £50,000 to complete the fundraising. I need to do whatever I can do to keep this going; it is not an option not too. My mind however still is calling me a quitter, despite my strong words! How does one stop that?

It's an excuse I know, but I'm not being allowed sleep at home and I'm not being allowed by my body to keep in the food I need. What am I meant to do? Quitter, quitter... shut up mind, just shut up.

Day 272 – Monday 13th June 2011

Five days since my swim was cancelled. Since then I have swum in the sea simply because I have needed to keep going, even though at the moment I am not sure what, when or how the swim will take place. I'm not sure about a lot of things at the moment. How can something like a swim, something I never even really knew existed two years ago, now be pulling me apart. It's nuts.

Over the weekend I thought long and hard and have had numerous discussions with Fiona, with Sharon, with my family and with some of my BSC friends. Ultimately I will swim the Channel, I've no doubt about that whatsoever. It is simply a case of when and how I do it. Fiona talked about a relay swim and after literally days of soul searching (still going on, truth be told) I think this would be the only way I could do it. The solo swim, although it is the only thing I have focused on, is simply not possible. Who knows whether I would have been able to complete it anyway, as I'm a crap swimmer compared to my BSC crowd, but I would definitely have started at Dover and done my very best (which is all one can ever do). However at around 9 stone I simply can't do more than three hours in the sea without a wetsuit - which the CSA does not allow you to wear for a Channel swim. (When wearing a wetsuit you are not able to judge your body temperature correctly - sadly, a swimmer - not with the CSA - died recently because he became hypothermic as he swam the Channel and his crew didn't realise in time. Also, the challenge has to be the same for everyone, except for the weather, of course, which is uncontrollable.)

With a relay I would do no more than around one hour at a time and then come out, warm up and eat and then go back in again with a clear head. Having read up over the weekend on relay channel swimming it is by no means an easy option and remains a huge challenge, albeit a different challenge. You have to be able to come out and be mentally and physically prepared to go back in. From what I can see, the success rate of relay swims is almost as low as that of solo swims, but it is one I think my lifestyle will allow me to do.

What now needs to happen is that my pilot needs to agree to move my swim to the end of the season (August-September), the CSA need to agree to bend the rules and allow other swimmers to qualify in June/July (rather than back in January) and then we need to get the other swimmers to agree to join me (hopefully some of my BSC friends). So not an easy job to accomplish in a short time but Fiona is doing her very best and I will do all I can.

At worst position it would mean a relay next year (2012: Olympic year),

175

but I am doing everything in my power to make it this year. Ultimately the weather conditions could call off my swim anyhow (Fiona waited three years before the weather allowed her to do her swim), so nothing has changed at this point apart from my swim moving back to the end of August and doing it with the support of others.

This swim will take place somehow, of that I am sure, but I have to accept that my illness is something I can only control to a degree. Over the last twenty-two years my Crohn's and I have battled constantly and I always win. This time will be no different. It is doing its best at the moment however and I have noticed that over the last couple of weeks I have been getting some very sharp pains in my groin/thigh area – sort of electric shocks that only last a few seconds but are so painful that I can't even speak. I've had these numerous times in the past and they have always been after I have dramatically changed my eating habits, which is another symptom of my Crohn's. So it makes perfect sense now to go back to my old eating habits, which have served me well for the last decade and have got me to this point in time. I need to get myself back to strength, get rid of these pains (mental and physical ones), get back up to 11 stone and get this job done. At the back of my mind are the 21 children's charities I have pledged to support and I will not let them down.

I am now waiting for Fiona to come back to me with the good news that we have an end-of-season slot and that the CSA are allowing us to do this. I can then get a team of swimmers together (somehow) and get back to the job at hand. Meanwhile I shall continue my training in earnest and keep everything crossed that everyone and everything allows me to do this.

Day 274 – Wednesday 15th June 2011

Mind now firmly back where it needs to be and forging ahead with training to complete my Channel relay.

Last night after work I had an hour at Falmer with Ross in the gym and boy, did he push me on those muscles! By the time I got home at 5.30p.m. my arms were literally down by my sides. However no stopping there, so on with the running shoes and a speedy 5km to finish off the night.

This morning I was back at the Arch for 7a.m. and a friendly greeting from two fellow swimmers who said they were relieved I was going for a relay and not the solo, as they were worried about my health. The temperature today was 13.8 degrees, so still very cold. Looking back over my blog to 15th June 2010, the temperature was 14.5 degrees, which is quite a big difference . So many supportive emails from people, some close friends and family and others simply people who have followed my blog and supported me on this journey. I am now starting to feel better again in my mind (at last).

Day 276 - Friday 17th June 2011

Feeling rather low today about the swim. Reg, the pilot of my boat, has confirmed he can let me have a mid September slot but it seems that the CSA won't allow me to register other swimmers this year. Also Reg's slot is on the second tide as a fourth swimmer, which basically means we miss the best first tide completely and then have to wait for three other swimmers to either succeed or fail in that week before we get our shot. If the weather is bad for any of those swimmers then they keep their position before me and I am moved on. With this being right at the end of the season and only having a single week as a window and three swimmers ahead of me it is like being at the back of the pack in a grand prix driving an old mini and expecting to not only win but also finish the race. Even forgetting the CSA's refusal to register more swimmers for this season for my relay, it seems taking this slot gives us the least possible chance.

What on earth does one do? I so want to complete this challenge, I've put more than a year-and-a-half of my energy, my time, my life into this and it's all I've been thinking about since I first stepped into the sea in April 2010. To realise I can't do this as a solo swim was both devastating and exhausting but at least I clung to the possibility of a relay this year. Now it seems that it's unlikely to happen.

Having read a number of Channel swimmers' stories and spoken to some real life Channel swimmers and future attempters, I have come across more who have not been able to swim on their first attempt than have been able to. It seems delays of years due to weather or illness is the norm. My plan of learning to swim and then successfully swimming the Channel in just over a year now seems crazy. I hate the word impossible, but it certainly seems that way.

I will have to give this some major thought over the weekend and then sit down with Fiona and see whether she thinks the CSA will refuse to let me do it this year with a relay and if I am being daft taking a fourth position of a second tide at the end of the season. I don't want to end up not only disappointing myself and my amazing supporters but also have a team of swimmers facing disappointment simply because *I* wanted to do it this year rather than plan it for next year.

I will not give up, however. If elements out of my control force me into next year then I have to be as strong as Fiona was and deal with it.

Day 277 – Saturday 18ᵗʰ June 2011

Father's Day weekend just gone and family time was the order of the day - ish! A day I miss my dad so much. God, I need him now even more than usual.

Saturday I did a solo swim in a rough sea, the tide like a monster dragging east to the Marina and the waves a constant barrage. An hour later, slightly battered and windswept, I was home and ready for the day ahead.

On Father's Day the kids were in bed with me, throwing cards into my face at 5.30a.m. I can't think of a nicer way to wake up than having my little stars telling me they love me, it's like winning the lottery a million times over. A day of family fun until 3p.m. when Sharon took them all to a birthday party and I put on my running shoes and hit the street. I did a 90-minute run through wind and driving rain and felt better for it.

Day 278 – Monday 20ᵗʰ June 2011

The CSA have confirmed to Fiona that they will not allow me to change to a relay and Fiona has said I would be nuts anyway to take that slot. So although I can try for a relay it will be in 2012 at the earliest, and possibly even later than that (god forbid!). So that is that. I have to accept it and move on. I need to forget the bad news and understand that I have a positive challenge in place for next year. I have time to find a new slot for next year (which might mean a change of pilot) and get a team organised as well as change my training to suit a relay rather than a solo attempt. All is good, then.

Day 280 – Friday 24th June 2011

Another day of bouncy water and once again a cold sea, circa 14 degrees. The cold today seemed to really get into my bones.

After work I went to the gym and trained with Ross who now trains with me rather than just trains me. We did an hour on lower body. After an hour of legs only, you really know it; they feel like ton weights. Tomorrow I'll probably be walking like Charlie Chaplin.

My training from now on is going to be focused on speed swimming and strength rather than just distance. I still plan some 3-and 4-hour swims but I need to get my speed up. I've a year now to nail that and nail it I will.

On the fundraising front things are still going forward. We are at around £54,000 and have plans to keep it going hard. At Falmer, my fantastic gym are now on board and have set themselves a target of £5,000. They have numerous events planned, including a very cool 21-day 'Tour de France' challenge on the spinning bikes. Very cool indeed to have such a great sports club helping us.

Day 281 – Monday 27th June 2011

Despite a hot day and a sky of blue I am not in the sea today. Great pity as the first day in a long time when it would not be nuts to go in. However this morning I was way too tired and this evening I will be working too late to venture out in the dark.

I managed a swim on Saturday, which was raining and foggy, although my legs were still hurting a lot from the Friday gym session. I did about 45 minutes in the sea to the West Pier and back, a hard but decent swim. On

Sunday I used the gym in the morning, trying to work out the still-aching legs, and then went to the beach with the family midday. We went to Hove rather than Brighton where the shoreline is much more level and there is much less movement by all accounts. I think our beach is probably one of the hardest in the city.

On a sad note, two men died swimming this weekend, both bodies found near the Marina. One was in his twenties and one in his fifties and they were unrelated. The sea is a dangerous place indeed.

On another note, Angus, who is swimming the Channel this July (the same week I was meant to and his third attempt to go in three years) is worried about the temperature and has said that it would be madness to go in two weeks with the temperatures as they are. Angus has been training so hard for three years and unlike me he has not had an eating problem and has been able to pile on the pounds as well as piling on the miles. He is an inspirational guy and certainly capable of completing the solo that eluded me. To think the cold temperatures might delay even him shows me that I would have lasted no more than a few hours.

Day 282 – Wednesday 29th June 2011
After two days out of the sea due to exhaustion from lack of sleep I was back to it today. The morning was dry, the air temp about 18 degrees and the sea still down to just under 14 degrees, very calm and the tide was midway through its change, so it was quick to get out of depth and the movement was very little; both conducive to an easy start. The whole swim was most pleasurable.

After my swim and two early meetings I headed to Falmer to present the Starr Trust and our fundraising to a meeting of 26 gym managers from branches around the south and east. The meeting, which Ross put together for me, was really good and we now not only have Brighton fundraising for us but also the other 25 branches! A fantastic result, and amazing support for the Trust. Afterwards I had a session in the gym with Ross for an hour, just on core and shoulders as I've had leg problems.

On the dark side of today I have suffered quite a lot with my leg pain – the electric shock variety I had a few weeks back. In the past it's been about two or three times in a row and about twice a day, each time lasting about twenty seconds. For some reason today I have had about six episodes, each with about five shocks and lasting about 30 seconds. To say it's been a painfully shocking day is an understatement. I certainly don't want to see the doctor or specialist as they will just say lay off the training for a while! Probably just the Crohn's and the tiredness getting together to tell me to have an early night and a healthy dinner!

Day 283 – Thursday 30th June 2011

Good news on the Channel front: I have a new date – way-hey! I have a week booked from 8th – 16th August 2012, Olympic year! I have the first swimmer spot, which is as good as it gets and means that for that whole week my team will get the first clear day to do the challenge. What I now have to do is get a team together. I'm not sure how easy or hard that will be but I am confident that in Brighton Swimming Club there are enough good swimmers who would like to join me. If not, then I will look further afield. In Brighton, especially with my connections at Falmer, there are a lot of swimmers and tri-athletes and amongst them I am sure there are people who would love to join us. This is not however a simple case of someone being able to swim an hour at a time. The relay has so many other challenges, including sea sickness, air temperature when you come out and try to warm up before going back in again, taking a year to train, taking a week off work awaiting your slot.... An easy option it isn't! However between Fiona and myself I am confident we will find five stars to join me. My boat pilot is Andy King and his boat is the *Louise Jane*. Now I have a new and confirmed date in place I am reinvigorated and excited about the swim again.

Day 284 – Friday 1st July 2011

An afternoon swim instead because of work meetings. I was at the Arch by about 4.15p.m. and went twice around the pier, beach to beach to beach.

Total swim approx 42 minutes. The sea was a little choppy, but not off-ensively so and the temperature was around 17 degrees, which was the highest it's been all year.

It was weird swimming at that time as the beach had a few people on it and both the prom and the pier had visitors. Being on my own late after-noon with all those people about was slightly uncomfortable but the actual swim was fantastic, much nicer than my morning swims. The sea was a lot warmer, I had more energy and had the Arch all to myself. I am certainly considering doing this once or twice a month if work allows.

Day 286 – Tuesday 5th July 2011

Air warm, sea up to around 16.5 degrees, calm, flat and jolly nice. Got to the Arch at a leisurely 7.20a.m. (late for me) and headed in alone. I didn't fancy a pier swim today, although I probably should have done a West Pier swim; instead I went around the three buoys on our beach, going around them four times in total, a nice easy enjoyable swim. The sea itself was really clear and you could see straight to the floor. Going around the buoy by the pier it was easy to spot the ride tokens that have dropped down (some people in the club dive and collect them by the pocket load) – good spoils for all! Going back along to the middle buoy I spotted half a dozen starfish of varying sizes, all having a morning nap. I love days when the water is clear like this, it makes being in the sea so amazing.

After my swim I spoke to Leo and Shoichi, who want to join me in the relay next year and who I would love to have on my team. Both of them are really good swimmers and very determined people as well as being fun to be around. So with three of us on board we are now going to get together and plan the rest of the team. There is a fourth person at the Arch who is amazingly fast and strong and super-nice and she has expressed interest, so I'll chat to her next week as well.

I have had a number of really supportive emails recently, once again giving me extra strength and confidence to carry on.

Day 287 – Wednesday 7th July 2011

No other country can change its weather like England can. Yesterday morning it was warm, bright and calm and this morning it was gloomy, raining and windy.

I was at the Arch by 7a.m. and decided to wait until others turned up. I didn't fancy swimming alone today. By 7.15am I was heading down the beach in a group that included Big Bob and Little Bob; seven crazy fools all fighting the wind to get to the shore. As for the rain, it was the cold type, big drops and rather icy. The sea was very choppy with some really big waves but luckily the breakers at the shore were not too bad so one could get in and out very easily. Big Bob and I headed out and around the three buoys but the first buoy seemed to take an age to get to. Halfway between the first and second Bob hit something. He thought it was me but I was a way away from him and later when we returned to the beach we saw a big pallet floating by, so it was probably that. I bet it made his heart skip a beat. Once we got to the third buoy we turned around and traced our way back around them and then headed back. By the time we got to the shore my arms, particularly my biceps, were really aching and an hour on they still ache.

Last night after work I headed to the gym and had an hour with Ross on shoulders and biceps, as I'm trying to now build up my strength for faster power swims. After the gym I did an hour in the outside pool and pushed myself as hard as I have done for months. After that I did a fast, 7-mile run around the streets. By the time I got home I felt physically sick and had to sit in the shower until it passed. I haven't felt that like from training in years. It's no wonder my arms and biceps ache after all that and then getting to the beach today and tackling a busy sea. That aside, I really enjoyed the swim today as not only did it stretch me out – a kind of 'hair of the dog' for exercise –but it was one of those swims where you were really battling the elements but in a fairly safe and comfortable way. More days like today (without the rain!) would be great.

Day 288 – Thursday 8th July 2011

First time I've done two swims in the morning before work, especially when neither have been particularly enjoyable.

The first started at 6.50a.m. and the wind was extremely strong. The waves at the shore were huge and the swell seemed unusually big. A sensible thing to do would have been wait for others to turn up and also to then go in on the girlie beach to the left of the pier but my middle name is not sensible, which sometimes is a great shame. I stood at the shore for about 10 minutes trying to find a way in and was hit by about six large waves big enough to knock me backwards and throw stones at me, nasty blighters! After a few big breakers I found my gap and went for it, jumping straight in and swimming as hard as I could to get away from the swells. I soon found myself being taken out quickly and was up near the silver ball by the helter skelter in no time. Looking back to shore I felt a little unsteady as the waves seemed to be getting bigger and bigger and at that point I decided to abandon going around the pier and to head back.

Unfortunately as I turned back around to face away from the beach I was faced with a massive wave that was about to break on me, so I swam down and under it. Swimming deep under the waves is much safer than trying to go over or through them, as you are the one in control and you can normally come back up cleanly. However today the undercurrent, or perhaps it was a massive rip tide, was so strong that as I went under it grabbed my legs and spun me over backwards. Before I realised it I was being spun in a ball and didn't know which way the sky or the sea floor was.

Calming myself I let my body float until it took me back to the surface. As soon as I broke through the sea I came face to face with another wave of the same proportions and the same thing happened all over again. Once again holding my nerve I let my body float up but I have to say that I was really quite scared I'd surface and it would happen for a third time... and again... and again. Luckily the next wave was only half the height and I was able to swim over it. At this point, with my heart in my mouth, I swam to shore as hard as I could but each stroke meant I was facing the beach and away from the waves and that in itself was scary. I did manage to get back to shore but it took longer than I wanted and was really frightening the whole way. This was the first time I found myself being turned under so far out to sea. It's happened a few times at the shore but all that happens is you get a few bangs and scrapes. Way out there, though, you genuinely wonder if you'll make it back. A couple of BSC swimmers on the beach were watching me and sensibly walked back with me to the Arch and saved their swim for another day!

The second swim was at about 7.45a.m. After my shower and change into civvies I was ready to go to work for a warming coffee and a couple of Nurofen Extra Strength but it struck me as odd that no one was at the Arch at that time, so clutching my bag of wet swimming gear I wandered over to the girlie beach - a more sensible place to go in - and there they all were. Bella and Big Bob were out in the ocean and made it safely back, but both were unnerved by the experience. Bella in particular seemed shaken by the intensity and strength of the waves and undercurrent. Rather than go back to the Arch they all stood looking to sea, where David and Martina were about a third of the way down the pier and not making much headway. David, whilst being the elderly one amongst us, is a very strong swimmer and managed to head back more quickly, and as soon as he was near the shore he called out that Martina was in trouble. Immediately Big Bob sprang into action and dived back in. Looking around, there really wasn't anyone else able to go in and help, so there I was stripping off my clothes, popping my wet trunks and goggles back on and heading out to help. Bob and I reached her pretty much together and took a position either side of her. Just having us there was support enough for her to swim in with more confidence and with us guiding her and shielding her as much as we could from the bigger waves we all made it safely to shore.

Walking back up the beach to the Arch we passed a council worker who was standing under the pier with fear in his eyes, clearly wondering what the hell we do this for!

Twenty minutes later, showered again, dried, dressed, hair gel in place and Clarins moisturiser reapplied to my salt-battered face, I headed off to work for that coffee and those headache pills. Thirty minutes later I was sitting at my desk realising that being a simple office worker was not such a terrible thing to be!

Day 289 – Friday 9th July 2011

Last night Asher was a right royal pain in the arse! He came in our room at about midnight and basically refused to lie in his own bed and whinged and whinged until we let him in our bed, where he proceeded to fall asleep whilst kicking me in the back and snoring, so very little sleep indeed!

Big Bob and I headed in on our beach to go around the pier with the tide but against the wind. As soon as we dived in we went straight into a wave and it was like running into a brick wall; it really winded me! But heads down we kept on swimming and headed out to sea. Unlike yesterday's madness, the waves were not breaking further out but they were very big swells and it was really choppy. When we got around the head of the pier we stopped for a breath. It's impossible to describe being so far out at sea right in the middle of massive walls of water that are crashing and swirling around you whilst you are trying to not only swim through them but also avoid being thrown into the razor-sharp legs of the pier. Even writing it down can't describe the feeling: the fear mixed with the adrenalin whilst trying to maintain a level breathing and an 'it's just a swim' attitude to keep yourself calm. I spent the whole time saying to myself, 'find the inner peace and relax' whilst taking in gulps of seawater and seaweed! This really is an extreme sport, no doubt about it.

Coming around the pier we fought on and went under the pier back to our beach and then headed in the straightest line to get to the doughnut by the groyne on the far side of our beach, where the shoreline is much flatter and therefore safer to land.

Another massive workout before work, adrenalin rushing around the body and a nice safe landing. Job done!

This was meant to be my Channel solo swim week and in this weather

I would not have been able to go. Next week I'm meeting with my possible relay team to start planning next year. I'm very excited by that.

Day 290 – Monday 11ᵗʰ July 2011

The twins turned three today. I really didn't want them to wake up this morning on the first birthday that they really understand and for me not be there, so no swimming today. Today is about Angus Macfadyen, though, the Brighton Swimming Club member who has been training for four years to swim the Channel, having missed his slots the last two years, once through unsuitable weather and once through illness. I don't know him that well as we've only swum together a couple of times but I have great admiration for him as he has stuck to this challenge. He has certainly put in the training needed (and then some) and has raised money for a wonderful cause.

He started his swim this morning and the weather leaving Dover sounded just about perfect, although the temperature in Dover is still low (around 16 degrees) and the Channel will be lower than that. So I want to take this opportunity to wish him well and to say that I for one have absolute respect for what he is putting himself through at this particular moment in time.

Day 291 – Tuesday 12ᵗʰ July 2011

Angus completed his Channel swim in 18 hours, 42 minutes. Or to be exact 4 years, 18 hours and 42 minutes. He has amazing tenacity and focus, the sort of focus I believed I had but which now leaves me questioning myself. Me believing I could achieve in a year what took Fiona and Angus many years shows me how naive I was. One could even say I was insulting the hard work and dedication put in by others, although if I did so then it was without intention.

Looking at myself, I find that whilst my respect for Angus has grown, my self-respect has shrunk. Sure I know in my head that my weight issue is medical and not of my doing but my heart still tells me I am a quitter. It's not an easy thing to deal with and to get positive about. However, positive I must be and I must focus on the fact that in a year I went from non-swimmer to being able to deal with sea swimming in all conditions and temperatures and I managed long pool swims of up to seven hours. With this is mind and if I stay focused, then with another year of training I should be a strong enough swimmer to compete relay level. The dream may still come true...

Last night I started the relay plan with a meeting of possible team members at my house over wine and snacks, where we got to know each other a little better. The mood was positive, if not perhaps a little too jovial for our first meeting. Some possible team members did not realise the reality of what a Channel relay involves. I'll be catching up with everyone individually over the next seven to ten days to see where everyone stands. Getting the right team together is everything at the moment. In the next couple of weeks I'll hopefully have a full team including two reserves. Once that's in place I'll need to get back to serious training as I will not allow myself to be the weak link amongst some very accomplished swimmers.

Day 293 – Thursday 14th July 2011
Today was back to the pool, yuck. I probably didn't need to do a pool swim as the sea time is so limited in terms of months in the year but it's been ages since I did one and I need to make sure I rack up long swims again. Today I did just 2½ hours but that's not to be sniffed at, as it's the longest one I've done in a while. I stuck to the outside pool for fear of getting ill with the chemicals again but I might try the indoor one in a couple of weeks just to see if I am any better in dealing with them now.

Day 294 – Friday 15th July 2011
The relay team is now starting to come together. So far Lindy, Shoichi, Paul F and Alex have said that they would like to join me on this adventure and all are decent swimmers. There is concern about seasickness on the boat – we may all need to go out on a fishing boat and test our mettle in that way. Also not everyone has done 2 hours of swimming, so I need to set up a training schedule for everyone. As we don't need to tell the CSA who our team is until next year it gives everyone time to decide if they will stick

with this or if it's not for them. They all need to be up for this to make it work for everyone, so it would be daft to rush and finalise the team before the year's end.

Fiona has been really taken up with Angus's swim and it must have taken its toll on her as she was the driving force on his team, but now that is over I remain hopeful she will join me on getting my team together and organised. Her knowledge and drive could be so very useful. All in all a great team is shaping up.

Day 296 - Tuesday 19th July 2011

Impossible to compare yesterday to today. Yesterday was a monstrous tide, howling wind and no chance of swimming; today was a calm sea, no wind and a perfect day for swimming. There is no way one can really plan for swimming days ahead, not with any real certainty. Total swim about 30 minutes and about 1 mile. Water temperature average 15.4 degrees, which is still too cold for this time of year, but not too cold for a short swim like this.

One issue that seems to be improving is my weight. I actually feel as though I've put on some weight at last and think I'm already back to about 10½ stone, which is where I am comfortable. It was clearly the 6-and 7-hour pool swims that were decimating me.

Day 297 - Wednesday 20th July 2011

A 2-hour pool swim at Falmer after work. Even though it's loads warmer than the sea it still felt cold, especially after 2 hours; probably not helped by the fact that as ever I feel exhausted after no sleep, a hard day at work, a morning swim and then an evening swim.

Last night was another restless child night, although Sharon did the bulk of it because although I was awake I couldn't move much, just too tired. Probably a total of 90 minutes sleep in all. Was at the beach by 6.50a.m., Big Bob and I pretty much did the same swim as yesterday, except in reverse – just over a mile and total time just under thirty minutes, so a pretty speedy powerful swim. I'm not completely sure how I do it sometimes with no sleep and feeling so tired, but there you have it. Tonight after work at 6p.m. I'm in the gym with Ross training on legs and lower body as I've still got skinny little legs and I need to start bulking them a bit.

On the relay front, I met with Shoichi yesterday and we talked about the swim in general and the training plans I want to set up. He is really excited about it, which is great. I also spoke with Alex and he also is definitely up for it; a wonderfully fast swimmer. I'm meeting Lindy later this week and Paul F next week to talk through things but I believe them both to be on board, so by next week the Starr team will be confirmed. If everyone is happy with the numbers then we may stick with five plus two back-ups; five feels like a good number to me; five Starrs seems to be a constant in my life. Saying that, six people on a team is the normal number and Fiona is pushing for that. I might let time be the dictator; what will be will be.

Day 298 – Thursday 21st July 2011

Sleep: Kids stole most of it.

Health: Not bad but electric pains again and too much ice cream for dinner (oh dear).

Swim: Mmmm, not exactly charming. After work last night I parked at Falmer, went for a 10km run and then ended up in the gym for 90 minutes with Ross. He pushed me hard; it was one of those sessions when I thought I might actually be sick but wasn't! We worked on core, abs, chest, shoulders and biceps – I didn't know one could do all that in a single session. Afterwards I headed home and got there at 7.30p.m., just in time for Sharon to dash out to get her hair cut, leaving me with teeth, books and bed for the little monsters. By 8.45p.m. they were all settled and I was in the home office on left over paperwork until Sharon got back for dinner at 9.45p.m. A nice meal of M&S paella, followed by a whole tub of Ben & Jerry's chocolate ice cream whilst finishing my paperwork – a mistake, I can tell you!

My night was basically filled with various visits from the kids and the in-between time was spent with my Crohn's complaining about the ice cream.

Total sleep approx 40 minutes.

The lack of sleep seemed to aggravate my rheumatism as well and the old faithful electric shocks were back in my inner thigh and my right leg was really burning up, until I went into the sea at 7a.m., and as usual it took away all the pain. Temperature in the sea down to 15.2 degrees but it was very still and very flat. Luckily Bob didn't fancy a mammoth swim today (I was certainly not up for anything huge), so instead we went around the four buoys at a leisurely pace, doing it in freestyle, breaststroke, backstroke and butterfly. A day like today does give you the chance to practice your stroke - or even all your strokes.

Tonight after work we have a Starr Trust CHOCS network event in Brighton, delivering CHOCS to some new schools and introducing them to possible partners and charities. I am desperate to stay awake for it.

Day 299 - Friday 22nd July 2011

Last nights CHOCS event was stunning, really invigorating. We were lucky enough to have with us the lead organisations from one of our existing CHOCS partnerships: Varndean School; The Grand hotel, Brighton; and Shika, our charity in Tanzania. The three of them have been working together on CHOCS for the last year and they explained to everyone what each one of them have got from being part of it. Varndean even presented Shika with her first fundraising cheque of almost £3,000. To hear first hand what CHOCS has meant to all three parties involved was incredible and a real testament to the Starr Trust that we have launched such an incredible educational programme, especially in such trying economic times. It really does make me so proud to be involved with something so life-changing to so many people.

My swim this morning was buoyed by last night's meeting. The conditions were almost perfect and I swam on my own to the fifth buoy towards the Marina and back again; a nice decent pace and a great start to the day.

Apparently a few sharks were spotted at the end of the pier; a fisherman even caught a couple and Damian swum back to the beach with one! One was around five foot long and the others half that size. First time since I've been swimming that that has happened and very pleased it wasn't me who spotted them!

For lunch I met Little Bob and Lindy and talked through the relay. I am thrilled to say that Lindy is definitely part of my team (what a strong team I now have) and Little Bob is going to be crewing for us; a fantastic crew to go with a fantastic team. Very exciting.

Day 300 – Monday 25th July 2011

Day 300 of my swimming career and I was pleased to be able to share that with my good buddy Timmy Piatt, who is doing a mini triathlon next week. Apart from training a lot on his bike, and running, he has hardly done any swimming - naughty Timmy! So this morning he joined me in the sea for a short swim before work. We went from the beach through the Pier and then back again, about 15 minutes and maybe 500-600 metres. I think Tim was a bit shocked at how different the sea is to the pool and that maybe he should have put a few more swimming sessions into his training but he did do brilliantly. He is planning on joining me Thursday morning as well, maybe without his wet suit! Actually, that would be daft as he's not used to the cold but if he's up for it I'll take him out to the second buoy and see how he fares with the depths.

Yesterday was my brother-in-law Darren's birthday; the big Four-Oh! He is also project director and co-founder of the Starr Trust and an inspiration to me since I first met him 13 years ago. He had a fantastic party with friends from all over the world turning up, bouncy castles, drumming sessions, a mini concert (he sings professionally as well) and far, far, far too much cake. Jesse ate so much that he was up all night and not all the cake stayed down!

Day 301 – Tuesday 26th July 2011

It was mackerel city down at the Arch. Walking down the seafront at about 6.45a.m. I could see literally hundreds of fish jumping from the sea. There were two large shoals about 10 square metres each, right by the shore line – and they were busy. David ended up catching nearly thirty and Yvo around twenty. The seagulls had a feast when the heads were being removed and thrown onto the beach. In fish terms it was a massacre, in bird terms it was a high holiday and in fishermen's terms it was the catch of the day.

I simply took in the spectacle and then jumped in the sea and had a swim of probably 1½ miles in about 40 minutes, following Big Bob all the way.

I have a gym session after work today with Ross for an hour and then I'll do a short 5km sprint around the park before heading home for books, bath and bed for the kids. I'm feeling a bit sluggish at the moment, possibly because I've pulled back on the training compared to the massive amounts I was doing earlier in the year. It's not a great feeling so I need to start upping it again. It's hard, though, to train in the evening, even though I've got a gym at home. Last night I decided to train at about 8p.m. after the kids were down, giving me an hour in the gym before we eat. The kids however had other plans and by the time the bed battle was over it was already 8.50p.m. and time to cook dinner. The will to do it is there, but time seems to be a constant fight.

Day 302 – Wednesday 27th July 2011

Day 302 – Wednesday 27th July 2011

Woke up this morning with a very scratchy dry throat, courtesy of young Jesse who has spent the last few days coughing straight into my face; my kids love to share. I did consider, very briefly, staying in bed this morning and not swimming but figured that whether I swim or not I will feel rough today so I may as well get in the sea anyway. Considering I wasn't feeling my best I managed a decent pace and felt quite strong and ended up going around eight buoys and the pier in 40 minutes. The temperature of course was still low at just 15.5 degrees and the air temperature (considering it's end of July) was a very poor 16 degrees.

What is up with people, by the way? By this I mean people who drop litter; why do they do that? The beach cleaners hadn't started as early as usual today and walking down the beach I must have seen around fifty empty beer cans and a dozen discarded beer boxes, not to mention the paper and plastic amongst them. There are massive dustbins at the top, how hard is it to use them? I just don't understand people's mentality.

Day 303 – Thursday 28ᵗʰ July 2011

Third day in a row that the sea has been flat, calm and a pleasure to be in. Had the pleasure of Tim Piatt swimming with me today, training for his triathlon at the weekend. I took him all the way out to the helter skelter; the boy did good.

Tomorrow, assuming the conditions are good, I'll swim to the West Pier and back. I need to get in a couple of miles whilst the seas are flat. Will aim to do a bigger one at the weekend as well, perhaps lagoon to pier, about four miles. Tonight after work I'm at the gym with Ross for an hour and then gonna do a 10km run as well.

A side note - kids slept in their own beds *all* night for the last two nights. Praying that they will do it again for a third in a row...

Day 306 – Monday 1ˢᵗ August 2011

Where is the year going? We are now a year away from my relay swim, though I remember saying that last year about my solo swim; time really is a weird concept. This morning I was in the sea by 7a.m., on my own although I did see others heading down to the Arch ready to come in. Sky very blue and no wind. The tide was very out, which meant I walked all the way out and could stand at the silver ball; very odd when that happens. Also the sea was so clear you could actually see every single stone, fleck of sand, fish, crab, starfish, bubble and bump all over the sea floor and was as clear around the head of the pier as it was at the shore's edge. In some respects this is really nice as it makes for an interesting swim, but ignorance is often bliss because when you can see everything your mind starts to wonder what else is down there! Total time about 39 minutes, so quite quick.

When I was back at the Arch I saw Little Bob and Lindy who had been attacked by a seagull and pecked on the hand. Must have scared the bejeebies out of her! If it's not the fish, or the sharks, or the waves, or the pier it's the blooming birds having a go!

Day 307 - Tuesday 2nd August 2011

A very sticky hot day, even though the sun wasn't breaking through the clouds. Meetings pretty much all day and then up to the gym for an hour with Ross at 3p.m.: shoulders, chest and legs = exhaustion! Afterwards I headed straight down to my beach, getting there about 4.15p.m. and despite the hard workout I was really looking forward to it.

After making my way through the crowds I jumped straight into the calm, clear sea and headed out around the buoys and then around the pier. Twenty-two minutes later I was heading back to shore but really not ready to so I turned around and went around the pier once more. After the second time around I really could have gone a third but I needed to get home, so reluctantly I headed back up the beach and scowled at those lounging on 'my' beach!

Swimming in the afternoon can be a real pleasure, as the sea has had all day to warm up and as such was around 17.5 degrees. If work would allow I would certainly do more of this.

Day 309 - Thursday 4th August 2011

After a few days of flat seas, blue skies and 25 degrees, this morning reverted to type with thunderous rain and cloudy skies - true English summer returns!

I waited in the Arch for Big Bob to turn up (a bit of rain wouldn't stop him) and around the pier we went. The waves were constant, as was the rain, but we carried on at a steady and decent pace. For no apparent reason I found a decent stroke early on and kept it up the whole time, fast and straight the whole way. The temperature was 16.4 degrees and the swim was about thirty minutes for the mile, which is good swimming in a rough sea. Come the winter I'll be in the pool a lot but swimming in the sea every day is making me a lot stronger and quicker and I don't think the pool would achieve anywhere near as much for me.

Day 311 - Saturday 6th August 2011

Sky very clear, little wind and nice and bright - a nice morning for a swim!

I was at the Arch by around 7a.m. and swam a decent pier to pier to pier, 1½ miles in around 50 minutes. Sharon is away in Spain with friends from tomorrow until Wednesday, so this is it for exercise until the end of next week as I have the three little kiddies all to myself. Am I feeling daunted by that? Maybe, but only a little!

A nice Chinese meal at the China Gardens with my good friends Dan and Nat will no doubt calm the nervous stomach.

Day 312 – Thursday 11ᵗʰ August 2011

After five days off from any exercise it was quite daunting getting up at 6.15a.m. and heading to the beach. It's funny how with just a few days of no swimming your confidence can be knocked, especially in a sea like this morning. The sky was very dark and the wind was blowing hard. I was tempted to not go in and also tempted to wait for someone, but standing there for a couple of minutes I thought 'What the hell' and went for it. I went in close by the groyne, swam out to the first buoy, which actually was quite tough in those conditions, and then turned and headed back to shore. I couldn't make it back to the groyne as the tide and waves were too strong, so instead I landed midway along the beach, just as the others were going in together by the groyne. Little Bob, bless him, waited by the mid section of the beach to ensure I got in safely. Tomorrow hopefully I'll be back to full power and the sea will have calmed its temper a little.

I certainly need to up my training again, as the last six weeks all I've done is a morning swim and a couple of gyms a week. That might sound a lot but compared to what I was doing it is pretty poor. I am currently feeling slightly overweight (which some would say is daft of course) and certainly not as fit as I was during the winter months. Tonight I will be planning out my new training regime for the rest of the year, which will include much more running (just got some fab new running shoes from Run in Blatchington Road - very exciting) and more core work as well as some 2-and 3-hour swims. Also I'll be plotting out the relay meets, as I really want to bring my team together now as it's officially just a year away.

Day 313 – Friday 12th August 2011

After a night of electric shocks in my leg once again I was wondering if I would be able to swim and run today but am desperate to try out my new running shoes. Luckily by the time I got to the Arch at 7a.m. my leg was 100% fine and I marched in for my swim. I was swimming on autopilot and planning my day ahead when Leo swam up behind me and grabbed both my legs and pulled me down. I can't say I jumped out the sea, but almost! Got to say though it was funny.

After my swim I dashed off home for a shave and shower and then got into my best suit and drove to Watford for a meeting. Then back to Brighton with a quick stop in Lewes for a short meeting and then back home for 2.30p.m., a quick change into my shorts, T-shirt and new running shoes and straight back onto the road.

The sensible thing of course would have been to have eaten and drunk something before heading out, especially as all I'd had was one cup of tea and an apple. In the past, when my years were less and I was not swimming or eating much, I'd have knocked out a decent run with nothing in me, but it seems that my lack of running recently, coupled with another year of grey hair and a thirst for more food (I have actually put quite a lot of on weight in the last month) have taken a toll on what I can do. By the 5km mark I was light-headed with lack of energy and had to stop at a Sainsbury's Express and buy a Mars bar and a Lucozade - a very new experience for me. Anyhow, I headed back out and finished my run, though I had to stop another four times and stretch a bit. It shows that I really need to eat and drink before I run. I ended up doing 16.85km in 1 hour 40 minutes; not a brilliant time, but considering my day already, my lack of intake and the 22-degree heat I guess I shouldn't beat myself up.

Day 314 – Sunday 16th August 2011

Whilst the run on Friday didn't affect my rheumatism problems, it didn't help, either. Last night the electric shocks were in my leg most of the night and my thigh was throbbing constantly, and so badly that for the first time in around three years I took one of my rheumatism pills. I'm not sure if the pill worked or if the condition was just playing around again but this morning when I got up it was fine. My legs and hips however were aching from the Friday run so I thought I'd try to stretch them out with a run and as such did a steady 30-minute, 5km run. Unlike a hair of the dog after a night on the town, though, a run after a previous run doesn't take the ache away! It also doesn't stop the rheumatism and my leg this afternoon has been really bad again. I probably should take another pill but I really don't want to go down the medication route again so I shall instead be a martyr to it and suffer in relative silence.

Tomorrow an early morning sea swim will do the job as it usually takes away the pain.

Day 315 – Monday 15th August 2011

Between the twins and my leg I simply have no idea how I will ever get to grab some sleep at night. My leg has been a constant pain now for a few days, last night being almost (not quite) unbearable. I am hoping, as has happened before, that the pain will just build up and then go away as if it had never been there. It's done that a few times so no reason to think it won't be the same now. As for the twins not sleeping, perhaps in sixteen years that will change!

This morning, with eyes half closed, I headed to the beach at 6.30 and swam with Damian around the pier, stopping for a nice catch-up chat at the head before a gentle swim back. Not necessarily great in terms of training, but just what the doctor would order on a Monday morning.

Day 316 – Tuesday 16th August 2011

A miracle indeed! My leg was pain free all night and here I am 5.30p.m. and still no pain today. It's such an odd illness, you never know when it's going to come or go. A great relief, though, all the same. Not such a miracle with the twins, but only three visits in the night, so not so bad.

The sea this morning was very choppy; lots of bounce and lots of face-slapping waves. I went around the pier again with Damian and was pleased to see Big Bob back at the Arch and also my relay buddy Alex. Strangely, these conditions are better for me than the calm ones. Yesterday in the calm sea Damian was ahead of me comfortably swimming around the pier but today I was waiting for him; he was not loving it at all. A very calm sea doesn't challenge me but a rough sea makes me work a lot harder and I push myself well beyond what the sea demands of me. Also I seem able to find the movement of the sea in my favour, grabbing the waves that go in and making sure I benefit from the tide movements, whilst in a flat sea I've nothing but myself for propulsion.

Day 317 – Wednesday 17th August 2011

Another night with no leg pains, so happy now that it has settled down. The last few days had clearly exhausted me, though, because I was asleep by 9p.m., which is not like me at all. Whilst I was still tired at 5.45a.m. I managed to roll out of bed without disturbing Mia who had somehow snuck back in. After a lethargic shave and slow dress I was in the car at 6.20a.m. A few small waves were breaking at the shore but the sea was flat and the tide was pulling slowly to the west. I swam under the pier towards the east (Marina) and went as far as the fifth buoy, probably just over a mile, then turned around and swam back, around the pier and into shore. Total time just under an hour, total distance probably just over 2 miles.

Back at the Arch Big Bob came in with a painful limp. When he was a few metres from shore he'd stepped on a weaver fish! Ouch! Foot in a bowl of boiling water seems to be the only way to deal with it; a painful start to his day. I wonder what the weaver fish has to do to get rid of the pain of being trodden on!

Days 320 – 322. Monday 22nd – Thursday 25th August 2011

Swimming – I swam Monday, Wednesday and today and it rained each day whilst I was swimming. The swims have been on average a mile per day and 35 minutes worth each time. Nothing extraordinary and that itself is not a good thing – I had planned to up my swimming again but haven't managed to. I need to get my mind back to it and start increasing them again. That may mean back to the pool, oh dread.

Running – Monday I did a 12.7km run in 1 hour 15 minutes; not bad as only just started running again. Today I did a run at lunchtime, a smaller 10km run in 48 minutes; again not great but not bad.

Gym – Tuesday evening I used the gym at home and did a 45-minute session, including my Vasa swimming trainer; need to do more of that. Wednesday did an hour with Ross at Falmer and he really battered my shoulders and abs. That's it for gym work this week unless I can find the energy and time for a quick home session Saturday night. Not sure I will though as I'm a guest in the director's box at the Albion's new Amex stadium on Saturday and it will involve wine and champagne!

Squash – A game with Ross at the weekend; turns out I have not lost my touch, as he didn't get a game and I was not exactly pushing it!

What else? Mmm, let's see? Oh yes, Jamie Goodhead, my swimming friend who I crewed for last year when his swim was called off. He managed last weekend to get his shot at the Channel and he took it with both hands and both feet. He got within a few hundred metres off France before they pulled him out; that as far as I and everyone else is concerned is a job well done and qualifies him as a Channel swimmer extraordinaire. His swim was so very tough; 6 hours of on-the-spot swimming, 9 hours swimming in gale Force 6, water on the lungs and eventual temporary blindness. Yet with all that he still managed to get within 300 metres of the shore. They had to pull him out at that stage as he was in danger of death, or at the very least permanent damage, but what an incredible swim. To say I am in awe of him and have massive respect for him is such an understatement; he has tried something that to date I have still not been able to. Jamie, my friend, you are a Channel swimmer and a madly brave one at that.

Day 324 - Tuesday 30th August 2011

Squash results from Friday - two games a piece (Jamie won the first two 10/8 and 9/7 and I won last two 9/7 and 9/2). A great game, totally at the same level, and massive exercise. Had to dive into the outside pool for a swim afterwards just to cool down and stop sweating.

This weekend signalled the last of the bank holiday weekends for the year, so summer (wot summer?) truly finished and autumn on its way. No exercise (other than chasing the kids) this weekend or yesterday as it was bank holiday and I am not so obsessed yet to give up a few days rest.

This morning, after three days off, it was once again not easy to get back into it. It seems that if I have more than a weekend of from swimming my mind and body simply want to stay in bed at 6a.m. and not even contemplate anything as crazy as heading for the beach. Full-on winter will clearly be a challenge again.

The sea was very far out today - it looked as though the plug had been taken out - calm and almost opaque. The air temperature was only around 14 degrees, which pretty much reflected the cool and sometimes cold weekend. The sea temperature hit 15.6 at one point and averaged 15.9 for the whole 30-minute swim. This is the first time it's dipped below 16 degrees since it warmed up from the winter. Being less than 16 degrees is really silly for this time of year but the fact is that the sea has never really warmed up this year. Last year it hit the heady heights of almost 19 degrees at one point; this year it never got passed 17.5 and that was only a few days. It seems likely that the temperature will now start to decrease week by week and it won't be long until I'll be wrapped up in hat, gloves and scarf, shaking like a blender on full smoothie mode and wondering what the hell I'm doing it for.

Day 326 - Thursday 1st September 2011

Back to the sea this morning, slightly achy from yesterday's 400-mile round trip to Bath for a meeting, then gyming, but nothing that the sea won't deal with.

Despite it being a bright start to the morning, the wind chill at the beach made it feel very cold and the sea had dropped down to 15 degrees. It was a low tide and Damian got bitten on the ankle by a crab walking out!

That is all the exercise I need today as I am now in the office putting finishing touches to a report and then of to Kent for meetings – busy boy at the moment!

Day 329 – Sunday 4ᵗʰ September 2011
Kids stayed at my in-laws last night, an unexpected bonus. It meant that we did manage to get some sleep at last, very welcome indeed! Unusual for me to swim everyday, usually I have a day off, but thought I may as well end the weekend on a high. At the Arch by 10a.m. and no-one there, although I know the early swimmers would have come and gone already and the later swimmers would be there just after I left; so I timed it nicely to be on my own. I swam once around the pier and back; rather choppy today and the sky threatening some very heavy rain. A bumpy, 25-minute swim all the way and very good exercise!

Later in the day, after the heavy rain had gone, we took the kids bowling and then down the seafront to play in the park. The rain had stopped and the sun was out, but the wind was quite strong. The sea was really picking up with very big swells and rolling breakers. I would have gone in if given the chance, but no way would have swum around the pier in that. Gotta know your limits.

Day 330 – Monday 5ᵗʰ September 2011
Pouring with rain this morning; still could have gone to the beach but just didn't fancy it. Instead was at the office by 7a.m. and worked through until 4p.m., then went home to an empty house and straight to my gym. Did 45 minutes level 9.5 incline 6 on treadmill, then 10 minutes on the Vasa swim trainer and 10 minutes on punch bag, then into pool for 30 minutes power swim. Extremely tired afterwards, but always good to be tired from exercise!

Day 331 – Tuesday 6th September 2011

Nuts out there today! Raining and windy and a very high tide; the sea was literally half way up the beach. The waves were monsters and they were breaking everywhere, especially in all the dangerous places. You could certainly have got in with the right timing, but I doubt you would have been able to get out safely, if at all.

By 7a.m there were a few more of us and we headed for the end of the groyne by the pier and I had my first ever 'groyne shower'. Sounds rude I know, but it's all natural! Standing right at the end of the groyne, the waves smash high into the air and come crashing down on you. After a few of those we headed to the girlie beach, which as always was not as mental as our beach, but still mental enough to not go in. Last year I definitely would have just gone for it but I think my respect for the sea coupled with the fact that I no longer need to prove anything to myself kept me at the shore. So there we were all at the shore and there was noting else left to do but 'pilchard' it. Picture the scene: Force 8 gale, mental waves, rain and wind, and seven of us lying down like pilchards being rolled around on the beach by the crashing waves. Certifiable, for sure

Day 332 – Wednesday 7th September 2011

Despite the continued wind we managed to get into the sea today. Our own beach was still far too dangerous to try, so it was straight to the girlie beach on the other side of the pier. The rain had stopped and the wind was about a third less than yesterday but even on the girlie beach there were massive swells. Shoichi, Alex, Big Bob and I swam out to around the first buoy before heading back. There were carpets of seaweed, some yucky brown bubbles and high mountainous swells that lifted you way into the air before dropping you straight back down. Even the pier with all its exciting roller coasters has nothing like the ride provided by the sea. Getting back was also relatively easy: all you had to do was hold your nerve, watch the waves behind you, feel the movement of the sea and choose your moment. When I got to standing depth I could feel the waves pulling me back in, which instantly tells you a big one is about to say hi. All you have to do at that stage is either run for your life (but that only works if you are well within the beach) or else do what I did today and that is turn back to face it and dive straight back into it and swim out the other side and start your return once again. Apart from a few small bruises from the stones being thrown at you when walking in it was a safe and energy-giving swim.

Day 333 – Thursday 8th September 2011
A cooling 13.4 degrees and, as per the rest of the week, very windy with huge swells!

Not wanting to wimp out again, Shoichi and I headed out on our beach whilst the others headed for the girlie beach. Due to the wind direction, the girlie beach had bigger waves at the shore, so very quickly the other lot were back on our beach. Shoichi and I got in fine and swam out to the first buoy. In these conditions it was a hell of a battle and what usually takes 3-to 4 minutes took about 15. The waves were all over the place and coming from the sides and the back and we were thrown around all over the place.

Having got to the buoy it was then a quick turn around to head back to shore. Shoichi, being a stronger swimmer than me, managed to swim against the tide back to the groyne, which is a safer place to land because of the way the beach is set under the sea. Unfortunately, I had to go where the tide took me, which was the centre of our beach. Ultimately I got out fine but it was quite hair-raising and at one point I found myself able to stand too far out, which meant that the sea had quickly pulled out, which in turn meant a huge wave coming in. Sensing this I turned quickly and saw a massive wall of water bearing down on me, so tall I couldn't see the sky above it. All I could do, which is the safest thing, is dive through it and swim out to sea again. Having done that I then turned back to shore and swam at full pace until I hit the stones safely, glancing behind me in case another one was coming. A swim not for the faint of heart! All done and showered, Big Bob, Little Bob, Mike and I headed to the Red Roaster for strong coffee, then it was off to London for meetings for me. Sadly the train was delayed because someone has been hit by a train; it seems my morning, however crazy, was somewhat safer than his. Once again perspective raises its head in the morning.

Day 334 – Friday 9th September 2011

Yet another wintry start to the day, gloomy, misty, rainy and windy. The sea was not quite as angry as it has been, although there were still some temper tantrums going on. A few down the Arch; it seems as winter comes closer more faces appear. A curious thing as you'd think the opposite would be true but I guess eccentrics such as sea swimmers don't follow expectations in the usual way. Shoichi, Big Bob and I decided it was time to head around the pier again as we haven't been able to all week and the conditions, whilst choppy, were not excessive. Saying that, I bailed out half way!

We got to the silver ball roughly half way up the pier and for some reason my breathing was really off. Every few breaths I would turn the wrong way and end up swallowing a mouth full of water. Most unpleasant, especially in such mucky-looking water. Mixed in with my breakfast of seawater were copious amount of seaweed that seemed to be grabbing at me from every angle. It actually felt like tentacles wrapping around and pulling you back. All in all between the drinking and the seaweed and my general lack of energy from little sleep last night I took the decision to let the two warriors carry on without me and I wished them a fond farewell and headed back to shore. Sometimes you need to follow your instincts; if it's time to go back then you go back. Swimming back through the waves and trying to stop the tide taking me too close to the pier was quite an exhausting swim and as I was walking out, a wave chopped behind my knees and knock me square onto my back and pulled me back in. It really does show you the power of the waves, even the smallest ones can be strong underneath.

After I was showered and dressed Shoichi and Bob came stumbling back into the Arch, slightly battered and covered in bits of seaweed. Apparently the same wave that took me out came back and landed Bob on his bum as well.

Now at work ready for the day ahead, just one 9a.m. meeting and then office-based to deal with a million emails and phone calls. A two-hour break in between however for a game of squash with Jon (not fancying my chances at all there), followed by an hour in the gym with Ross. I cannot imagine a two-hour training session midday going overly well but perhaps a large espresso might change my mind.

Happy Birthday to my mum, sixty-five today and still looking fifty – amazing lady.

Day 335 – Monday 12th September 2011

A nice weekend, devoid of exercise apart from massive BBQ arms! On Saturday I did a BBQ for my mum's birthday and cooked for fifty people, which is a lot of food turning and equal to at least one swim(ish). Then Sunday afternoon I ironed two weeks' worth of adult and kids clothes; again at least equal to one swim(ish). So no real exercise, but fake exercise of sorts.

This morning it was back to it and in the sea by 7.15a.m. A very windy morning indeed but as it was low tide the waves couldn't get the height they would have liked. Big Bob and I crashed and fought our way through, doing fifty strokes at a time without a break and then being able to put our feet down for a rest. A couple of times I almost lost my goggles and my swimming cap - it has to be pretty strong to rip a swimming cap from you.

After work I hit the streets and did a fairly long run, 16.6km to be exact, but in this wind it really felt a lot harder than usual. Tomorrow it'll be another sea swim in the morning, then after work an hour with Ross in the gym and then hopefully an hour in the pool. Tomorrow should be interesting, as I've got a lunch meeting with Robin Cousins the ice skater to talk about the Starr Trust; he's one of our patrons. As for the rest of the week, it's going to be grabbing exercise when I can as I am in Burnley and Blackpool on Wednesday, then in Watford on Thursday and Cardiff on Friday. The time is fast approaching when I'll be back to my winter pool sessions; not a bad thing as I need to start doing some long and fast swimming sessions again.

Day 336 – Tuesday 13 September 2011

Another windy start to the day, although no rain and slightly brighter. Big Bob and I decided to try to go around the pier, but spent about half-an-hour swimming on the spot, being bashed by wave after wave. A fantastically good workout, though, as well as being fun (if you like that kind of thing!).

Afterwards I had coffee at Browns with Robin Cousins who has amazingly agreed to be an Ambassador for our CHOCS project. It is such a fantastic project and one we are aiming to take national and then international. Having Robin Cousins as our ambassador is fantastic, as it could really help promote the project.

Afterwards it was back to the office for another meeting, then off to the gym for an hour with Ross (now my arms are really aching) and then into the outside pool for a 45-minute speed swim session (I need to be doing more of these now). Then back to the office to pack my briefcase with the reports I need for Burnley and Blackpool tomorrow.

Day 337 – Thursday 15 September 2011

Today's sea was the reason one swims in the morning; just beautiful.

After a 17-hour working day yesterday I was in bed by 11.30p.m., then fully awake at 2a.m. due to the usual visit by the twins. We took them both straight back, but 10 minutes later they were with us again. At this point Sharon vanished to another room and I was left with the coughing of Jesse and the twisting and turning of Mia until about 5.30a.m., when they both went to sleep. That left me half an hour of lying there waiting for the 6a.m. alarm telling me to stop being lazy and get down that beach. Despite that long day, no food for 24 hours and no sleep I dragged myself up and got to the Arch. And boy, am I glad I did.

The sea was a mid tide, which meant a short but enjoyable walk out just past the pier sign, then a gentle swim in a still and flat sea around the pier and coming head-on into the rising sun over the Marina. Just perfect. I lay on my back, arms and legs spread out, for about ten minutes, just letting the sea take me along to wherever it wanted. Despite my tiredness I felt alive and awake in ways you could only understand if you were to experience it for yourself.

As for the rest of the day... to the office to clear work, then to the gym for an hour with Ross at lunchtime, then back to the office and then into the pool at home for 45-minute speed sessions and then rest, assuming the kids allow it.

Day 338 – Monday 19th September 2011

At the Arch by 7a.m. and swam well, maintaining a good speed the whole way.

After work I headed up to Falmer for an hour with Ross; back, shoulders, chest. My right shoulder is slightly strained, I can really feel it pulling as I move, so I have booked in to see my physio Kim on Thursday. It's the first session with her for months, so long overdue. The body is a machine and needs to be MOTd every now and then.

Trustees meeting tonight as almost ready to dish out some of the funds raised through Swim4Smiles. Although I am swimming next year and will continue to fundraise for our projects, we did tell them originally that they could expect money this year. Therefore on 28th October we are giving out the amount we have raised so far towards the £100,000: around £65,000, so fantastic by all accounts. We're also going to choose our 'Starr Scholar', the child who will get the £2,100 cheque to help them achieve their dream - very exciting.

Day 339 – Tuesday 19th September 2011

Having a 7.30a.m. meeting in the diary, I had to be at the beach and in the sea by 6.15a.m. I was a tired, lonely soul walking down the beach in near darkness and building winds. I got to the middle of the beach and tried to wade in and as soon as a gap appeared I headed in. The next wave was a bit of a monster and before I had a chance to dive in I was knocked off my feet onto my bum and dragged up the beach. Anyone watching that would have no doubt had considered me a mad fool. Picking myself up I headed to the doughnut groyne, where the waves are never as crazy. From there

I swam against the tide and managed to make it to the Brighton Centre; not an easy swim. It took me about 35 minutes of hard battling but only 5 minutes to get back!

The 'Starr Scholar' has become 'Starr Scholars' plural. We couldn't separate two of them – they were both so different but both so worthy. Seeing how we can support the other nineteen projects from our current funds was incredible, although fundraising needs to continue in earnest. We still have so many more children we can help smile and I must hit our £100,000 target.

Day 341 – Thursday 22nd September 2011

A morning of sunrise and Littlewoods catalogues.

Had a fantastic evening last night at the O2; we were guests at the Peace One Day annual concert. Got home and into bed at 1a.m.-ish and the kids let us be for a welcome change.

Still getting up at 6.15a.m. was not an easy task. Big Bob, James and I headed out around the pier. We headed east against the tide (anti-clockwise around the pier) and swam hard and fast all the way around the head and then paused on the other side to take in the sunrise. It was magnificent, to say the least; no word in the dictionary could describe the sunrise over the Marina viewed from the end of the pier in a moving sea.

Then we continued our swim back down the side of the pier, being held back by waves heading out and then thrust forward by waves going back in a kind of slingshot movement. Coming down around to the steps of the pier we swam into Alex and Crazy Leo coming the other way. Alex, always one to have his camera on him even in the sea, decided we should climb the stairs and jump in with James treading water and taking the pics. Apart from the barnacles and rust on the steps causing blood to be spilt it was a fine idea. First shot was Alex and me in a 'Littlewoods swimming trunks' pose; very much catalogue boys!

Then after a gorgeous cappuccino I headed off to the Withdean Sports Stadium for a session with my physio-terrorist Kim. After 40 minutes of pulling and pushing my shoulder was certainly better, even if the rest of me was feeling somewhat battered.

Day 342 - Friday 23rd September 2011

Sea swim (7.15a.m.)

Big Bob, Damian and *moi* around the pier in good time, rather cold at 13.6 degrees but flat and yet another incredible sunrise.

Squash (1.45p.m.)

Against Jon, and I shan't report the scores as I was annihilated.

Pool Swim (2.30p.m.)

Fifty cool down lengths after squash and before gym.

Gym (3p.m.)

An hour with Ross, and halfway through my energy levels dropped. Could be because up to that point all I had eaten since getting up was a banana and all I had drunk was a Red Roaster cappuccino. I am determined to sort out this ridiculous eating.

How did I manage to fit in any work? I did though, in fact I landed two really big accounts today for the company, so a good day in many ways.

Tomorrow, Saturday, there is a BSC Marina swim (one way only) at 11.30a.m. and as long as my arms stop aching I really hope to join them. Then tomorrow night it's our Starr Trust Barn Dance, the last one we shall do for a few years as it's our third year in a row. So far out of the 200 tickets we had hoped to sell we are up to 198! A great fundraiser and a lot of fun (if you like that kind of thing). Although a quiet evening and early night should be on the cards, it's dinner out with my Sharon for her birthday; life may be tiring but it ain't so bad!

Day 343 - Saturday 24th September 2011

An 11.45a.m. BSC swim today. About twelve of us took part and luckily the sea was calm and the air was dry and the tide, whilst fairly still, was not against us.

Dressed in our finest swimwear we walked to the Volks Railway (the first public electric railway in the world) and purchased tickets to the Marina. We got some interesting looks from seafront visitors as to why a dozen semi-naked men and women were queuing up to get on the old train. With exact fare in hand we made our way to the seats and enjoyed a leisurely ride to the Marina. Whilst this was going on, poor old Fiona was on the kayak and making her way across the ocean to the Marina so we had a guide/helper in case of troubles.

At the Marina we disembarked we lined up against the Marina wall awaiting Fiona's instruction to dive in and swim, swim, swim. This was *not* a race, it was a 1.5 mile swim to get from the Marina to the doughnut groyne on our beach in under 14 degrees.

As this was *not* a race, why was my heart beating a hundred miles an hour and why did I spend the whole swim worrying about being last? This is exactly why I don't swim fast, because I am so tense in these situations. As it turns out I wasn't last but nor was I near the front!

Day 344 - Monday 26h September 2011

The sea was churning and the waves bouncing around. The BBC were at the Arch filming Paul, as he has recently had a lottery grant to preserve the BSC's 100-plus years of history. (There is now a permanent exhibition about the history of Brighton Swimming Club at Brighton Fishing Museum, documenting the many roles of the club between the 1860s and the present day, called Floating Memories.) They filmed us walking down the beach and diving into the sea and it's going out tonight on BBC1.

A relay attempt was called off last week due to the adjudicator falling down on the boat and being injured. This was their third attempt at trying to go and as such, two of the six-person team had to fly back to the USA, leaving the team two people down with one final slot on Wednesday (28th). Big Bob and Alex were asked by Fiona to stand in and they both agreed. It was fairly surprising Bob went for it as he seemed so against doing this. Anyhow, both are fantastic swimmers and totally capable and the relay team are extremely lucky to have them. If the weather holds they will hopefully be successful Channel swimmers by Thursday – good luck to them both!

Day 345 – Tuesday 27ᵗʰ September 2011

Today would have been my dad's sixty-sixth birthday. Five years on and I miss him more today than I think I have ever done. Time heals – apparently. I don't know who said that but they were wrong. What heals is a large glass of Jack Daniels with plenty of ice and remembering what a lucky, lucky boy I am to have been born to Edward and Trish Starr. I was blessed the moment I was born and I even got a fantastic sister as well. Sure as hell miss him, though.

I didn't sea swim today. Instead I had my first TI training – TI stands for 'Total Immersion' and is an alternative swimming training. I found this system while trawling the Internet for help on bettering my swimming technique and speed. I am so fed up with not getting faster and my technique not looking or feeling better and I need a radical change. The more I swim and the harder I push myself through the water, the more exhausted I get: my speed is only marginally quicker than eighteen months ago. Something has to change and it seems to me that traditional swimming training of 'working harder' and 'pushing the muscle' is counter productive. Maybe more efficient swimming with slower, more controlled strokes will be better than brute force. Looking at TI it seems this is worth a try.

I met Toby, the TI instructor, at Queens Hotel opposite the pier and he talked me through how TI works and what I can expect. It seems there is a lot of mental preparation and that I will have to totally undo all the swimming skills (or lack of them) I have built up over the last eighteen months. Once again here I am realising that if I had not rushed headlong into the traffic I could have done this first and been a decent swimmer by now! As ever, more lessons for me on being impetuous.

The lesson was interesting as it was an hour in the pool with little swimming in the traditional sense. It was all about how I lay in the water, my bodyline, my kick, my head position. I will certainly stick at it and give it as much a go as I can, although I think I will find sticking at it rather tough. Toby was not – I'm not sure exactly what to say – inspiring. I'm sure he's a great TI teacher and a splendid chap but just didn't seem to motivate me personally. Perhaps at my age it's a case of not being able to teach an old dog new tricks.

Day 347 – Thursday 29th September 2011

At the Arch by 7a.m. and Little Bob and Damian there, no-one else. I've never seen such a low tide before – so low that we walked past the Brighton Pier sign and the sea was not even up to my ankles! Every day is so different, it's amazing. Little Bob went to the end of the pier (shows how long the walk was) and Damian and I carried on around. The air temperature was at least 16 degrees (meant to be 26 degrees by this afternoon) and the sea temp 14.4 degrees, so up a bit.

Once more no words to describe the sunrise other than simply a marvel.

Channel relay by Big Bob, Alex and four others was completed success-fully in perfect conditions at 12 hours 23 minutes. Apparently the conditions were freakishly freaky – not a ripple anywhere in the Channel, just flat, flat, flat. Well done them. Now we have to hope our conditions are as good and aim for 12 hours 22 minutes!

Day 348 – Friday 30th September 2011

No sea swimming today, Crohn's playing up.

Yesterday after work I did an hour with Ross in the gym and then a 30-minute pool swim going over the TI exercises Toby showed me. Not easy to master them on your own after one lesson but I gave it a go nevertheless.

I hadn't been feeling terribly well all day so it was probably daft to have used the gym and the pool, and on the way home I had to pull over to the side of the road a couple of times; not good. After getting changed I headed off to Sharon's parents as it was Jewish New Year and Sharon's mum always does a big feast. Sadly I sat there with a completely empty plate, as there was no way even a morsel could cross my lips the way I was feeling!

Having not slept a wink last night (not the children's fault this time!) I got up at 6a.m. but decided not to go to the sea. I feel massively better this morning, but best to be sensible. If the day goes well and I feel better I'll try to head to the gym for an hour but I'll see how I feel.

Day 349 – Tuesday 4ᵗʰ October 2011

Good news for the day: This afternoon I have a meeting with boxing promoter Frank Maloney (he was boxer Lennox Lewis's trainer when he was world champ and he is a patron of the Starr Trust). He's coming to Brighton with an event's company to meet me about them putting on a golf tournament in Portugal in Frank's name in aid of a fundraiser for the Trust. Mind you, sometimes very cool things are suggested that ultimately do not end up happening, so I will keep a level head on this one as it probably won't happen – not me being negative just me being honest.

There is some disappointing news for the day too: As you know I was already sceptical about the new swimming training, Total Immersion. It was pretty much the opposite of everything I had been doing in swimming. However, I am desperate to get my speed up and thought I should give it a go, so last week I had my first lesson and I took it very seriously and then in the week went to the pool twice and practised it. I felt very foolish doing these exercises whilst everyone else was swimming but I did them all the same. This morning at 10a.m. I went for my second lesson. After such a long day yesterday and a full diary today it was hard to schedule this lesson in, both workwise and mentally, but there I was at the pool at 9.50a.m. ready for my second dip of the day and with an open mind. By 10.45a.m. I was back in my car and really disappointed that not only did Toby the instructor not turn up, but he didn't phone, email or text! I have since had an email from him saying he forgot to put it in his diary; apparently I should have emailed him to remind him! How about, 'Sorry, Rob, my fault. It won't happen again'.

When I met him last week there were two of us waiting; he apologised to the other chap saying he was expecting him next week and basically tough luck. The chap was insistent it wasn't the next week but ended up leaving very disappointed. Seems Toby has form... It's a great shame, as TI was hard enough for me to mentally commit to without being left standing, embarrassed, in my trunks and goggles next to a pool. This is the second swimming teacher who has let me down but all I'm trying to do is get a little help - not for free, I am very happy to pay, but I can't seem to find the help anywhere. Think I'll bin that idea and stick to learning to swim by swimming!

Day 350 - Wednesday 5th October 2011

Where's the weather gone? After being spoilt for a week with magnificent weather here we are with darkness, wind and a little rain. This morning I was at the Arch by 7a.m. and heading into the sea with Big Bob and Lindy. The waves were quite big and the swells high. Lindy went around the pier whilst Bob and I headed west against the tide to the Brighton Centre; we seem to like that swim. I still find I swim better in rougher waters; perhaps it's because everyone else is a little more cautious whilst I stay the same whatever and hence come into my own. Saying that, Bob copes with all weathers and on a day like today it's good for me that we swim together; safety in numbers as well as someone to enjoy the crazy experience with. This was not the only challenge of the day for me; in fact I would say this was the easiest part of my day.

Day 352 - Friday 7th October 2011

Another dark and cold start to the day. How is it possible that a week ago I was sitting on Lancing beach in 24 degrees and taking the twins for a dip in a sparkling sea, and this morning it is about 8 degrees and very stormy looking? The sea was showing some quite big waves at shore and some monster swells way out to sea. Big Bob and little me headed out from our beach and straight out to sea. On reaching the helter skelter, having already been thrust feet into the air numerous times by massive swells, I stopped for a second and called out to Bob that perhaps we should turn back. Naturally in such a busy sea he didn't hear me so on we went. (Funnily enough, when we got back Bob said he considered stopping at the helter skelter as he fancied turning back but he didn't think I would want to.) Getting to the end of the pier and heading around we stopped for a moment to enjoy the calmer water before going back around and into the walls of water heading to shore.

We decided to land on the girlie beach rather than go under the pier and back to ours as the waves would have made it very hard and dangerous. Back at the Arch, Alex complained that we shouldn't call it the girlie beach just because it's safer; actually he is spot on, as the BSC ladies are a tough bunch and often have bigger b***s than the boys! We should rename it the safer beach to be politically and factually correct!

The whole swim took about 26 minutes and felt like a massive workout; my shoulders are still aching. Bob remarked that we sometimes forget the enormity of swimming in the sea and around the pier, let alone in conditions such as these. He is absolutely right; we do take it for granted because it's what we do, but for most people it would be unthinkable.

Day 353 - Saturday 8th October 2011

A happy Yom Kippur to you today, although I am not sure if one is meant to be happy on the Day of Atonement? However, in my world we should always be happy, so happy wishes to you all. This morning Sharon took the three little Starrs to the synagogue (unlike me she has no sins to atone for) but being one not to follow any organised religion I decided not to join them; support them of course, but not join them. Instead I put on my running shoes and did a nice 12k run in 1 hour and 2 minutes. My knee was aching at the end, so there was penance involved!

Day 354 - Monday 10th October 2011

Last night we only had little Mia join us in bed, so how come I was still shoved out? Considering she is only three, she sure has a lot of strength in her legs and arms. I spent the whole night fighting to just stay on the edge rather than the floor. By 5.45a.m. she had won game set and match and I was on the floor feeling rather sad to have been beaten once again.

On the positive side I needed to up and about early as I had an important

8a.m. meeting to get to, so an early swim was needed. I was at the Arch by 6.30a.m. and met with Shoichi. The wind was really pushing and the sea was a mass of waves. Luckily it was low tide, which meant we could get in; if it had been high tide it would have been suicidal to have even tried. After 25 minutes of battling we got safely back to shore and headed up the beach, both of us swaying with dizziness from the pounding and the crazy movement of the sea. I headed straight into the shower, holding onto the sides as I was still swaying.

Next week before I go away on a much-needed week's holiday I am going to arrange a meal out with my relay team so that we can be regaled by Alex's recent relay swim and understand a little more of what we are heading into. It will also be great to meet as a team again because time is marching on and I want us to be very prepared; we can't expect the same perfect conditions that Alex and Big Bob had on their swim and need to be ready to take on the elements whatever they throw at us.

On a final note, I really must start running at least once a week. After my shortish Saturday run, my thighs are really tight, though I should be able to knock out these runs without any problem at all. Surely I'm not thinking a marathon could be done as well, am I? Not with my rheumatism problems; surely?

Day 355 – Tuesday 11ᵗʰ October 2011

Have you ever swum backwards doing the front crawl? No? Well if you had joined us this morning on Brighton beach then you would have done. Luckily it was a low tide again but just like yesterday the sea was wave upon wave and the tide was pulling so fiercely to the east that even a herd of wild pilchards fitted with Ferrari engines couldn't have made headway against it. A fair few of us down there today and all went in at the doughnut groyne, furthest away from the pier at the other end of our beach. Little Bob, needing that extra power and oomph, even wore my trunks but sadly they didn't help.

No matter how hard we all swam it was a case of one second by the groyne and the next by the pier. We kept having to get back to the beach and walk on the stones back to the shore to just stay away from the pier. The harder we swam the more the tide fought back. A massive morning of exercise, for sure, and a lot of fun. Big Bob and I ended up being in there for over 45 minutes, which for us in the morning at the moment is a decent amount of time.

After work I was meant to be at the gym, but instead thought I'd do another run and did 14km at an average of 5.25 minutes per km; a much better performance and I'm most pleased (and most tired).

Day 356 – Wednesday 12th October 2011

Once again down my favourite place in the morning, beautiful Brighton beach (written without sarcasm). No-one at the Arch at 6.45a.m. so I went in alone. Still dark, I headed around the pier. It was still a bit lumpy out there and a couple of times I looked up and found myself facing one of the razor-sharp stanchions; really heart-stopping stuff, especially when you see it that close and feel a wave behind you about to thrust you forward! Coming around the stairs I opted for going under the pier against the tide; my reasoning was that my shoes were on my beach and I was too lazy to walk from the safe beach to my beach afterwards. Of course I then had to battle very hard against the tide to get back instead of just letting the waves take me to shore. Under the pier the sea seemed to be coming straight at me at massive speed and no matter how hard I swam I couldn't break free from the pier and eventually landed on the beach next to the groyne by the pier, feeling rather nervous as the groyne is not something you want to swim into. It was nice to be back at the Arch greeting my friends with all limbs intact!

Day 358 – Friday 13th October 2011

I wasn't planning on swimming around the pier today as my shoulder is still swollen from my session with physio-terrorist Kim yesterday, but with so few days left at this temperature it felt a waste not to. As it turned out

I felt strong today, despite my shoulder, and swam at a really good pace. The temperature was 12.9 degrees, so we are now below 13 and I am sure it won't be long before Big Bob and I will be in there complaining about it being under 6 degrees.

Having had a text from Fiona yesterday I am hopeful that next week or the week after she and I can get together to talk about next year's relay. I am desperate to get my team together and actually have a 'team' rather than a group of people. The problem is that Fiona is always in great demand and I am not one to badger people, so whilst I am hopeful she will be on board I can't keep pushing her as it's not fair to either of us. Hopefully she'll be with us and I don't have to do this alone although if I do have to then I will.

Day 359 – Monday 17th October 2011

That was a looooong day. It started at 2a.m. with the terrible twins turning up in our room, jumping into our bed and falling fast asleep longways. Within five minutes I had no room and was uncomfortably lying in Mia's bed waiting for the morning. By 6a.m. I was in the car heading for the beach in the pitch black wondering what the hell I'm doing it for. Seeing Lindy, Dr Mark, Shoichi and Paul F already wandering down the beach at that time at least made me feel I was not the only madman in the town. A quickish 30-minute swim around the pier later I was back in the Arch (pleased that the others had only just got back as well as it meant I did a decent speed) and showering to warm up (12.4 degrees) and then dressed in my best suit I headed off to Brighton station for my 7.33a.m. train to Middlesbrough.

Now it's 9.05 p.m. and I'm on the underground heading back to Victoria hoping a Brighton train is there to get me home by 10.30p.m.

The one thing I dislike about days like today is the eating. As expected I had my usual little to eat during the day and now no doubt I will find myself standing at Victoria station waiting for a train and gorging on a rubbish Burger King and chips and then will regret it for the next day whilst my Crohn's complains!

Day 360 – Tuesday 18ᵗʰ October 2011

Back to the gym later to see Ross and work off that awful Burger King I had yesterday; my Crohn's was certainly complaining about it this morning by giving me some quite severe stomach cramps. Must avoid the rubbish food when I'm travelling for work. It seems like a good idea at the time but boy, do I pay for it later!

Tomorrow is my last day at sea for a week as we are off on a much-needed week away. A week in the sun and with little or no exercise will be a treat and will do my shoulder the world of good as it's still not right.

Wednesday 19ᵗʰ October 2011

No swimming today as Asher not at all well and Sharon needs me around in the morning to help out and to try to keep the twins away from him so that don't catch anything so close to our holiday. Everything crossed that they stay healthy and we get to go!

Thursday 20ᵗʰ October 2011

We almost never left home today for our holiday! A very close call indeed.

Asher stopped being sick yesterday afternoon but was naturally tired, so we felt confident we could still go. By 7p.m. Ash was in bed but Mia throwing up for England. She was still throwing up at midnight, by which time we had decided not to go away on our holiday. By 2a.m., with us still awake and Mia fast asleep and Jesse only falling asleep by 11p.m. (he simply refused to go to sleep) we had decided definitely not to go as no doubt Jesse will be ill when he wakes up and Sharon and I were only feeling 75% well ourselves (probably just exhaustion, but could have been sickness bug as well). I turned off the alarm and resigned myself that I would be back to the beach and to work tomorrow as usual. However at 4a.m. Sharon woke up, woke up me and the kids, and said she had decided we should go for it. By 5a.m. we were handing over our car at Gatwick, by 6a.m. we were checked in and now at 9.30a.m. we are at 30,000 feet! So far, no more sickness and everyone in good spirits. I need a holiday!

Thursday 27th October 2011

A fantastic holiday; truly fantastic. There was no more illness from the moment we reached Cyprus and the kids have been a dream all week. The weather was a constant 22 degrees, so not too hot to sit out in. Food wonderful, place exceptional, kids a dream; all in all just what was needed. I did go into the sea one day; it was about 25 degrees, yummy! I also managed to use the hotel gym twice in the week but apart from that it was no exercise at all (apart from keeping up with the kids). Definitely doing to make family holidays a priority in the future. Heading home later this morning and not looking forward to the cold sea that awaits me!

Friday 28th October 2011

Safely home and not swimming today as needed to be at my desk early as there were over 500 emails for me to look over. Holidays are great but one has to pay the price on the return!

Tonight we have the Starr Trust Swim4Smiles Presentation at the Sussex County Cricket Club. We have about 130 people coming; some from the projects we have supported, some of our donors, some friends of the Trust and some new friends. I can't believe that a whole year has now gone since we launched Swim4Smiles and in that year we have managed to raise around £70,000. An amazing achievement by the Trust! Tonight we celebrate by giving out the £70,000 to our projects and hearing exactly where the money will go and how it will help children smile. For me of course the challenge continues because I do not complete my swim for another ten months, but for now it's time to enjoy the amazing work that the Trust has done in the last 12 months.

Day 361 - Monday 31st October 2011

Back in the sea today after twelve days away; a rude awakening. The temperature was 11.9 degrees, which is remarkably warm for the last day of October and it means that we can still swim around the pier, something we couldn't do last year due to the temperature. It was not an easy swim today for me though as it was really choppy and even out at the end of the pier we were being hit by the big waves. The hardest part was getting from the silver ball to the helter skelter as the waves kept fighting us back, but eventually we broke through and made it around. I think that having not swum for nearly two weeks, still being in holiday mode, having a chesty cough and the sea conditions made it much harder than it probably should have been. However it was a decent start to the day and hopefully tomorrow I'll feel more able and strong and can enjoy it a little more.

Day 362 – Tuesday 1st November 2011

A day much like yesterday. Sometimes I forget that it is quite an achievement to swim in November in the sea without a wetsuit about 1/2 mile out to sea in very choppy conditions – and all before work. As we do it every day we don't think about the enormity of it, but actually every time we do it we face life- threatening danger and physically and mentally push ourselves, all at 7a.m. when most people are just waking up. Interesting to think about!

Wednesday 2nd November

No swim today, which was a great shame as I really fancied going, but I was heading to Sheffield for a meeting and my train was leaving Brighton at 5.45a.m!

Coming back on a late train I was sitting in first class (every now and then you have to treat yourself) and I witnessed another one of those 'lack of common sense' moments. Two ladies, probably mid-fifties, sat in the chairs next to me and were laughing about the crazy train journey so far; they had missed three trains, got on two wrong ones and had missed four meetings. They were now heading to Brighton for a conference that finished at 5p.m. (it was 6.30p.m. at this point). They were laughing so much it made me laugh with them. They decided to go to Brighton anyway and have a drink and they felt they deserved to go first class to end the journey on a high (not that first class on trains is much of a treat, in all honesty). So when the inspector turned up they requested an upgrade to first class and asked the cost.

He advised (or should I say spoke down to them) that they could not upgrade on the train. Laughing with disappointment, they got up to move. He told them he had to fine them £60 each for sitting in first-class with standard tickets! They explained they thought they could upgrade otherwise would not have sat there, and (between bouts of laughter) told him about their mad journey so far. He didn't crack a smile and insisted they pay. It was clear they were not trying it on and had planned to upgrade, but he would not listen. They ended up having to pay £120 fine between them and were also made to move. Absolute nuts! What is wrong with the world? Good for them though; not only did they not give him the satisfaction of getting upset but they paid up laughing even more and to his horror they both gave him a kiss. He looked mortified! Good on you, ladies.

Day 363 – Thursday 3rd November

Off to Exeter today for three meetings, what a glam life I lead – but time for a morning swim. Very choppy indeed; just getting in was challenging. Damian ran back three times, to the amusement of those standing on the beach watching him. Total swim about ½ hour and very up and down with the waves. Back to shore was a real timing issue to avoid being bashed; we all made it apart from Alex who was grabbed by a very heavy wave and spun over. He was fine luckily.

Day 364 – Friday 4th November 2011

After getting home so late yesterday I didn't want to do a big swim this morning, especially as I have another busy work day and also an hour in the gym after work. Luckily the weather helped me out by being windy and rainy. Once you were in it was wild but totally swimmable. I just swam around for a bit and then body surfed back to shore. Dentist James and I timed it just right because as we were leaving the sea the next wave that hit was a true monster and no doubt would have drawn blood.

Day 365 - Tuesday 8th November 2011

Monday came and went and I never made it to the sea. Tuesday however was a much better start; at the Arch by 7a.m. and in the sea by 7.15a.m. Big Bob and I swam around the pier - pretty impressive stuff in this weather in November. The air temperature has dropped and I would guess the sea temperature is in the low 11s. You could really feel the difference today but by the time we were into the swim and near the end of the pier we had warmed up enough to keep going; up to then though I really felt the cold in my breathing.

How long will it be before it'll be too cold again to swim around the pier? I'm not looking forward to it as that will mean short sea swims followed by pool swims. It's almost seems impossible that I'm now into my second winter of training!

Day 366 - Wednesday 9th November 2011

Sentiment of the day: 'So pleased I'm back.' I said this at 7.50a.m. with utter sincerity as soon as I was able to stand again by the shore.

James, Bob and I headed straight into the sea, diving through some fairly big waves to get away from shore. The air was probably under 10 degrees and it was raining lightly again; the sun not quite breaking through gave it a slightly eerie feel. The water temperature was 11 degrees exactly. Today it was very rocky out there, with waves constant and high and building by the minute. The swim out was good; I felt strong and able and was enjoying the battle against the waves to make it forward. Heading around the end of the pier was harder as the waves were bigger by then and you often find that at the end of the pier it's quite a tumble of waves from all directions and a lot of peaks and troughs as the waves crash into the pier head. Coming around the other side I started to feel tired and the cold was settling in a bit. By the time I had cleared the pier and was around the steps heading back under the pier to our side I was really feeling it and having to battle. It was at this point I looked around for Bob and James, just to see if I was keeping a good speed or not. Luckily for us James wears a wetsuit and a

224

bright orange hat so is very visible and I could spot him quickly and then see Bob next to him. They were parallel to me, further along to the groyne, whilst I had stayed closer to the pier. By the time I got to the pier sign I was really shattered and could easily have got out though being in the sea in a high tide there is nowhere to go! So on I had to plod until I was able to put my feet down at the shore. Was I pleased to be back.

Once again another crazy, energetic (and somewhat risky) start to the day, and once again another victory against the sea and against common sense!

Day 369 - Monday 14th November 2011

This morning I woke up in Mia's bed, Sharon woke up in the spare room and Mia, Jesse and Asher woke up in our bed. Now how is that for strict parenting? You can see who's in control in the Starr house, and it isn't me!

I hit the beach at 7.15a.m. with Big Bob, Damian and Shoichi. The four of us walked in and within about 50 metres we were off and heading around the pier. Damian and Shoichi are quick and were probably 25 metres ahead of us all the way. We met for a quick chat at the head of the pier and watched the starlings doing their morning dance, then headed down and back to shore. Coming back around the stairs and under the pier to our beach Big Bob got stung on the top of the right leg at the back! Upon inspection later it looked like a jellyfish sting; a line of dots with a circle of dots above and quite sore. In this temperature I was amazed they are still there and with that amount of open water it was millions to one to that it would sting someone.

It's still warm for November in the air; last year on this day the air temp was just 6 degrees, yet it is double that today. The sea temperature however is almost exactly like last year on this day. Last year the snow hit at the end of November and the sea temp dropped to under 9 degrees.

Day 370 - Tuesday 15th November 2011

Air temperature this morning shouted 'Wiiiinnnntttterisacoming'. Sea temperature down to 10.7 degrees and shouted 'Gonna start hurting you anytime soon'. The joy of sea swimming...

Actually despite the cold it was a nice swim today. The sea was calm all the way out and just a little choppy on the way back. It was so clear that the whole way around the pier you could see the sea floor and all the crustaceans crawling around and hanging onto the pier.

Day 370 – Wednesday 16th November 2011

I went solo around the pier in a flat sea, pretty much like yesterday's conditions, although the temperature was down to 10.2 degrees, which is a massive 0.5 degree drop overnight. I could really feel the difference; my forehead hurt for a good minute when I got in and my fingers were slightly bent when I came out. At this rate it will be in single digits by next week; then it really starts to hurt.

Day 372 – Friday 18th November 2011

A rough night at home and a rough sea; I genuinely could not say which was the rougher.

A cacophony of coughing from around 11p.m. until early morning, with all three little Starrs (bless them) coughing all night. Mia the minx came into our bed from 11p.m. and despite us taking her back a half dozen times she never gave up. By 2a.m. she was coughing loudly right into my ear and spent the next two hours pulling the duvet off me until I got so fed up I had to leave the bed and sleep on the floor. A cold, uncomfortable and sleepless night.

The sea was about as unwelcoming as my bedroom! We made it as far out as the silver ball but the waves were fighting us all the way and turning us over, swishing us around and throwing us into the air like we were badminton shuttles. On getting to the silver ball (about half way along the pier) we decided to head straight back to shore. The ride back (and it was a ride) took a fraction of the time, but it was physically challenging just to stay on top of the water rather than being pulled under and as we got closer to the beach it was a case of holding tight and hoping the waves didn't pummel us too much. Certainly one wave took us all under and over just to make a point as to who was the boss! Safely back on shore my head felt a little shaken about but the job was done and the day ahead now beckons.

Day 373 – Monday 21st November 2011
Two very different evenings, one giving a good night's sleep and one a good night's pacing!

Saturday

Sharon and I spent the night in London, seeing a show and staying over-night. We checked into the Hilton Park Lane and were told we had been upgraded from a standard room to the executive floor. How kind, we thought. A quick shower and change and we were off to see the show (Ghost - well worth a see). Afterwards it was to a bar for cocktails and some snacks. On returning to our room at the Hilton we found neither of the keys worked, so at half past midnight I was back at reception asking for new keys. The receptionist presented me with new keys for a different room, explaining that they had to give our room to another guest and had moved us! I was a tad confused and a little annoyed until she explained they had moved all our stuff to the Presidential Suite on the very top floor. To say I was surprised was an understatement; the room is the biggest in the hotel and can cost more than £5,000 a night! She had no idea why this had been done but the First Lady and I found ourselves in a suite with a massive bedroom (you could land a small plane in it), three lounges, two bathrooms, a steam room, a dining room with table for twelve, a balcony, views over the whole of London and a butler call button. One of the most random things to have happened to me in many a while. To say we slept well is an understatement.

Sunday

Back in our own room (all feeling rather small now) and I ended up taking Mia back to her bed five times before giving up at 4a.m. I also took Jesse back to his room four times, eventually giving up at 4a.m. That is nine bedroom visits between midnight and 4a.m. The First Lady slept on!

Monday

Back to the Arch to find it very busy for some reason. Big Bob and I swam to the helter skelter, drifting to mid beach with the tide, then swam back towards the pier, under it to the other side, then down the pier to the café, back through and headed to shore. Total swim, 24 minutes against a strong tide. A good strong swim but temperature starting to bite now.

Day 374 – Tuesday 22nd November 2011

A rough night with my Crohn's. I was OK all day at work, then after work I used the gym at home for an hour and again was fine. I possibly worked too hard, because when I was finished I was sweating like a sweaty thing and my stomach muscles were feeling very contracted. About two hours later the pains started and continued until the morning. It naturally deprives you of sleep and leaves you feeling very sore, but worst than that is the lack of energy; it really does deplete you.

As such I didn't want to do an around the pier swim this morning as the fear factor for me is getting half a mile out to sea and then the pain starting again and taking away what little energy I've got, especially in a cold swim which depletes you anyway. Luckily Big Bob was kind enough to stick with me and we headed out (in a calm, flat and tide-less sea) to just past the silver ball, on pretty much the same route as yesterday. We got back in about sixteen minutes, which was bit too quick, so we took another ten minutes to swim (right at the shore) to the doughnut groyne and back; total time about twenty-five minutes and sea temperature up again to 10 degrees exactly. Sea swimming, especially in cold water, does wonders for the Crohn's and takes away the pains, which is a welcome thing.

After work today I've got an hour in the gym with Ross. I'll still do that but if it starts to cause pain I'll have to give my apologies and end it early. Hopefully though by the end of the day all will be fine and I'll be back to strength.

Other news is that Richard Bates, my solicitor, completed his Death Valley cycle ride (cycling through the deserts of Nevada) for the Trust. A massive personal challenge for Richard and an incredible fundraiser; he's almost at his £6,000 target. He's such an amazing chap, a great supporter of the Trust, a good friend to me personally and an inspiration to anyone who wants to take on an extreme challenge.

Day 375 – Wednesday 23rd November 2011

I so should have had my camera with me at the beach this morning. Coming back from our swim, literally standing in the sea by the shore with the sea up to my chest, we watched the sun rising in the east with the pier between us and it. It was so quick to watch, as the sun started its climb seemingly from beneath the ocean until it was a full round ball of light against the backdrop of the criss-crossed pier legs. It really was an incredible sight.

The swim itself was the same as yesterday; cold for sure but the sunrise was enough to warm your spirits.

Day 377 – Friday 25th November 2011

A wavy day at sea with white horses galore. We went in on the girlie beach and swam out just past the café before heading back. The waves were breaking high and fast way out past us and raising us high into the air and dumping us back again. A strong tide to the east made staying near the pier impossible. A fun swim and certainly a challenge, but unfortunately a short one and not as satisfying as one would hope sometimes. Gym after work so will work up some sweat and some aches there instead.

Day 378 – Saturday 26th November 2011

Unusually I decided a Saturday morning swim would be good, especially as yesterday wasn't as full as I'd have liked, so I convinced Big Bob to join me and we braved the storm! It was one of those seas where it was rough but enjoyable. There was a very strong tide pulling to the east (Marina) and a lot of very high swells. It took about a quarter of an hour to just get from the middle of our beach to the groyne; usually this is about a 1-minute swim. We kept heading west against the tide until we got passed the Thistle Hotel (about 25 minutes in total) and then we turned around and headed back to our beach, the swim back taking about 2 to 3 minutes only as a massive tide shot us back. The swells were big, which gave it that feeling of one second being higher than the other and the next being lower, a real roller coaster ride. Scary at times, dangerous at times I'm sure, but a great, invigorating swim all the same. Total swim time 32 minutes; air temperature around 8 degrees and sea temp 9.4 degrees.

Afterwards we headed to the Red Roaster for a glorious cappuccino and met with five other morning swimmers who had already been and gone before we even got in. Brighton is full of crazies!

Day 381 – Friday 2nd December 2011

Wednesday

I needed to be in London for a 7a.m. start and didn't leave London until after 7p.m., so no chance to swim or train that day. Having not swum in the morning left me in rather a foul mood, which was not good as I was at a conference and was a guest speaker! Oh dear.

Thursday

I was also in London at the same conference and was a specialist guest speaker again; luckily I had a swim first thing so by the time I got to London I was buoyed up and raring to go. A morning swim really changes one's mood. The rain was pouring down, the wind was up and the sea was throwing big and strong waves at us. As it was a relatively low tide it meant that it was dangerous but was more of a play than a swim. The temperature felt really cold even though it was still 9.5 degrees; a great start to the very long day ahead.

Friday

I was planning on a swim today and by all accounts would have enjoyed it as Big Bob and Shoichi swam around the pier. A December pier swim would have been great, especially as last year it was not possible. Unfortunately Sharon was really ill overnight and I had to get the three kids up, dressed, breakfasted and to school and then dash back home to get Sharon settled before heading off to work. It is so unlike Sharon to be ill, so I feel really bad for her. Blooming shame to miss the swim though as really could have done with it. Also going to miss gym with Ross today as need to get home sharpish for Sharon. Hopefully if I can get everyone to bed and settled tonight I'll use my home gym for an hour. Roll on an illness-free Monday!

Day 382 – Monday 5ᵗʰ December 2011

5th December seems to come around so quickly for me; it is the anniversary of losing Dad. It is inconceivable that it's been five years, so very much has happened that it's hard to think Dad wasn't here for it: the twins being born, the Starr Trust being set up, house moves, the changes at Seico and my swimming career, just to name a few. I hang onto the fact that whilst he's not here with us he still participates in it all. I miss you, Dad, and I always will.

The beach was cccccold today. Air temperature about 2 degrees and sea temperature just 8.3 degrees. Unusually there were more non-swimmers than swimmers, with just three of us going in and six others standing on the shore in their costumes. We swam as far as the café and then headed back in. Coming back up the beach afterwards my feet were really starting to ache from the cold and my hands were slightly numb (still are, in fact). I fear my swimming around the pier days are over now until next May, which is a long time to wait. Hopefully, though, a day will appear when it's not too cold in the air and the sea is pancake flat and I'll persuade Big Bob to join me for a fast swim around. Until then, in the wise words of Little Bob, 'It's micro-swims for all but the very hardy and the very lardy'.

Other news is that today I sign a significant contract for work, something that is rather life-changing in many ways, especially after twenty years. Sometimes one needs to take the leap and see if one can reach the other side safely, so here I go, best feet forward. Funny how it has fallen on 5ᵗʰ December; divine plans maybe ?

Trust news includes two exciting events. First, I have a meeting today with the jazz supremo Claire Martin. She has agreed to be a Starr Trust patron and wants to really get involved and help us; very exciting for me, especially as Dad was a great fan of Claire's. Second, and this is really something, our CHOCS schools project has taken a massive leap forward. As from next year Shoreham Academy are not only joining us as CHOCS partners but they are actually including CHOCS as part of their curriculum. This is astonishing! I planned (hoped) for this by 2015 at the earliest, I never expected we would get there this quickly. It is the start of us taking CHOCS nationwide and having it included as a chosen subject in schools. Now the hard work starts, but boy oh boy, it is exciting!

Day 383 – Tuesday 6th December 2011

After a rather emotional and stressful day yesterday my stomach was some-what topsy-turvy last night, which in turn plays a little with the Crohn's. However it's all a state of mind so one has to refocus, get the mind back on the road to smiles and we are back in business.

Big Bob and I headed to our beach for a short swim west. The sea was choppy again but lighter than yesterday and the temperature was about 8.5 degrees. We didn't waste time getting in as we had to literally just run and dive to avoid being held back by waves. Really it's the best way of doing it, but it is a shock to the system. It always gives my face the worst shock and it takes a good couple of minutes to become bearable. The tide was mid change which meant it wasn't pulling either way, so in terms of effort it was only a case of having to deal with the cold and the waves. We stayed close to shore and headed to the west, reaching the end of the Thistle Hotel in about nine minutes, then turned around and headed back in similar time. The cold started to get to my breathing but only as we reached shore. In fact the most painful part of the swim was the walk up the beach to get our Crocs back on; walking on the cold pebbles after a cold swim is extremely painful; I imagine it's way worse than walking on hot coals.

Day 386 – Friday 9th December 2011

Yesterday afternoon the wind was ferocious, with much of the country getting battered; in some parts the wind turbines were spinning so fast that they caught fire! Driving down the seafront in the afternoon I had to pull over and watch the sea, the same sea we braved that morning. Only now it was as if World War Three had started under the surface; magnificent to watch and deadly to be in. Leaving the seafront, I took myself to the gym and did a massive 90-minute work-out followed by a 30-minute swim.

This morning, with the wind almost gone, I headed to the Arch to find that even though the wind had gone the sea was still kicking up a fuss. Waiting to get in, I stood watching for about twenty seconds too long and by that time (and it can happen that quickly) the waves suddenly opened up and I was faced with two minutes of just standing there trying to find my moment to get in. Meanwhile Big Bob and the others had been spun a couple of times and were now out in the depths waiting for me. I found my moment and went for it; the cold hit me like a brick wall. I had to keep going or I would have been hit by the next succession of waves, but it was painful and hard to do. Not only was it extremely cold but the sea was getting bigger and bigger by the second. Safely landed on our beach a few minutes later (total swim about fourteen minutes and temperature under 7 degrees) we painfully walked up the stones to the Arch. After we were all showered and dressed it was off to the Roaster for the best coffee in Brighton and a reflection on yet another crazy start to the day and another crazy end to the week.

Tuesday 13th December 2011

Sunday and yesterday was my annual Crohn's tests at the hospital. Sunday just horrible with the medication, felt sick and in pain from about 10.30a.m. until about 2.30a.m. the next morning. Then yesterday were the more invasive tests, which meant a hospital stay. Unfortunately they didn't give me enough anaesthetic and I felt a lot of the poking around without being able to say anything; boy, was it painful. Torture would be a word I would use. I got home hoping that a night's sleep would help, but three children and 100m.p.h. winds put paid to that. As such, no way I could go swimming this morning and no way I can use the gym today.

Day 387 – Wednesday 14ᵗʰ December 2011

The pains have not gone – they are worse today than yesterday. The doctors took around fifty biopsies from inside me, so no wonder I'm sore. The gym is certainly out of the question until next week and if I listened to the women in my life (wife, mother and sister) then so would the sea be. However, I don't listen (some say brave, some say foolish) so I was at the Arch at 7a.m. awaiting my swimming buddies for our morning dip.

The sky was an ominous colour, threatening not just rain but sinister things to boot. The wind was still strong enough to give the sea a hard time. A relative low tide meant it was safe to go in but it was more a play than a swim. The temperature was a shocking 7 degrees and having been out of the sea for four days made it really uncomfortable when I got in, to the point where I almost came straight out. But Big Bob and my crew went in so who was I not to join them? The cold totally numbed my pains and it wasn't until about an hour afterwards that they returned, so once again the sea helped rather than hindered. Now, being 4p.m. and after a long day in London, I am about to head home as I need to rest, otherwise tomorrow will be a hard one.

With Christmas just around the corner I am going to cut down on the gym and avoid the pool until January and stick solely with my fun in the sea until then. Come January I'm going to get in the pool and work on my speed and strength. What I can't work out is if it is normal or somewhat crazy to enjoy the sea in these temperatures. Have I officially joined the crazies at Brighton Swimming Club as one of theirs or is this a temporary blip on my sanity chart? I guess once my Channel swim is done next year I shall be able to answer that; until then, insanity prevails.

Day 389 – Friday 16ᵗʰ December 2011

Got back from London after 7p.m. and went straight to the local pizza pub to join the thirty-plus Starr Trust volunteers for a Christmas get-together to thank them for all their hard work. The Trust volunteers are just incredible and give of their time so freely; without them the Trust couldn't grow, so thanks to them all.

I had another one of my train moments coming back from London yesterday. I was sitting next to a chap who engaged me in conversation about business, the economy and world politics. At the end he said, 'Can I buy your company?' Normally someone may suggest buying you a coffee after twenty minutes but not your company! Turns out he is a venture capitalist from Japan who wants to bring Japanese technology into the UK insurance market and needs a UK-based insurance company to facilitate this. After my 'Thanks, but no thanks' he suggested a joint venture instead. An hour later, after bidding farewell at the station, I receive an email from him suggesting a meeting, an offer that I will gladly take up. Life is so funny, you never know from one minute to the next what will happen and what doors will open. Just like the sea... you never know which wave will turn you over and which one will lift you up high.

Can starfish commit suicide? If so, then how? And more importantly, why? This week the beach has been littered with starfish. Just this morning I walked passed twenty-three of them (I stopped counting at that point) on the beach and on Wednesday I counted over a dozen. Maybe it's annual starfish suicide day or maybe it was a starfish sacrifice to the great seagull in the sky; either way it was an oddity. I think I need to call my relay team 'Team Starrfish' out of respect for those fallen starfish on today's beach.

This morning it was raining cold raindrops on the beach (and apparently snowing on the outskirts of Brighton). Not many at the Arch once again, but enough of us to make a happy bunch. The sea was playing nice today with some very decent high waves, but at the same time feeling safe. A lot of fun if you can forgive the cold (6.8 degrees). The worst part for me was the cold on my face. I am taking the cold hands, body and feet cold OK but for some reason my face is really finding it hard, to the point where I almost couldn't stay in for more than a Little Bob (my term for a minute - sorry LB, just a joke). We stayed in for maybe 15 minutes, which was enough and then off to the Red Roaster for a gorgeous chill-out warm-up. No London today, so a nice easy day at the office. All good for the swimmers, but sad for the starfish.

Day 390 - Tuesday 20th December 2011

No swim yesterday for me as exhaustion won out. I hate using the 'e' word as I so rarely lose energy to that extent, but I think a very long and busy weekend, plus lack of sleep, plus a lot of pressure at work, plus pain from the op last week just took me over the limit. I did get up in time for my swim but Jesse (who'd joined us in the night once again!) pulled my arm, told me he loved me and snuggled back in and that along with the 'e' word was too much. I fell back to bed until 7.30a.m. and then headed off to the office.

This morning however I was down the Arch by 6.45a.m. (too early as it was pitch black still). I was soon joined by Little Bob and Lindy and then by Big Bob, Shoichi, Damian and a couple of others; not a massive turnout, but it is winter! Big Bob and I went in on our own and headed west in a flat-ish sea against a fairly weak tide. The temperature (my watch showed 6.3 degrees) certainly slowed us down; it isn't long before your arms really feel heavy and your mind starts to wonder a little. We swam from the middle of our beach along the coast past the groyne to the next beach and then turned around and swam back along our beach to the pier and then back to the middle again to collect our shoes. Total swim 11 minutes. A good cold swim to energise one before work. A very painful walk up the beach with frozen feet on freezing stones to remind us the madness of winter swimming.

Off to the gym at lunchtime for an hour with Ross. Looking forward to it as I have not been in the gym for a week, although the area around my kidneys is still hurting so I hope a gym session doesn't aggravate it too much, otherwise it'll have to be a complete rest from the gym for a couple of weeks.

Day 392 - Thursday 22nd December 2011

A nice warm end to the swim today, courtesy of Paul Smith and Captain Morgan. Big Bob and I headed to the pier, then back to the groyne, then back to our landing spot mid beach. Total swim eleven minutes, temperature up a bit today to 6.8 degrees - cold but bearable.

Afterwards, a few of us headed to the Red Roaster for our usual coffee. Paul Smith (from Swim UK Ltd) joined us and sneaked a spot of rum into our drinks. Rum at 8a.m. is the start of a downhill slippery slope, but far easier to slip downwards than struggle upwards!

As I won't be swimming on Christmas Day (it's the kids' time, not mine) it means tomorrow is my last official sea swim before Christmas. I might do Saturday morning (24th), but we shall see !

Now nice and warm I shall head off to the office and get some strong coffee inside me.

Day 394 - Wednesday 28th December 2011

Back to work today and therefore back to the sea (with some trepidation; it's always like that when I've been away from the sea for a few days).

Walking down the seafront at 7a.m. in the dark and getting soaked and windswept I did get that 'What on earth am I doing?' feeling again. However once at the Arch with my BSC friends it felt as naturally crazy as ever! Walking down the beach meant we were cold and soaked before we even hit the sea. The wind made it crazy rough but it was such a very low tide that even though we did the long, long walk we never made it out of our depth. I think the total swim (if one can call it a swim) was no more than maybe 10 to 12 minutes, but it was refreshing, mind-clearing and fun. Great to be back to it.

As from next week I'll be back to my Channel training, which means at least twice a week in the pool for 2-hour swims (including speed swimming - very needed), plus two to three gyms, two runs and four sea swims a week. In an odd way I'm looking forward to getting back to really challenging myself physically and wearing myself out, whilst still getting my early morning sea swims in (very important for the mind).

An exciting year ahead: I am definitely going to get my Channel swim done and dusted and move on!

Day 395 - Thursday 29th December 2011

Who turned the wind machine on and turned the temperature down? We were literally pushing against a wall of wind just walking down the beach.

Once again a low tide meant it was safe to go in but the actual swimming was almost impossible. As for the cold, the wind had such a chill in it that my whole left hand side (the side that I kept to the waves) was actually starting to ache. I think the total time in the sea was no more than minutes but it was enough to hurt. Getting back to the Arch and into the shower I was so numb that I couldn't even tell if the shower was hot or cold.

Day 396 – Friday 30th December 2011

Another year over, another year perhaps a little wiser, and the last swim of 2011. The wind kindly left us alone this morning, although it was still very cold in the air. The sea was relatively flat with some rogue waves coming along every now and again to add some sparkle to the morning dip. I stayed in for 15 minutes this morning and swam to the doughnut groyne and back and then played a little in the waves before heading in with slightly bent hands – sea temperature around 6.7 degrees – cold, yet a lot warmer than this time last year. Great shame Big Bob isn't around because if he was here then no doubt he and I would have pushed each other for a longer swim today, which would have been good for the body, mind and soul. It's too easy when you're unchallenged to just go in for a quick dip.

Come on 2012, let's be having you!

Day 397 – Tuesday 3rd January 2012

What a start to the New Year! Heavy rain, ridiculous, almost hurricane-force winds and very gloomy; sounds more like a day in the Houses of Parliament rather than the weather.

I did (rather stupidly) head down to the Arch this morning at 7a.m., hoping it would be a very low tide so that we could go in and have a workout against the elements. But it wasn't to be; it was a medium tide and as such way too much water to make it safe, so it was straight to the office instead.

After work today I've got training with Ross for an hour. Then it's back to the pool and some proper training. I'm planning a 2-hour pool swim today, which will be my first pool swim since June last year so it may be a challenge. I need to spend the next eight months really working on my swimming ready for our August relay Channel swim and it has to start now; no excuses. It'll be more of a mental challenge for me at the moment but once I get back into the routine I'm sure it'll quickly become normal once again.

Day 398 – Wednesday 4th January 2012

Return of the Magnificent Seven (pilchards, that is), a stunning cast to behold:

* Lead pilchard played by the Arch's own leading man, Little Bob Pilchard
* Second pilchard played by the six-foot crazy dentist, James
* Third pilchard played by our own Brunel engineer, pilchard Mike
* Lady pilchards played by the gorgeous Bella, the health-crazy Martina and the ever-smiling Charlotte pilchard
* Final pilchard played by the new pilchard on the block, Robbie '5-Starrs' pilchard

A fine cast on a not-so-fine day!

Another crazy day at sea saw just seven of us braving it down to the shore. There is something rather scary about standing right on top of a swirling sea and watching the waves build up just offshore and then come crashing in succession down at you, especially when they are turning right on the shelf and curling under. We stood there watching for a good ten minutes trying to decide whether or not to give it a go but every time we thought the sea had settled we were confronted by at least three monster waves one after the other. Therefore it was down to our leading man, Little Bob, to show us the way! One after the other we found ourselves as pilchards, lying in a row being washed over by a freezing cold sea. The sensible mature James stood and watched in amazement whilst we lay down in the wash and questioned the sense in it; of course, a minute later he was lying down with us and understanding that there is no sense in it and that is the whole point!

Yesterday afternoon was back to the pool for me, something I have put off since last August when my Channel swim was postponed. I wanted to use the outside pool but the lashing winds and rain meant that the lifeguards refused to go outside and the club therefore shut the pool. Utter nonsense, as I don't need a lifeguard in a pool that is only five feet deep. I shall bring this up with the management! So I was stuck in the inside pool instead, far too hot and chemical-ly for me, but no choice in the matter. The other problem I now have is that I am now far too fast for the slow lane but not really quick enough for the fast lane and need my own in-betweeny lane! So I was in the fast lane for two hours and conscious the whole time of who was around me and trying not to slow them down. I guess it does make you swim faster, which is only a good thing. I did an hour of just lengths and then an hour of speed interval lengths (stopping each 50 metres to rest and then starting again). Afterwards, feeling a little waterlogged, I dried off and went straight into the gym for an hour with Ross on abs, shoulders and legs. A tough 3 hours of training, but a great feeling afterwards.

Day 399 - Thursday 5th January 2012

Sadly hurricane weather continues to batter the coast so rather than waste my time heading to a sea that doesn't want visitors I went to Falmer for the pool. While I will miss the morning meet with my friends at the Arch, I need to get as much pool time in as possible now.

I was at Falmer and in the outside pool at 7a.m. I was pleased to find only one person in it. Grabbing my favourite lane by the far side I did an hour of constant lengths, followed by 30 minutes of speed lengths – two lengths then a 30-second rest and repeat. At the start of the speed lengths I was doing about 24 seconds per double length and by the end I was doing 19 seconds per double length. It was good that despite getting tired I was speeding up. As the outdoor pool is only 20 metres it equates to around 10 seconds per length. I have no idea though if this is quick or slow or quick, quick slow or otherwise. When Big Bob is back I'll have to find out what he does (probably twice that speed).

After work today I'm heading to the Arch to meet up with Jamie

Goodhead, my Channel swimming friend (the one who did the Channel in 19 hours last year but got pulled out a few hundred metres from landing). He's trying again next year, the crazy fool. We are going to go for a long run (probably 10 miles or something) then off for a drink so I can hear all about his swim.

Day 400 – Friday 6th January 2012

Oh my goodness, my legs! Last night I met with Jamie at the Arch and we went for a little run. I say 'little' with as much sarcasm as my fingers can type. Not only can the boy run distance but he can do it at speed as well; for my part I did all I could to keep up. We ended up at Shoreham Harbour wall before running back. Not sure of exact distance but most definitely well into double figures and fast. Having not run for about three months I am this morning walking like John Wayne after he's crossed the deserts on his trusted steed without stopping for three long nights! Perhaps a 2-hour pool swim earlier that morning added to my aches. Afterwards we grabbed a much-needed cold beer and had a long chat; Jamie is very much an inspiration when it comes to someone who has the ability to just keep going.

This morning I was still back at the Arch for 7.10a.m. and pleased to see a decent number there (four lovely ladies, four of us chaps) and a relatively calm sea at long last. For the first time this week we could actually swim in the sea, but boy was it cold. When I went to go in I was faced with quite a large wave so there was no time to gingerly acclimatise, it was dive straight into it or be swept away. This resulted in an 'arrgggh' shock to the system and woke me up! I did a fairly quick swim – it was good to be back in and for a short time it took away the pain from my beaten-up legs.

After work I've got an hour in the gym with Ross, so I'll have to make sure we do no leg work at all and that we use at least half the session for stretching only, otherwise tomorrow I doubt I'll even be able to walk! Afterwards I may head into the pool for a 'slow' 30-minute set of lengths just to warm down. On the plus side it's been an extremely good week of exercise and has got me both back into the pool and into my running shoes. I am sure, though, that I'm much too old for all this!

Day 403 – Wednesday 11ᵗʰ January 2012

Today saw the return of Big Bob. Sounds like a horror film, but far from it! Very nice to see Bob back after a long break, and with Little Bob, Mike, Charlotte and Bella the sea was full of smiles – until we went in, of course! Actually whilst it was still cold, it was in fact a little up on earlier in the week (6.7 degrees instead of 6.3 degrees) and the air temperature was a stunning 9 degrees. The sea was flat and it was a low tide; bring on the long cold painful walk. With BB there it meant I actually swam and we stayed in for a whopping 12 minutes and 42 seconds. When you compare that to Damian and James yesterday apparently swimming around the pier it sounds a bit nothingness but swimming around the pier in that temperature takes a much bigger (in rotund terms) and braver man than I. At my speed and my weight I think swimming around the pier without a wetsuit would be suicidal. I can imagine getting to the end of the pier quite easily and then swimming around the head of the pier with tired arms and my heart beating way too fast, but then the swim back down the side to the beach being undoable and me sinking fast. I shall leave that to those bigger, braver and faster than I.

Day 403 – Thursday 12ᵗʰ January 2012

In the words of Little Bob, 'Shall we go for a deep sea hike today, chaps?' The tide was so low this morning that swimming was only possible after a very long walk out through the waves. What made it interesting was a very strong tide pulling to the east and a strong wind adding to the pressure. Big Bob and I eventually got chest-deep but after a few minutes swimming we found ourselves dragged back almost to the pier and then having to walk through the waves back to the middle of the beach; probably a better cardio workout than you could ever get on a running machine. The only real problem, apart from the 6.7 degrees, was that the waves were then crashing in at below waist level and smashing into one's private areas; it meant every other step felt like a ice boot being kicked into your bits. Twelve minutes and many bruises later we were back walking up the beach. That is enough water for me today.

Last night I met Fiona at the gym before my one-hour pool swim. We went over my relay team, discussing all the strengths and weaknesses, and came to the conclusion that it's a good strong and fun team. The work certainly starts very soon and I am sure that my team mates are up for the challenge ahead; and a challenge it really is. The more I talk about it, the more excited I get.

Day 405 – Friday 13th January 2012
And the ice man cometh. This morning the air temperature (as predicted by the weather gods) had dropped from yesterday's high of 10 degrees to a much chillier 2.5 degrees. The sea, not to be left out, dropped from yester-days 6.7 degrees to 5.8 degrees. All in all a chilly start to the day for those daft enough to jump in the sea before work.

Big Bob and I walked until we were out of our depth and then swam to the groyne and then to the pier and then back to the middle before emerging chilled seventeen minutes later. It was great though to be actually doing a proper swim; very good for me to have Big Bob back and pushing me on. A 17-minute swim in those conditions is easily comparable to over an hour in the pool and much more challenging in every respect. It took a while to warm up afterwards as my hands really suffered the cold today. They were very painful for a while and then went white (normally only the older folk suffer the white hands).

Day 406 – Monday 16th January 2012
Another cold week just gone; air temp in the morning around zero. On Sunday I hit the streets and did a 12-mile run, including two rather large hills, in 1 hour 49 minutes. Not a tremendous time but still a half marathon run on a cold Sunday morning is not a bad effort. Did I use the word 'marathon'

again? I'm getting a little too tempted! Do I really want to run a marathon this year as well as do a Channel swim? Surely not. Sharon would go nuts if I suggested that.

This morning, with slightly achy legs, I headed down to the sea. The air temperature was registering blooming cold (thick ice on the windscreen kind of cold) and the sea was a low of just 5.2 degrees; another massive leap down. Big Bob and I headed straight to the pier, then under the other side, then back around and back to base. Total time about 12 minutes and in that time I lost feeling in my hands and feet. My feet didn't stop hurting until about 9.30a.m! I looked like I was doing hopscotch on the way to the car.

Day 408 - Wednesday 18ᵗʰ January 2012

I was in London early today so no beach or early pool. At midday I met a chap called Dan Bullock from SwimForTri. A really fantastic guy, he had offered to give me a free swimming lesson whilst filming my technique. I met him at his gym in London and we did an hour in the pool with him looking at my technique and filming me where necessary. Interestingly he thought that my upper body swimming was pretty good and needs some tweaks but nothing major. However my lower body, particularly my legs, were shocking. It is not a case of me just not kicking, it is a case that each time I take a breath my legs do some ridiculous splaying dance that looks like a giraffe on heat. Dan reckons I am using my legs to try to stabilise myself whilst I take a breath. Interestingly all I could feel was me kicking, I had no idea it looked like that! The end result is that my legs, being the two largest muscles, are basically causing so much drag on the water that each time I breathe my arms and legs pull in opposite directions.

We continued the hour working solely on that and he gave me loads of exercises to go away with to correct it. This is a priority now, because if I can get my legs to stay straight it could speed me up by 50% and save buckets of energy. Dan is a great guy and this has really helped me, I'm very grateful to him. It's always a good day when one finds out one's faults.

Day 411 – Monday 23ʳᵈ January 2012

This morning (waking up in the spare room as ever!) it was dry and still out there, albeit dark and cold. Down at the Arch it was the usual magnificent seven and at last an unusually flat and calm sea. Big Bob and I headed out to the pier, under and back and then off to the groyne the other side. A total swim of 13 minutes, which in 5.2 degrees it pretty good going. Apart from the extreme pain in my face for the first few minutes it was a good strong swim and a good start to the week.

No more exercise today but some strong gym, running, pool and sea this week for sure.

The relay team has its first official meet on 7ᵗʰ February, which is great as the weeks will now start to fly by .

Day 413 – Wednesday 25ᵗʰ January 2012

This morning I used the outside pool at Falmer rather than the sea and swam for ninety minutes. I still find the outside pool a bit too warm at 20 degrees but it's way, way better than the 28 degree inside pool! I spent the first hour on gentle lengths and then the last hour kicking up and down the pool. Bloomin' tiring to just kick for half an hour, especially that time of the morning having had little sleep, no food and no drink, but no-one said this would be easy!

Day 415 – Friday 26ᵗʰ January 2012

How exactly is one able to function with zero sleep? The body and the mind are incredible that they allow us to continue. Last night, after banishing Sharon to the spare room to get some sleep, I was faced with all three children. Asher from 10.30p.m. with a very bad ear, Mia at 11.45p.m. feeling hot and unwell and Jesse at midnight, not wanting to be left out. By 3a.m., having taken Asher back and forth to my bed, his bed on my floor, his bed back in his room and so on, Sharon eventually came and got him and took him downstairs. Throughout this time Mia was kept awake by all the comings and goings and she in turn was keeping Jesse awake. By the time I got up exhausted at 6.50a.m. I had had exactly zero sleep! I probably should have skipped exercise but the guilt in me got me up and drove me to Falmer for an hour in the outside pool. In truth the hour was only about 40 minutes, as I spent some time simply standing in the water and yawning.

The swim was legs only today, though; flippers and a float and just up and down and up and down and up and down and up and down and yawn, yawn, yawn, yawn....

At the office now getting ready for a very interesting Starr Trust meeting that could be the biggest single development in the Trust since we started. Then it's back to the office for normal work, then off to the gym for an hour with Ross (might cancel that if the yawning continues). Please children, give us a break tonight.

Day 416 - Tuesday 31ˢᵗ January 2012
Twins unwell on Monday so not only was I unable to grab a swim, but I ended up skiving from work and staying at home to help Sharon. I probably ended up taking more calls and answering more emails yesterday than I would usually do at the office.

This morning, with just 1-degree air temperature, I was tempted to head to the beach as I've not been in the sea since Thursday but headed to Falmer as planned and was in the outside pool by 7a.m. I was planning an hour but after 40 minutes I was done; my shoulder is hurting again and probably needs some physio and that along with a general cold and bad throat made that enough today.

Day 417 - Wednesday 1ˢᵗ February 2012
More pool and less sea makes Robbie a grumpy boy! Yesterday after work I hit the gym with Ross for an hour, working on every arm, back and shoulder muscle I posses, and boy did I know it. Afterwards I had about 90 minutes before having to meet Sharon and Asher at the Nuffield (poor Asher having ear problems), so rather than hang around I jumped back into the outside pool and finished off what I didn't bother to do in the morning. Another hour

of lengths meant two swims and one gym yesterday, a good day of exercise.

At the Nuffield we met a wonderful consultant who made Asher so comfortable; these guys have a tremendous skill with kids. Sadly he is going to need an operation to help his breathing and hearing; fairly routine for the surgeons of course, but not something a parent takes so lightly. If only a parent could take the illness and pain from the child and suffer it them-selves. It's really horrible not being able to do anything for them. We're not sure when, but probably at the next school holiday break, but meanwhile the banana medicine takes away any pain.

Now to today. While I had planned to be back in the sea, Big Bob sug-gested we pool swim together, so at 7a.m. on the dot we were in the outside pool (-1 in the air but warm in the pool) and Sergeant Major Bob set up the drills! He really did push us, like boot camp in the water. Ninety minutes later, exhausted but exhilarated, I was in the car heading for Middlesex for a meeting and then onto North London, probably getting back to Brighton by 6p.m. A long, hard, busy morning following by a long, hard, busy day no doubt followed by a long, hard, restless night. Living the dream baby, living the dream!

Day 418 – Thursday 2nd February 2012

After having restless children until about 10p.m. and then having to sleep in the spare room because my bed was too busy, I was desperately ready for the sea. Despite the –2 degrees in the air and no doubt 5 degree sea I was still raring to go. Sometimes being in the sea in the morning, despite the pain of the cold, is the most alive you feel all day.

By 7.15am, Big Bob, Little Bob, Mike, Paul, Flick and I had all tried our keys in the door, but *nada*! The lock just wouldn't budge. The only swim-ming option left was a change on the beach, but being the wimp I am I said that in this temperature I would want to warm up afterwards so I'd have to go home and shower after, which I simply didn't have time for as my first meeting was 8.15a.m. in the office. Wimp maybe, but sadly true. It seemed my influence over my fellow swimmers is greater than I thought and they all too quickly agreed and headed off to the Red Roaster to drown their sorrows! Come on guys, you could have talked me out of walking away if you'd tried a bit harder!

So sadly (and I truly mean that) I headed to work. My next sea swim will be on Monday (which will mean nine days out of the sea, as I've been in the pool all week). Tomorrow morning at 4a.m. I shall be flying off with Sharon and two friends to Stockholm and taking a short flight to the Ice Hotel. Just two nights but one of them sleeping in an ice room on a block of ice. Despite that, I reckon the fact that we have no kids with us will give us the best night's sleep we've had all year. Very exciting to see the Northern Lights (hopefully) and to have a reindeer ride (or sandwich).

Had a call from Big Bob. He and Martina went back and changed on the beach and had a swim. Afterwards, sitting on the beach trying to get dressed, he realised the madness. He was so cold it made him feel sick and shivery and that even walking to the Roaster afterwards was a challenge. Madness for sure! Big up the pair of you!

Day 419 - Monday 6th February 2012

On Friday morning I headed off with Sharon and good friends Claire and Kieran to the Arctic Circle for two nights. We stayed at the Ice Hotel in Jukkasjarvi, Sweden, and the temperature was -45 degrees Celsius. I cannot even tell you how that feels! Despite layer upon layer upon layer of clothing, covered on top with the heaviest windproof suit as provided by the Hotel, the cold still got through and it hurt!

The first night, after dressing in so many clothes it took over an hour to get dressed, we climbed onto snow bikes and followed a tour guide out across the frozen lakes, through a dark and wondrous forest and to an eventual stop near some wilderness huts. Inside we sat around an open fire drinking hot berry juice and eating reindeer stew. I sat so close to the fire that my socks caught alight! Then it was back onto the bikes and the hour's ride back at midnight. Total time four hours, but despite the layers of clothing (five), pairs of gloves (three), face mask, and two hats, the pain in our feet, hands and face was so bad we could not have gone on much longer. A bottle of water in my rucksack was frozen into a solid block after twelve minutes. On returning back we headed straight into the main building, got changed into less clothing and then trekked across a short expanse of ice and snow to the Ice Hotel, carrying just our sleeping bags, to try to sleep on a block of ice in a ice room which was -5 degrees. The second night we thankfully had a warm cabin to sleep in!

The trip involved riding reindeers, husky rides, more snow bikes and temperatures ranging from the hottest at -27 to the coldest at -45 degrees. Probably the most nuts thing I have ever done. I would recommend it to anyone who is adventurous and daring and not recommend it to anyone of any other disposition. As for going back there... not in this lifetime!

Sadly I was not able to swim today as I needed to take Asher to school and then be at the office straight after. Tomorrow I have to be in London for a meeting at 8.30a.m., so again no swim. Then Wednesday and Thursday I have meetings in Gibraltar, so again no swims as I'll be over there! I will manage to get in three gym sessions and a 2-hour pool swim but sadly no beach. By Friday, when I'm back and at the beach, it will be a massive shock because I will have been out of the sea for ten days in a row by then, my longest since taking on this challenge.

Day 420 - Friday 10th February 2012

First day back in the sea today and it was not easy! Over the last ten days I have gone from -1 in the UK, to -45 in the Arctic, to 0 in the UK, to +18 in Gibraltar and then back to -2 and snow in the UK and a cracking 5.1 in the sea this morning. My body must be wondering what the hell is going on!

It was bright and warm in Gibraltar and it meant that after my meetings I managed to stick on my running things and head up the Rock. Last year I ran all the way to the top in about 25 minutes and then the same back down. This year, probably because I was so tired by the time I got there, I found the run really hard and only ran about halfway up and then had to power walk the rest, which was frustrating. Still, it only took me 30 minutes and then I sprinted down in about 20 minutes, so decent exercise, I guess. Getting back to the UK last night and only getting about four hours sleep, it was not easy to leave the house at 6.30a.m. to head to the beach and was not made easier by another fall of snow last night.

Being away from the sea for ten days made it harder than usual for me but everyone felt the pain today for sure. My watch showed 5.1 degrees but I'm not convinced it wasn't under 5, the lowest it's been since this time last year. It was debilitating cold and each step I took was slower than the last. Eventually, having got to chest deep, Bob and I plunged in and swam for a few minutes but the cold in my head was ice-cream headache severe and I couldn't do much more. Total time in the sea 9 minutes and total pain well over an hour. Craziness!

This afternoon after work it's back to the gym with Ross for an hour and then an hour in the pool. Afterwards I doubt I'll be awake long enough to experience a Friday night.

Day 421 – Monday 13th February 2012

A cold and gloomy winter's start to the week. No rain or wind, which was a blessing, but just 1 degree and dampness in the air with a slight haze. The sea however was very flat and calm, which if this had been the summer would have been a perfect sea to swim to the West Pier and back, or twice around the pier or even the Marina and back (yucky swim). As it was, being the winter still, it meant about 10 minutes only.

We headed straight in (mid tide so not too shallow) and Big Bob and I headed over to the doughnut groyne and then turned back to the pier, making it only back to mid beach before we had enough. It was the lowest temperature so far for over a year, just 4 degrees; once it goes under 4 degrees then it is officially freezing and certificate worthy! It was so cold that as soon as we started swimming I felt physically sick from the cold on my neck; it didn't last long, but long enough to be unpleasant. Apparently at the weekend one of the members brought their daughter with them (grown up, not a kid and a decent swimmer) and she was only in for a minute or two but coming out had to be helped up the beach because she couldn't walk. You have to be so careful in these temperatures and that even though we can do 10 to 15 minutes, most people can't. Saying that, James and Shoichi (two of my relay team) swam around the pier on Saturday, taking 20 minutes. I don't know if they are brave or just plain daft!

By the way my relay team is currently:
Lindy Dunlop
Alex Downey
Shoichi Yanagasi
James Hooper
Rob Starr

The way the weather is at the moment we might need to up it to six people, which is the standard number. The difference between five and six may seriously be the difference between success or failure. I would like Leo, but he has been up and down a lot lately and I really need commitment and to feel secure in my team. We shall have to wait and see what occurs!

Day 422 – Tuesday 14th February 2012
Before I started my sea swimming, Valentine's Day used to bring a nice warm start. Now it brings a shockingly cold wake-up call! Big Bob and I did much the same swim and suffered much the same pain as yesterday. For me at the moment the most painful part is actually when I'm back in the Arch in the shower and the blood returns to my hands. My hands throb so badly that it is like being back in the Arctic Circle.

The Arch this morning seemed surprisingly busy. No Mike today as he was kayaking from Brighton to Peacehaven last night and then camping out on the beach in Peacehaven and kayaking back today. Considering he is into his later years (me being kind here) it's amazing really. You find that the people at the Arch really do have big whatsits and aren't afraid of extremes.

This afternoon after work I'm back to the gym once again and then back in the pool and then tomorrow morning Big Bob and I will be in the pool for an hour's hard graft. With the marathon coming up in April and then the Channel swim in August, I really need to keep the pressure up and increase my training weekly.

Yes, I did say Marathon! I have entered myself into the Brighton Marathon (now in its third year). I know it's not good for my rheumatism and it is likely that halfway around I will have to quit and do the walk of shame back home, but I thought that as I'm doing the Channel this year I might as well do the marathon as well; two challenges in the same year as the UK Olympics seems fitting.

Luckily I have nothing else in my life to focus on! For instance, can you imagine how crazy it would be if apart from swimming the Channel and running the Marathon, I was already in my forties, had three businesses to run, three children to bring up, a household to keep going, a children's charity to run, a theatre building project on the go and was writing a new book. Wouldn't life be a bit extreme then?

Day 423 - Wednesday 15th February 2012
Boot camp with Big Bob; or more precisely Speedo camp with Big Bob.

7a.m. in the outside pool at Falmer, Big Bob in second lane, me in the first lane and off we go. Twenty lengths warm up followed by 10 lengths non-stop, with the final 2 lengths of each set being at full pelt. Then a 15-second pause and off we go again, 10 lengths with last two quick and so on. Final set of the morning, after an hour, he ups it to the last 4 lengths at full pelt. Boy oh boy, that was a wake-up call. My arms and shoulders already ached from an hour in the gym the day before and I was tired from lack of sleep, so this really was a challenging start.

Tomorrow will be back to the beach and then Friday back to the pool.

Day 424 - Thursday 16th February 2012
What a lovely start to the day. My usual 7a.m. swim with Bob and the boys,

cold as ever, and then our usual coffee in the Red Roaster. Why was it so lovely compared to other days? I've no idea. It just felt like a relaxing way to start the day and I went to the office with plans for a nice pleasant day, and a pleasant day it was. More like that please!

Day 425 – Friday 17ᵗʰ February 2012

I guess one has to pay the piper! I don't know why, but it just seems that way – a good day has a cost later on it seems.

After my swim yesterday, whilst the mind was fluffy and happy, my left shoulder blade was causing me pain. It might have been the morning swim or the swim the night before but whatever it was it was rather painful. Then last night, despite absolutely knowing it would happen, I had a takeaway pizza that upset my Crohn's. Sharon was out and after settling the kids I went to the kitchen to cook something and found it very dusty and messy; the builders had been in to lay some new floor tiles and had left it is a state that was not conducive to cooking. So despite my knowing the dangers, I ordered in! The result was that within the hour of finishing it I was doubled over in pain and it continued through the night. The annoying thing was that it was completely my fault and I should know better. Luckily I do have an answer to my problems; it is called the sea!

So this morning, struggling out of bed still in discomfort, I headed to the Arch and met up with my usual crowd. About thirty seconds after being in the 4 degree sea all my pain had vanished and I was thinking about nothing else other than how far out am I drifting and whether I can get back in before the cold stops my arms working! With those thoughts in mind there is no room to worry about anything else. After about 7 minutes Bob suggested we head in but I was way too happy to not be in pain and I stayed in for a few minutes more. So much better that a handful of pills!

This afternoon after work I have a gym session booked in but I think I will cancel it as my shoulder is still not settled and I don't want to aggravate the Crohn's again. Hopefully by the time I've got the kids settled (Sharon out again; every night this week I have been a widower, what is the world coming to?) I'll be feeling on top of the world and I'll grab an hour in my home gym and then have a nice piece of healthy grilled fish and rice.

Day 426 – Monday 20ᵗʰ February 201 2

Another week gone and another one starting; time really does march on at a pace. The marathon is now only a couple of months away and the Channel swim only about six months. What will I do with myself when they are done?

Yesterday was the Brighton Half Marathon and a beautiful bright chilly day it was. We have about a dozen runners running for the Starr Trust, which was brilliant. I personally didn't take part in the official race, so instead went out at 8a.m. and did a 12-mile run around Hove. In fact I did eight times around Hove Park and then down to the seafront, along and up Sackville Road and then along and up King George, so some good hill work. Total time about 1 hour 50 minutes, so not too shabby.

This morning was the usual quick dip in the sea; although nine minutes in 4.5 degrees is not exactly quick. Usual crowd there and a flat sea and astonishingly beautiful sky.

If kids behave tonight I'll grab some home gym time tonight.

Day 429 – Thursday 23ʳᵈ February 2012

The hottest day in February for years and years and of course I choose to use the pool rather than go into the sea; typical me! Saying that I would assume that despite being a massive 10 degrees in the air, the sea is still probably a chilling 6 degrees.

With Big Bob heading to France for a few days I thought it would be good to get back to the pool today and tomorrow and knock some decent lengths out. I used one of Fiona's training regimes today; a 2-mile, 1-hour swim. I did it in 1 hour 5 minutes, so a decent pace but not the hour I wanted. I am thinking that a night of very broken sleep and no food or drink means that 65 minutes rather than 60 minutes isn't bad for 2 miles; perhaps with the right conditions of sleep and sustenance I should be able to knock 5 to 10 minutes off this. No gym or run planned for today, which is good as I do feel tired but tomorrow I'll head back to the pool and try to get this same swim down to 60 minutes, then I'll hit the streets after work for a 12-15 mile run; then the weekend, thank the lord!

Day 430 – Friday 24ᵗʰ February 2012

Whilst I quite fancied the sea today I thought another day in the pool would be better for training, and of course that is what this is still all about. I got to the pool at 6.45a.m. and I got straight into the 2-mile swim from Fiona's list. Sadly, I didn't make it in the hour but I did do it in 1 hour 4½ minutes. So very nearly there.

Then straight to work for what is going to be a crazy busy day of lots of meetings – one particular one with a staff member is not one I want to have, but sometimes people do the most stupid things and it is me who has to mop up the mess! Afterwards I aim to grab a 10 mile run to get rid of the frustration, then it's off to Asher's school to pick up Ash, grab the twins and then on my own once again as Sharon is her usual busy self. Oh the joys.

Day 431 – Sunday 26ᵗʰ February 2012

What a glorious summer's day today. The fact that it's February doesn't mean it can't be summer; it's sunny, warm, dry and simply beautiful out there. By 8a.m., running shoes firmly tied in place, I was on the streets – so important to get some miles in now that the marathon is nearly here. It's a real balance to try to get enough training in to satisfy the Channel swim (being the most important of course) and the marathon (not exactly an easy challenge). I decided today to go for the enjoyment factor rather than watching distance or time, which is how I expect myself to run the marathon itself. It's quite tough, as instinctively I want to check both time and distance, but I kept my iPhone on silent and hidden away and only checked it when I got home.

I ran all around Brighton, most of it along the seafront of course. My god, it was beautiful. The sea was absolutely flat and a kind of sky blue and seagulls hovered around whilst others were floating on the sea. Being still quite early meant that whilst there were a few runners and some early risers looking for coffee and toast, the seafront was relatively quiet. It made it quite a personal run, which was a lovely start to the day. Watching the sea all the way down the seafront made me almost desperate to strip off (not in public of course) and head straight down the stones and dive in. I don't know if only I get this as a sea swimmer or if other runners feel it as well, but I seriously don't remember ever feeling like that before I started sea swimming. There really is something about being in the sea everyday that becomes almost habit forming, a drug of sorts; very odd, but in a good way. Maybe all addicts think that!

Back to the run; 15.93 miles in total (although I think it was a bit more than that as the iPhone app does drop off sometimes) and a time of 2 hours, 9 minutes and 48 seconds. I'm certainly racking up some miles, but I have no doubt at all that I am doing nowhere near enough to run a marathon. I should be doing 18-20 mile runs at least twice a week, not 15 miles once every few weeks. But then I should be doing 10-mile swims by now each day and I'm not doing them either - just not enough time in life to do everything and somehow not enough dedication either, it seems! That does annoy me to write but sadly it seems true enough when I search deep within my soul.

Day 433 - Tuesday 28th February 2012
Another night of ups and downs, although mostly with the twins.

Back to the Arch by 7a.m. and some usual peeps: Little Bob, Mike, Shoichi, Damian, Flick, Martina, Charlotte, Big Bob, James and finally after many months of extreme illness and operations, David. He is quite something, the oldest member of the club, and has suffered illnesses that would stop most elephants. A recent virus meant a hip replacement, yet he is back at the Arch and heading into a 5.5-degree sea. Some people are truly incredible and can make you realise that limitations are simply things that society place on us and it is our choice as to whether we buy into it or not.

Day 434 - Wednesday 29ᵗʰ February 2012

Come on, push yourself! Get up Starr, get working! What is this, a playground? Move, move, move! That is swimming boot camp talk with Big Bob, as tough as it gets!

6.45a.m. at Falmer and 7a.m. in the outside pool. A grey morning but warm in the air and by the time we finished a bright blue sky. Seventy minutes of non- stop pool lengths and sprints; about 2,000 metres in total with no break. As tough as it is first thing in the morning having had no sleep and a child throwing up all over you during the night, a swim like this with Bob is brilliant. It really challenges and pushes you to the limit. I certainly think that maybe food or drink before the swim would make me go faster but I kept up with Bob most of the time and hopefully challenged him as much as he challenged me. Tomorrow the sea calls.

Day 435 - Thursday 1ˢᵗ March 201 2

A swim in the sea was very refreshing after yesterday's beating by Bob. Temperature up to around just over 6 degrees, so still cold but the face not hurting quite as much.

The big news for me is that after twenty-one years of trading solo, I have now completed both a merger on one of my companies and an acquisition on another. Doing both on the same day was not for the faint-hearted, but the time was right for both and sometimes you have just go to dive in with eyes wide open and hope for the best. I guess time is now my judge as to whether I made a good or bad decision. Either way the ink is dry on both, so no turning back.

Day 437 - Sunday 4ᵗʰ March 201 2

Raining hard, sleeting hard (actually snowing) and cold! Where did that come from?

Yesterday, Saturday being my day of rest from exercise, I had my three kids, my two nephews and one of their friends - a single parent of six! After lunches and then dinners I was pleased to see the back of them all and head to bed! Actually they were all great and a lot of fun.

After lunch I deposited the kids at my sister's and hit the streets for my Sunday run. As it was around 2 degrees, raining and snowing, it had to be a quick one, just 5 miles and all at a run. Did I feel better for it? Of course!

Day 439 – Wednesday 7th March 2012

A glorious swim this morning. Cold in the air and dull in the sky, but the wind was kicking up a storm and the sea was reacting to it. A low-ish tide meant it wasn't dangerous (at least not for experienced sea swimmers – pool swimmers should not attempt such antics). Big Bob and I went in right next to the groyne where it was safest and we headed out rather than along. A great fun swim amongst some big waves; not for the faint-hearted or the less experienced, but great for us.

Day 440 – Thursday 7th March 2012

Bloomin 'eck, it's cold this morning. If I was a turtle I would wind my neck back in and hibernate.

The sea was chilly, down once again to 5.4 degrees and the air temperature must have been around 2 degrees. The wind had died down, which meant a calm-ish sea with just a few large swells and a strong easterly tide left over from yesterday. Big Bob and I swam for around 15 minutes and an hour later my hands are still a little numb! Tonight I'm at pool boot camp with Bob again; be weird to do it in the dark of night rather than the dark of morning but it's gotta be done.

Day 441 – Friday 8th March 2012

I'm still not sure how I sometimes function being so busy and having so little sleep, but then again who cares how as long as it continues. Last night after dinner I headed to Falmer and joined Bob in the outside pool. We did exactly a mile in lengths and then some speed exercises. Before starting the swim we both looked like we were sleepwalking and energy-less but an hour later we emerged wetter, tired yet energised. Exercise is like Duracell for the body.

If it had just been the night swim then I would have woken all refreshed and ready for the day ahead but Mia decided to play up. Bless her heart she wasn't well, although she was also being minx-y. By 2.30a.m. I was still sitting in her room and sending work emails on my iPad (my clients must think I'm a workaholic). Each time I went to leave she screamed. I should have left her but I didn't want the boys waking up, so it wasn't until around 4a.m. I got to sleep in my own bed. By 4.30a.m. she was with us along with Jesse, then Asher. So basically no sleep.

By 7a.m., dressed and sleepwalking again, I was in the Arch with Big Bob, LB, Mike, David, Flick, Martina, Charlotte and Lindy - a large crowd at last. The sea was relatively warm (up to 6.5 degrees somehow) and it was a low tide. For a nice change Big Bob and I headed out rather than along and went to the silver ball and back.

Then it was a fantastic coffee in the Red Roaster with my boys, then off to work for one of the most manic days I can remember in years (all good, thank goodness) and then an hour in the gym with Ross to beat up my biceps.

Now, 8p.m., at home and still trying to get the kids to bed. Roll on the weekend!

Day 442 - Sunday 11ᵗʰ March 2012

No exercise Saturday (this is always my day off). I did however exercise my stomach by taking on a massive plate of Chinese food for dinner. Probably not the greatest idea in the world as although I love Chinese it has been a while since I've had it and it's not great in any quantity for my Crohn's or the best preparation for a long run the following day.

On Sunday morning the sun was already shining and it looked like a glorious one. A bowl of Rice Krispies later and I was on the road at 8a.m. for my run. I ended up doing the longest one I've ever done in terms of miles and time: 3 hours 9 minutes, 20.01 miles. All was fine until about mile 16 when my right knee became so painful that I had to walk for about a mile; really annoyed about that. After the mile it still really hurt but I got going again and made it home. I will not run now anyway for another week and will take that time to get some treatment. I want to do it again next Sunday if possible, so need to have the knee sorted by then. I think it was just an IT (iliotibial) band issue, so stretching and foam roller, however painful, should do the job. Another thing that would help is if I take some drink and food/gels with me; as usual I am probably the only fool not eating or drinking on a 20 mile run!

The run itself was great though (apart from the pain). When I was heading towards Rottingdean I bumped into Fiona cycling the other way, which was lovely. Then when I was back on Dyke Road heading home I bumped into Little Bob and finished my run with him. It was like Brighton Swimming Club running section! LB and Lindy are also runners; LB does marathons in under 4 hours and Lindy in under 3½ hours. They are an amazing couple in so many ways.

After getting home and having a 30-minute lie in the spa pool to rest the legs it was back up on them and back to the seafront with the kids on their scooters. The rest of the day, although glorious weather and wonderful kids, was somewhat painful on the knee. Hopefully tomorrow the sea will help that (freeze away the pain!).

Day 443 - Monday 12th March 2012
My knee wasn't so bad this morning. Very encouraging.

At the Arch this morning and the sea was being lazy, as it was nowhere near the coast; a long walk out in perfect flat conditions. When you add in the morning sun, clear sky and no wind then it makes a beautiful scene to behold. Big Bob and I walked out until we got to chest height and then swam out all the way to the helter skelter. It was the perfect day for going around the pier, but still at 6.5 degrees just a bit too cold for us two to want to risk it. A good long swim though and lovely to get out near the end of the pier again.

Day 445 - Wednesday 14th March 2012
Gym yesterday with Ross was an 'uber session' (his words, I'm not entirely

sure what uber means, although I assume it means tough as my arms, shoulders and chest were all feeling it and still are).

Was at the Arch by 6.50a.m., Big Bob and Shoichi waiting there and the three of us in the sea by 7a.m. Temperature almost 7 degrees, which whilst a rise is still chillingly cold. We swam to the helter skelter at the end of the pier, Shoichi absolutely motoring, Bob at a decent pace and me way too slow compared to them! When I got back to the beach Bob was just walking to his shoes and Shoichi was already back in the Arch in the shower. Why oh why can't I get my speed up? To say it frustrates me is the biggest understatement since the last biggest understatement I made. Total swim 17 minutes exactly, which in 7 degrees is pretty good going.

Day 447 - Friday 16th March 2012

This morning was back in the sea, and a choppy sea it was too. Temperature still hugging around 7 degrees, which hurts the face when you swim, and the air temp was around 5 degrees. The flat calm sea had gone and in its place was a much choppier sea that was slappy and annoying. Big Bob and I headed along the coast to the Thistle Hotel and back, the tide dragging us here quickly and the wind taking us back almost as quickly. Total time a poor 11½ minutes. I even wore my flippers today (they are micro flippers, just ankle and a little in front); I need to get my legs working and also keep my body straight, and flippers really help that. They also add to the speed, which at the moment I need from a mental perspective as my slowness is really starting to grate on me!

We have a name chosen for the relay team, courtesy of Little Bob and the starfish suicide of a few months back: Team Starrfish. Come on Starrfish, rah, rah, rah!

Day 448 - Sunday 18th March 2012

Mother's Day today, so I decided on a shorter run than last week and then home to look after the wife. The plan was a 10-mile run but it ended up being 13.28 miles. It was slow, arduous and painful. Slow because we had gone out for dinner on Saturday night with friends to a restaurant over an hour-and-a- half away and didn't get back home until well after 1a.m. Then by 5a.m. the kids were in our bed and being way too noisy, so by the time I hit the road for my run at 7.30a.m. I really didn't fancy it and as such my pace was the slowest I've been since records began averaging over 10 minutes a mile, well above what it should be. Painful because my right knee went again, this time only after about 8 miles; exactly the same spot as last week.

I'm no expert but I really think it's my IT band and unless I can get some treatment on it I will be in a lot of trouble for the marathon, way slower than I should be and probably not make it around. Some people have a time aim for a marathon but mine is just to get around and to do it without causing any injury that could affect my Channel swim. Really, it's mad to do a marathon and risk the Channel swim (as Sharon has said a few times), but I've committed to it now and when I commit to something...

Day 449 – Monday 19th March 2012
Knee still hurting this morning, so it was a limp to the Arch and a limp down and back up the beach. Shoichi was already there waiting for company, so we swam, him way faster than me of course, to the helter skelter and back. The sea was perfectly flat and the sky was completely clear and blue, but it was cold, the air around 3 degrees and the sea round 7 degrees, and it took a while to warm up afterwards.

Swimming Day 450 – Tuesday 20th March 2012
Bob's boot camp was hard. I got to Falmer at 8.30p.m. after a long day and was hardly enthusiastic. Bob turned up bright as a button and also Shoichi was waiting for us and ready to rock and tumble. So in the outside pool we went and proceeded to spend the next hour bashing out 2,800 metres. A decent swim and very energising; it certainly woke me up.

After getting to bed at about 11p.m. it was great that we had no visitors until 6a.m. At the Arch by 7a.m. and in the water – total swim time about 15 minutes and temperature usual 7 degrees.

Afterwards it was a dash home to get into a suit and then off to London, getting back to the office (just now) at 6p.m. ready for another hour of paperwork. Anyone fancy swapping lives with me?

Day 451 – Wednesday 21st March 2012

A Scooby Doo morning with fog over the pier hovering just above the surface of the sea. I slowly lowered myself into a very calm and flat sea at 6.45am. It's been a while since I swam on my own and it was quite weird to be the only one in the sea, especially when it was so foggy you couldn't even see the shore when you were a few feet out. I swam out to the silver ball and then diagonally along to the doughnut groyne and then back along the coast to my blue Crocs patiently awaiting me. Total swim 15 minutes 7 seconds; sea temp 7.1 degrees by my watch.

At the office now and ready for my first early meeting of the day, then it's a half day of Starr Trust work and then a half day of Seico work, variety being the spice of life! Tonight, after the kids are in bed and Sharon is out at her concert rehearsal, I shall either (a) fall asleep on the settee at 9p.m. (b) use the gym at home then fall asleep at 10p.m. (c) have a very large scotch and pretend I used the gym and then fall asleep. Hopefully (b), possibly (a), more likely (c)!

Day 452 – Friday 23rd March 2012

This morning it was with a smile on my face that I headed down Brighton beach with Big Bob at 7a.m. and into a very calm and beautiful sea. The sky was seriously clear, the sea was seriously calm and Bob and I were seriously heading for the helter skelter at a decent pace. In truth we could have gone around the pier today as the conditions were perfect but at 7.2 degrees it was just a tad too cold for us to want to. Total swim over 19 minutes, and as the pier only ever takes us about 20 minutes it shows we can do it now, so next week is definitely around the pier and then that means we are firmly heading towards summer and the buoys will be back in the ocean very soon; can't wait.

263

Rest of today, ignoring the work in between, I have a 1.30p.m. physio session for half an hour on my running knee problem, then 3p.m. - 4p.m. session in the gym on shoulders, chest and back and then 6p.m. - 8p.m. swim in the outside pool with my entire relay team. So a very busy day trying to get my work done around all that and a decent physical day to end the week. Even though it's a lot of exercise in one day and that sounds extremely tiring, I'm pleased to be doing it as I am feeling like I've put on a bit too much weight. That, of course, is a stupid statement as I am meant to be putting on weight for my Channel swim, and I spent all of last year stressing about not putting weight on so I should be pleased - and by the end of today I will probably have lost all the pounds that are bothering me anyway. I guess it shows my weight is still a mental issue for me, and that even after forty-two years I have still not come to terms with it. I certainly don't have an eating disorder but I think the line between having an eating disorder and not having one is very fine, otherwise why do I look in the mirror and think I look fat when clearly I am not, and why can I not recognise that if I'm to cross the Channel I need to put weight on? A confusing dilemma, for sure.

Day 453 – Monday 26th March 2012

Friday's training day went well: swim in morning, physio and gym in afternoon followed by 2-hour pool swim in the evening with the relay team, who all performed brilliantly. It was very inspiring to be in a pool with such amazing swimmers.

The weekend was great. It was Asher's sixth birthday and the sun was shinning throughout. Saturday was BBQ time at home (amazing to again open up the garden and crank up the BBQ) and then Sunday we all went to Beaulieu Motor Museum. No exercise at all for the weekend, which I hope has helped my knee and allowed my shoulders a rest.

This morning, with the clocks going forward, it was slightly darker than it has been but still light and clear. 7a.m. at the Arch with Big Bob, Little Bob, Lindy, David and Shoichi. Last night the kids (all three) played up and I'm not sure I had more than an hour's sleep and even that was broken. At the Arch

I must have looked about as enthusiastic as I felt; amazing that I managed to drag myself there, to be honest. However with Big Bob ready to swim I gingerly followed him in and it wasn't long before we were at the helter skelter and contemplating carrying on around the pier; which was do-able, if the truth be told. However despite the very warm weekend weather the sea didn't warm up at all and was still 7 degrees; if you mix that in with sleep deprivation then it brings it down even further! So rather than go deeper out we headed over the pier and swum under to the other side, down a bit and then back through and then straight to the shore. Total swim time 19 minutes and a decent steady pace. Tonight I'll grab an hour in the gym at home, then that's an easy break into the week.

Day 454 – Tuesday 27th March 2012

Today didn't quite go as planned after all! Mia ended up in hospital late Monday night with breathing problems and as such I had to cancel my London work plans. Early the next day, out of hospital, she was tearing around like a crazy girl without a care in the world - the parents, of course, are left with the high blood pressure. Thankfully, she seems fine.

I ended up on the beach in the morning as usual and headed to the helter skelter with Bob. A windy, coldish morning to start with, but a flat sea and about 7.5 degrees. Total swim around the pier 23 minutes and a decent pace - fantastic to now be around the pier again, a month earlier than last year; both of us very proud and pleased as punch.

As Mia was back on form, Sharon took the kids out and I decided to go to the gym for an hour, which I did and worked bloomin' hard. Afterwards I planned to grab the afternoon to get loads of jobs done but not all plans go to plan, do they! Sharon called half an hour after I got home, saying she had a flat tyre and was sitting on the motorway with four kids in the car! Thirty minutes after that she was driving off into the beautiful, sunny day with the kids in my car and I was stuck sitting at the side of the motorway with her car awaiting the AA. After three hours they turned up and towed me home. Oh well.

Day 455 – Wednesday 28th March 2012

I was at the Arch by 6.45a.m. but not feeling the best. My throat is sore, my right knee aching (probably because Mia kicked me out of my bed and I spent a restless night in her small bed with my legs hanging off the side) and my stomach is in knots (maybe Crohn's again or just the anxiety of Mia being unwell yesterday). My speed slower than yesterday as I felt sluggish because of not being at my best, however after Shoichi raced home I landed seconds after Big Bob and we waited a couple of minutes for the others, the first time for a long time I have been with the front pack!

Swim time 23 minutes (again, but felt slower), air temperature maybe 6 degrees, temperature in sea 7.8 degrees. It still felt cold and after heading around the top of the pier I lost all feeling in my feet!

Day 456 – Thursday 29th March 2012

Woke this morning unable to breathe from my nose and with a very sore thouroat. At the Arch, coughing and spluttering, and in the sea a few minutes later. My breathing was really making it tough so instead of carrying on around, we headed through the pier and down the other side then back through to our beach and to dry land. Total swim about 15 minutes, temp in sea dropped to around 7.5 degrees, flat sea and blue sky but with a sticky south easterly tide – basically felt like swimming through mud coming back under the pier.

The rest of the day was much more relaxing and totally stress free, although that didn't improve the nose and throat. I headed to London with Sharon, and we spent the day in Greenwich meandering about, then had a fantabulous Chinese in China Town before heading off to see *Warhorse*, a long, long play.

Now at 1.20a.m., I am back home coughing and sneezing. Definitely not going to sea swim tomorrow, it would be crazy. But I do have a late afternoon gym session and then dependent on how I feel I will try a 2-hour pool swim.

Day 458 - Monday 2nd April 2012

April already, where did the winter go? Yesterday, feeling 50% better, I hit the treadmill rather than pounding on the streets. With just two weeks to go before the marathon, now is the time to start pulling back on the training and to make sure I don't aggravate the knee any further. Treadmill running is so much gentler and even though I did 2½ hours on it I had hardly any pain at all. I might stick to the treadmill now until the big run, that way I'm still holding my fitness but not causing any damage.

This morning I headed to the Arch and was in the water by 6.50a.m. With Big Bob away for a couple of weeks I am now Billy No Mates. I headed out and around the pier with no fear and no crazy racing heartbeat. It's still cold, in fact slightly down on last week (eight degrees by my watch), but still warm enough to whizz around the pier. Total time 24 minutes and I enjoyed the whole swim; even feeling bunged up and throaty didn't matter, it was just a beautiful morning to be swimming solo around the pier.

Day 460 - Wednesday 4th April 2012

Woke up once again with rasping cough and very blocked nose - it really needs to go now!

Sea was flat with a very slight wave and the temperature had dropped to 7.6 degrees - only 4 degrees in the air. They actually have snow up north so we should be pleased with a sunny sky and some lower temperatures! I swam around the pier feeling very sluggish indeed but somehow getting around in just 22 minutes - I guess the tide pulled me around quicker than I thought. Energy levels really low at the moment and need to get them back up fast; marathon in under two weeks and need to be back to form!

Day 461 - Thursday 5th April 2012

This morning I skipped the sea and went straight to my physio-terrorist Kim. As ever she was painful but great. She worked for an hour on my leg and then wrapped it in a special runner's band and gave me a spare one for the marathon. She insisted would be better if I don't swim, run or go to the gym until the marathon next weekend. She said if I feel restless then a 5-mile run mid week is fine but that is all.

Day 462 – Friday 13th April 2012

I've done no swimming, no gym and only two runs since last Thursday. My body is screaming at me for resting and my skin is confused as to where all the salt water has gone. On the plus side my cold is a lot better although not cleared completely. This is really important, because Sunday is the marathon and I need to be as healthy as possible for it.

I did a 2½ hour run last Sunday on the treadmill at home but stayed off the road to rest my knee and avoid the cold air in my throat. That much time running on the spot can be somewhat boring but I had Denzel Washington on the DVD to keep me company and the time flew by. The beauty of the treadmill is that not only does it help you keep your pace and pull you along, but the impact is so light that after 2½ hours I had no leg pains at all.

My last run was yesterday after work and I went outside to test my knee on the street. I did a 5-mile run in 35 minutes, so quite a speed, but just a short distance. Again no leg problem, which is a good sign. That's definitely it now until the marathon in two days.

I am almost looking forward to the run, although I am also very nervous as I've never run in crowds before and certainly never run that distance. However I'm looking forward to the finish line and being able to cross this one off my list and then give my full concentration to my Channel swim, as that is only a few months off now.

Monday I will be back in the sea, which after ten days off will be very difficult, but hopefully the body and mind will respond positively to it!

Day 463 – Monday 16th April 2012

And the marathon is done! I crossed the finish line at 13:44, total time 4.23.57 and position 5433. I was expecting (hoping) for 4.30, so I am happy with that. In truth the idea of time vanished completely when I got to the 20-mile marker; at that point I couldn't care less how long it took, I just wanted to finish it. Lindy finished in 3:19:00, what a remarkable lady, and LB in under 4 hrs.

I had a good start and was steady up to the halfway point (13 miles) and was at 1 hour 57 minutes, but by the time I reached mile 18 my legs were starting to burn and by mile 20 my thighs were in serious cramp. It was interesting though that I saw a lot of people throwing up and plenty at the side of the road being helped by physios and ambulance men, yet at no time did I feel tired or in trouble, apart from the pain. My only problem was my thighs at mile 20. I think if perhaps I had taken the training more seriously I could have avoided that and would easily have bettered the time, but what with training for the Channel Swim and everything else it would have been impossible to have done any more training than I did. That aside, I am really pleased to have completed it and in the time I wanted and without any injury at all. I can now throw all my efforts into my swimming; the Channel is calling!

This morning I was back at the Arch by 6.50a.m. and was in the sea with Big Bob, Lindy, LB, Mike and David by 7-ish. The air temp was a chilling 1 degree (I had to scrape ice from my windscreen) and the sea was back down to 7.7 degrees. It was painful getting in after a week off but when I settled in it was good on the aching legs. I was going to just float around a bit but Big Bob wanted a swim, so we headed along the coast. Not a massive swim, but much more than I planned. The sea was extremely flat and calm and despite the cold the sky was deep blue and the sun was out. I now need to really focus my training in the sea on technique and strength.

Day 464 – Tuesday 17th April 2012

The sea this morning was nuts! Shoichi got in at the girlie beach before we got to the shore and was almost dumped a couple of times trying to get out. I tried a few times to get in while Bob and Martina went straight for the pilchard position (lying on the beach being washed over by the waves). But the waves were so big and so inconsistent it made it impossibly dangerous. They were crashing in from every angle you could imagine and were so powerful and on top of that the wind was hitting you full on and freezing rain was pelting down on you! Tomorrow I am heading straight to the pool. There's no point heading to the beach like this when I need to be training for the big swim.

Day 465 – Wednesday 18ᵗʰ April 2012

Yesterday after work I had an hour in the gym with Ross. He also ran the marathon (in 5.33 hours) and he was walking like he'd ridden a horse for a month – in fact, he swears he's broken both his feet, which of course he hasn't, the wimp! He did amazingly well considering he trained as a runner even less than me, although I am of course twenty-six years older than him. I have to say that using the muscles again, after two weeks away from the gym and having just done the marathon, was harder than normal although it did energise me, which I definitely needed. At night, when I was reading to the twins, I just couldn't stay awake and they kept questioning me on why I was missing out pages. Doh, caught out again! So I downed a Red Bull to pep me up but the bloomin' thing didn't kick in until about 9p.m. and then I was sitting there all buzzed up!

This morning, knowing the sea wouldn't be swimmable due to the weather, I headed to Falmer to meet Big Bob for one of our swimathons. We did about 1½ miles in the hour (outside pool of course – wind and rain on us), a mix of distance and speed. I am now done with exercise for the day.

I'm pleased though that after a marathon on Sunday I was still able to swim in the sea Monday, then sea swim and gym Tuesday and then a big pool swim today. I might not be Superman but I'm pleased to see people half my age crashing out after Sunday and just lying around complaining whilst I can just keep going.

Day 466 – Thursday 19ᵗʰ April 2012

The waves were fairly big and the tide was coming in this morning, which meant it was pulling really hard to the east. Big Bob and I went in at the doughnut groyne and headed straight at the groyne towards the thistle.

The tide was strong enough to mean that about 15 minutes later we were only just crossing over the beach to the other side, very much swimming on the spot and being bashed by big waves every few minutes. I don't think either of us enjoyed it that much. The temperature was down once again; just 7.5 degrees. It's amazing to think that just a few weeks ago we swam around the pier day after day and I was going around on my own with no fear. I wouldn't have done it this morning; too rough and too cold. Apparently May this year is going to be the coldest May in over one hundred years – what's that about?

After work today I'll at the gym for an hour on shoulders and biceps; all strength stuff for my swimming.

Day 467 – Monday 23ʳᵈ April 2012

As expected no training on Friday or Saturday but on Sunday I went for an 8-mile run, which took about 1 hour 10 minutes. Annoyingly my right leg hurt from the start of the run. I guess I need some physio on it to get it better before I get back to some longer runs. Do I even need to do long runs ever again?

Last night I went to London at 7p.m. to see the UK premiere of an amazing project called Step by Step. It's a collaboration between an Israeli school and an Arab school where forty teenagers have got together to write a musical about the madness in the Middle East and how it affects them and what life should be like rather than how it is. It showed that the kids do not want the fighting and want to convince the older population to listen to them; not an easy task of course after hundreds of years of fighting but it has to start and the best way is one kid at a time. An amazing group of individuals, and very inspirational to anyone who wants to see peace anywhere in the world. I felt honoured to be asked to go along and see it as one of their guests and I'm hoping that the Starr Trust, especially our CHOCS programme, can work with these amazing people in the future.

Day 468 – Tuesday 24ᵗʰ April 2012

What a crazy day. It's 6p.m. and I'm just squeezing in a couple of minutes to write this up before I dash off to get to my next meeting.

No sleep last night as usual; Mia and Jesse in our bed with Mia coughing all night and Jesse bashing me in the head with his elbow. I left our room about 3a.m. and sat in Mia's bed reading a book until Asher called for me at 6a.m. – so a normal night for me then!

At the Arch by 6.45am and the sea was flat and calm (yesterday and tomorrow apparently rocking in the sea with big waves!). I had planned a lazy, easy swim as I was dead tired but Big Bob had other plans. So exactly 25 minutes later, in a cold 7.8 degree sea, we were back on shore having swum around the pier; a slowish swim, but better than it should have been with no sleep or food behind me (in fact it's 6p.m. now and I have still only had a single cup of tea today and nothing else to drink and nothing to eat – appalling behaviour). Oh yes, I also crammed in an hour with Ross in the gym on back, shoulders and arms – this was a lunch hour I managed to sneak into my day; gym instead of eat, not a good lunch!

Day 470 – Thursday 26th April 2012

This morning was pool morning with Big Bob. I met him at Falmer and we did 120 lengths in an hour, with 40% being speed swimming and 60% normal stroke. It really is bloomin' good exercise and fantastic swim training for me; I leave there really knowing I've worked out! Straight afterwards I headed over to physio Kim and she punished my bad legs with an hour of solid thumb pressure – owwwwch!

That is certainly exercise and pain done for the day! Tomorrow, whatever the weather, I shall be at the beach and enjoying it!

Day 471 – Friday 27th April 2012

A great sea this morning. Just over 8 degrees, no rain but a strong wind which meant decent waves. Big Bob and I were in the sea before 7a.m. (so we would have time for a Red Roaster coffee afterwards) and headed straight out. The waves were frequent and big but manageable (if you are a competent sea swimmer – certainly not a sea for a pool swimmer). A couple of times both of us had the extra heartbeat moment when the waves got big and you wondered if you would have been sensible staying closer to shore and Bob got rolled over once, but it was basically a lot of fun. Way too much seaweed though; sometimes it felt like hundreds of hands tying ropes around your ankles and pulling you down, but a couple of shakes of the legs and it soon fell away.

Sadly on the next beach along we could see a number of police vans and police officers, including one officer guarding a white sheet, which clearly was covering a dead body. From where we were just beyond the groyne we had a clear view of what was happening but of course it wasn't 'just a body', it was a person; someone's friend, lover, brother, sister, parent – who knows? Whatever the story, it is very sad.

Day 472 – Monday 30th April 2012

A grim weekend for rain and wind but this morning a bright sky brought hope. Getting to the beach by 6.40-ish (after another restless night) it was dismaying to see such massive waves. There were about nine of us this morning and we headed over to the girlie beach, which was better but not necessarily safe. Getting in was easy enough as you are facing the waves and can choose your moment easily enough; getting out is the challenge and the heart-stopper. I swam in with head down and legs kicking until I was as close to the shore as I could safely get without the waves crashing me. This is when the heart really steps up a beat! It is a case of swimming with one eye firmly behind you so as not to get caught out; by the time I was almost there the waves had picked up again and were crashing in a big dip. You need to avoid the dip as that is the 'suck and pull down' area and very dangerous. I thankfully timed it well and was on the beach milliseconds before a monster wave curled in, grabbing the back of my legs as I escaped. Safely back on land, the heart returns to normal and the endorphins kick in to give you that high; the one adrenalin junkies start to crave, the one that you need to somehow keep in check!

Day 474 - Wednesday 2ⁿᵈ May 2012

If yawning were a sport then I reckon no one could catch me today. Another pier swim today, two in a row and both so different. Big Bob, Shoichi and I headed out into a very flat sea; no wind, no rain and a strong westerly tide. It felt 'sticky' coming around the head of the pier and for some reason the beach seemed a lot further away than usual.

Day 475 - Thursday 3ʳᵈ May 2012

Last night's pool sessions went from an expected 2-hour swim to a sad 1½ hours - all down to me. Big Bob was up for it but having had only a couple of hours' sleep, then swum in the morning in the sea, then worked all day, then done an hour's run after work to clear my head, I found that two hours in the pool was pushing it a bit. We still did well over 2 miles, so a decent swim, but I am a bit annoyed with myself for calling it early.

A very quiet Arch this morning. Big Bob and I headed into a completely flat sea, with very little movement at all. The only problem was the colour, a murky brown. The recent weather conditions have brought in a brown algae in and it is not only horrible to be in but gives a fishy taste and smell, which is not pleasant. I don't think it's dangerous but we need to keep an eye on it - if it turns red we should probably avoid it for a few days. We hadn't planned going around the pier today but with a sea so flat, despite the yucky colour, we just had to. Bob is really motoring at the moment (training for a gala swim) so I am having to swim as hard as I can to keep up with him, which is proving impossible as he is constantly about 100 metres ahead of me all the time now. The good thing is that it pushes me to swim harder each time; the bad thing is that I remain frustrated that I can't keep up again!

Best news of the day for me was that the buoys are back in town; or more accurately, back in the sea. It is always great to have the buoys back as it means the summer is on its way and they give you a point to swim to. Also, on those occasions when the heart is beating too fast because of the nerves, it allows you the comfort of knowing that you could have something (rather than someone) to hold onto.

Day 476 – Friday 4th May 2012

It's a conspiracy! Last night Jesse stayed in his bed the whole night, not a peep from him. Mia however turned up at midnight and by middle of the night I was turfed out again! It must be a twin thing that they instinctively know whose turn it is to kick me out of bed.

Dragging myself to the Arch once again it was at least good to see the sea once again as flat as a flat thing and no rain or wind. I hadn't planned going around the pier as I was not only sleep deprived but I hadn't eaten anything for around 24 hours and was starting to feel depleted (no one to blame but myself, of course, for that). However the sea was too flat to ignore and Big Bob was keen to swim, so swim we did, once around the pier, around 23 minutes, I think, and 9 degrees. Only downer was the amount of brown algae once again; disgusting.

This week so far (and it's only just Friday) has seen five sea swims (most around the pier), two gym sessions, a 2-mile pool swim and two 1-hour runs. This afternoon when work is done I will top it off with an hour in the gym on shoulders and abs with Ross. That is enough to warrant the bank holiday weekend as a rest.

Day 477 – Tuesday 8th May 2012

My bank holiday weekend was somewhat of a surprise and involved a lot of exercise, although not in the usual sense. I got home from work on Friday afternoon and was presented with an early birthday present: a weekend trip to Barcelona without the children. At 8a.m. on Saturday morning we dropped the kids at my mum's and jetted off (if you can call Easyjet jetting) and were in Barcelona at the hotel by 2.30p.m., just the two of us as Sharon and Rob rather than Mum and Dad. Joyous! At 3p.m. we went for a little walk to explore the city and ended up walking for eight hours solid (apart from a 40-minute break for food at 6p.m.); boy, did we sleep well that night. The next day we hired bikes and went on a 3-hour bike tour around the rest of the city; again lots of sleep that night as well. A fantastic city and one that I could easily live in although it was wonderful to get home late on Monday and have the kiddies back again.

This morning was a shock to the system, having gone from a sunny 20 degree Barcelona to a raining 5 degree Brighton. The sea was totally flat and the tide was so far out it was almost a run rather than a swim. We walked right up to the silver ball (half way along the pier) and then Bob and I swam around a decent pace. Tomorrow back to the beach and then the pool on Thursday morning and the gym and the pool on Friday after work.

Day 479 – Thursday 10th May 2012

This morning was going to be a pool morning but with the weather being turbulent it was just too good an opportunity to miss a raging sea at low tide. I was at the Arch, already soaked, by 6.50a.m. and found a few of us fancied a rough water day. The low tide meant that the waves only ever attained so much height and whilst they were full and strong (and rapid) they were safe (assuming you know how to handle them). Big Bob, James and I headed out to the buoy by the silver ball and then back across the beach to the next buoy and then headed in. Bob and I hung around a bit more and did some speed swimming, as much as the sea would allow. Total swim 30 minutes and sea temperature just 9 degrees. A really good workout, a very good swim – and a lot of fun. As we missed the pool this morning it will mean a punishing session tonight at 8.30p.m.

Having had a rather turbulent (that word again) day at work yesterday it made me think that sea swimming and life in general are so very similar. This morning we aimed for the buoy by the silver ball and then intended to swim either through the pier or across to the other buoy. We started out strong and determined with heads down. Every few feet a wave would hit us, some at the side, some straight in the face, some with little power and some so big that we were pushed back almost to our starting position, yet we forged on regardless. Despite being hit time and again we made our way forward. Lessons were learnt though; it became clear that unless we swam slightly at an angle and towards the tide we were simply not going to make headway, so we adjusted our course and headed out. When we got to the first buoy we had a decision to make; go left or go right. We floated a bit and discussed the options and then decided that going to the other buoy meant going with the tide rather than against it and therefore that was the decision we made. It was based on the fact that the other way, whilst do-able, would have been very strenuous and possibly fatal, and going with the tide was safer and quicker.

Is that like life? Maybe it is and maybe it's not. All I know is that yesterday I had a plan at work and along the way I felt like I had been punched in the face numerous times. Yet I carried on with my day and eventually hit my target. Sure I ended up taking a different route and certainly it was more stressful and tiring than originally planned, but I learnt a lot along the way and eventually got to where I needed to be. The sea and life, life and the sea; both different and yet both the same.

Forty-three years old tomorrow - where did those years go?

Day 480 - Friday 11th May 2012

Last night's pool swim; 8.15p.m. - 9.15p.m. in the outside pool in the rain, 2,200 metres in an hour. A tough and tiring swim but fantastic exercise.

My birthday morning was spent with my new favourite friend; a friend who is sometimes welcoming and who is sometimes vicious - the big blue sea! Another day very similar to yesterday; big waves and strong tides, the difference today being that the waves were not breaking a lot, they were just very high and towering and it was a high tide, which gave them a lot of weight. Also the tide was pushing heavily to the west whilst the wind was strong to the east, creating a bumpy washing machine effect.

After yesterday's sea swim followed by a tough day at work, then a big pool swim in the evening and then a sleepless night last night, it made for a tiring and hard swim this morning, although it was satisfying when we safely landed back on the beach. Afterwards it was off to the Red Roaster for a lovely birthday coffee; yum, yum, yum.

Day 481 - Monday 14th May 2012

If it's possible to swim in the sea on autopilot, in fact a very bouncy rough wave filled sea, then that is exactly what I did this morning.

We had a great weekend, but tiring. A fantastic dinner party for twelve on Saturday night and an impromptu BBQ for fifteen on Sunday afternoon, which along with the usual weekend running about made for an exhausted fall into bed on Sunday night. Sadly, by 2a.m. Jesse was with us, and not lying still for a second. I took him back at 4a.m., by which time Mia crossed me in the hallway and was firmly fixed in the middle of our bed by the time I got back. Then at about 5ish Asher called me (unusually early for him, to be fair). By the time I helped him down his ladder from the bunk bed and walked him into our room, Jesse was already back and lying next to Mia on my pillow. On seeing us come in, he says, 'Asher, I've saved you a place - quickly.' I couldn't believe it, he saved *my* place for Asher! In jumps Asher and there I am, at 5a.m., having been bumped by Jesse for Asher - charming!

I was at the Arch by 6.45a.m., eyes still closed and not engaging with anyone, and by 7a.m. was sleep swimming, following Big Bob on autopilot out into the huge waves. About 25 minutes later, heading up the beach, I swear I was still not fully awake.

Day 482 - Tuesday 15ᵗʰ May 2012

Bob and I decided on a pool swim this morning because we both need some speed work - him for his gala and me for the Channel. We did the following:

20 length warm-up

5 length sprint repeated 10 times with 10 second rests between sets

2 length fast sprint 12 times with 10 second rests between sets

20-length cool-down

A very good set of sets by all accounts but rather exhausting at that time of the morning.

At the office by 8.30a.m. and unusually needing food; skipping breakfast (obviously) and a very small dinner the previous night clearly meant the swim had depleted me. So a quick round of toast at the office, then a stack of paperwork before heading back to the gym for an 11a.m. session with Ross. Weights and more weights and by the time I finished and was back at the office at 12.30p.m. it was straight into a meeting. It was 3.30p.m. by the time I resurfaced and had to get a sandwich and a piece of fruit down me pretty sharpish as the energy once again crashed.

Day 483 – Thursday 17th May 2012

Sadly, I never got to the pool yesterday as planned because my first London meeting was moved to an earlier unsociable time of 8a.m. By the time I got back home in the evening it was too late to do much more than give the kids a good night book.

This morning was however successfully back to the pool and the same set as Tuesday:

20 length warm-up
5 length sprint repeated 10 times with 10 second rests between sets
10 length cool-down
2 length super fast sprint 12 times with 10 second rest between sets
10 length cool-down

Job done!

Day 486 – Tuesday 22nd May 2012

Once again warmer than yesterday; in fact the air temperature this morning was topping 15 degrees (which is a lot for 6.40a.m.) and the sea hit over 11 degrees. Bring it on!

Big Bob and I swam around the two buoys near the doughnut groyne, then headed around the pier, then to the buoy the other side, then back to the buoy on our side and then back in. At last a longish, decent swim in the sea. Very flat surface, quite a strong tidal pull to the east (Marina), which made the swim back to our beach challenging. Simply a fantastic swim and the reason we go to the beach in the mornings (sadly not like this every day).

Headed to the gym at 1p.m., then back in the office by 2.15p.m. and straight into next meeting – unusually I grabbed a sarnie on the way into the meeting (yesterday I ate nothing all day again!).

So much amazing news to talk about on the Starr Trust that I don't now where to begin. I guess the biggest news is the best and that is the fact that we are working on building our own incredible performing arts centre in Brighton, The Lyrics. Our sights are drawn to the King Alfred, a monster site in the city and with good tides it may just come to us! The plan is not just a theatre though; it's combining leisure with art and culture – swimming pool, gym , climbing wall, diving, theatre, film, music, art, relaxing, restaurant. A real community hub for leisure and arts – what do you reckon? It's a crazy idea for little me to try to get the city's most valuable bit of land and build on it, especially as we have no money and no experience as contractors; I reckon it'll cost over £120 million to build, utter madness as I can only just afford a cappuccino at the moment. However, I am surrounded by brilliant and talented people, some with masses of experience and some with deep pockets, so who knows what the next turn of the corner will bring. Channel swim first though; come on concentrate, Rob, concentrate!

Day 488 – Thursday 24ᵗʰ May 2012

Another beautiful day ahead and Bob and I decided to head to Falmer for our weekly boot camp. Due to the warm weather the outside pool was even warmer than usual and that meant more people in it, even at 6.45a.m., which meant Bob and I had to share a single lane. We did a similar routine to the last couple of weeks, although we definitely worked harder once again. This time on the 50 metre speed swims, instead of having a dedicated 10 seconds rest in between each set, we allocated 60 seconds per set. This meant that the quicker we went the more rest we got and the slower we went the less we got. On some of the sets we had a massive 11-second rest, on others though it was down to just 3 seconds; a tough workout.

Day 489 – Friday 25ᵗʰ May 2012

And it gets better and better; the weather that is. A proper summer's day at last, just what we have been looking for and please, please many more like it. Despite the beautiful weather the Arch was quiet when I got there at 6.40a.m., in fact just me. You can't get much more quiet than that. Paula, who hasn't been around the pier in ages, decided to join Bob and I this morning and considering she is slight of frame and swims just backstroke, albeit with flippers, she was hard to keep up with, so our usual 'Easy Friday' swim turned into more of a swim than expected. Chasing the gorgeous Paula around the pier was a pleasure not a chore for both Bob and me, so we didn't complain (and it certainly beats chasing each other, I can tell you!) The sea was flat up to the pier head but got quite choppy and splashy going around and down and back. A completely wonderful start to the day all the same.

Day 490 – Monday 28th May 2012

The weekend was simply glorious; the sun shone, the sky was blue and everyone I met seemed to be happy and smiling; you can't ask for more than that. Mia had been unwell but she perked up and joined her brothers staying the night at my in-laws', which meant I would have the house to myself as Sharon was singing in a concert choir. A treat I rarely get. Of course by 11p.m. my house was filled with the entire choir of about twenty, who Sharon invited back to ours after the show for a party! So my quiet evening in ended up seeing a dozen pizzas, a hundred chicken wings, garlic bread and copious amounts of alcohol being delivered at 11.30p.m. and the last of the revellers leaving at about 3a.m. At least Saturday morning without the kids gave us time to recover! My plan of a long run on Sunday didn't materialise as the Jack Daniel toll from Friday were still ringing slightly in my head and the sun was beating down just a bit too much to force me into my shoes.

This morning however I was up bright as a button and walking the seafront at 6.10a.m. waiting for Bob and others to arrive at the Arch. We did our round the buoys and round the pier swim as usual and took about 40 minutes between getting in and getting out. Probably about a mile I would guess?

Will be June 2012 by Friday; just two months from the swim. Time to get my team together again and start the serious planning.

Day 491 – Tuesday 29ᵗʰ May 2012

Another night of not too bad from the kids – it seems letting them stay up late has its advantages, although I am behind on the ironing.

This morning was again a beautiful one, with sun shining and about 16 degrees in the air. I keep forgetting to take the sea temp but it is probably 11.5 degrees. Bob and I swam to the silver ball then through the pier to the buoy the other side, then around and back to the silver ball, then along to the next two buoys and then back in. Total swim about 40 minutes and non-stop at a very good pace indeed; probably over a mile and quick (for us). I wore my mini flippers, which meant we stayed together the whole way, which made a nice change!

4.30p.m. – After a hot, sticky day in London I headed back to Brighton, arriving at 3.30p.m. Rather that go back to the office with no energy, I headed straight back to the beach and with wet trunks back on I repeated this morning's swim (minus Big Bob), and then at the head of the pier headed along the buoys and along our beach and over to the next one and onto the Brighton Centre. Then I retraced my route along the buoys and back to shore. On the way back, at the buoys near the silver buoy I heard someone calling 'Excuse me' in a rather strong Asian accent and saw this chap a few feet away bobbing about in the water. He was looking relaxed but was a little unhappy about being there although he very proudly said he was fine. However he wanted to talk whilst he swam back, so I swam next to him and calmly talked about where he was from and how long he was in Brighton for etc, etc. We stopped a few times so he could get his breath and then carried on and he asked me how often I swam here, was I training for anything, how nice Brighton is; anything, I think, to take his mind from where he was. When we got back to shore he asked me how old I was. Forty-three, I replied. Rather than saying 'Thanks for sticking with me', or 'It was nice to talk', he simply said, 'Wow, you're old'. Then he sat down on his towel next to his friend and closed his eyes. Charming! I almost replied saying that unless he took care in the sea he'd be lucky to reach half my age. Instead I just smiled and wandered back to the Arch.

Day 492 – Wednesday 30th May 2012

In the pool this morning with Big Bob; considering it was a cooler, foggy day it was good to start in the pool rather than the sea. We did the usual 20-length warm up, followed by 5 lengths at speed allowing 2 minutes in total for the lengths including the rest. This is hard because is means that when you start to slow down you end up with less rest and that makes you even more tired. We did six of these sets, then an easy 10-length swim, followed by 20 (yes 20) 2-length sprints in a minute, including rest. The first two sets I managed to do in around 50 seconds, giving a 10-second rest. That soon turned into an average 5-second rest! As soon as you stop and wipe your goggles it's 3,2,1 and go again. The last few I pulled back 2-3 seconds thankfully. This worked out about half a mile in 20 minutes; quite tiring. Then, to finish, an easy 10-length swim.

A very hard workout and the heart was beating like a jungle drum. After the shower it was to the office where I downed a Red Bull (sadly no wings appeared), followed by a massive glass of Mars Bar chocolate drink, so healthy, not! Tomorrow the sea beckons again and maybe (hopefully) a 10-mile run after work.

Day 493 – Thursday 31st May 2012

Tomorrow is 50% of the year gone already. I'm not sure whether it was stolen or just vanished, but I do know that somehow it feels like I missed it!

Back to the sea this morning with aching arms from yesterday's pool beating and all the other swimming and gyming from the week so far. Last night after I got the kids to bed I picked up my saxophone and my clarinet for a very quiet play. Having not played either for well over a year it was funny to feel them in my hands again and my shoulders seemed so stiff from all the exercise this week that I found it hard to hold them correctly without my shoulders bunching up. I think perhaps it's time for a massage (also some music lessons, if last night's notes were anything to go by!)

This morning the sea was back to being choppy. It wasn't exactly rough, but it was definitely bouncy and the tide was pulling hard to the west whilst we of course were swimming to the east. We got around the pier in decent time, rather bashed about and tired but pleased to have done it. It's quite something actually when you think about the fact that we swam non-stop from the beach all around the pier, back under it and back to the beach, bashed about by the waves and pulled by the tide, and all before 7.45a.m. I'm not bigging us up or anything, as there are plenty of people I am sure who do so much more, but it certainly feels like an achievement.

Day 494 - Friday 1ˢᵗ June 2012

Pinch punch, white rabbits and all that. Also good luck to Lizzie for her Diamond Jubliee - go, Queenie, go!

Today the sea was back to an eerie calm. There was an almost tranquil 'calm before the storm' feeling in the air. No air movement, no waves, only a minor tide to the east and a greyish sky. On top of that there were dozens of yachts languishing out near the buoys all ready for their annual sail over to France. Bob and I decided to avoid the pier today and head west. The sea temperature was almost exactly 13 degrees, which is almost comfortable and the swim was a real easy one with no mid-week rush. Back on dry ground in our civvies we headed to the Red Roaster for what will be my best coffee of the day.

After work I will be at the gym with Ross for an hour, then home to pack for our pending hols. A week with the kiddies in France! I can't wait, very pleased to be getting away again.

Day 495 - Monday 11ᵗʰ June 2012

One day I was on holiday in the south of France in 25-degree heat and sunshine and the next I was standing in Brighton in rain and greyness. After a wonderful family holiday, which included swimming in the water of Monaco with lots of big fish, I was back at the beach today at 6.30a.m. I almost didn't go, though, because my mind was going around and around; swim/don't swim/swim/don't swim, what's one more morning off, go on, lie-in, no I can't,

I must swim, I must swim... and on and on and on. By 5.30am I was up and dressed and totally fed up with the endless arguing in my head. Sitting in the car in my drive at 5.50a.m., having has a glass of orange juice to settle my nerves (Scotch not allowed before 6a.m.) I decided swim had to win. I was therefore at the beach by 6.15a.m. and sitting once again in my car outside the pier and looking at a wet and raining sky, a semi-rough sea and only one or two drenched runners. The mind was once again busy; swim to the first buoy and back, don't swim just get in and out, go to work why bother swimming, swim around the buoys and on and on.... you get the picture! 6.30a.m. in the Arch and in my trunks and all alone again; should I wait for Big Bob etc or should I go now, or should I go to work, or should I go back to bed... arggggggghh!

6.40a.m. in the sea, not as cold as expected, and headed on my own around the pier. I really didn't expect to do that but all the arguing in my head had to stop and the best way to do that was have a decent swim. If only I realised it was that easy I would have gone at 5a.m.! Hopefully, now I am back in the swing of things tonight will be a sound sleep and I can join Big Bob for a gentle, normal morning.

Day 496 – Tuesday 12th June 2012

After my gym session yesterday I had to get back to the office to finish some reports and then onto a meeting; ended up getting home 9.30p.m. with a raging headache and feeling a little sick (probably caused by a long day, exercise and little food - I *still* haven't learnt re the whole eating nonsense). After a handful of headache pills I hit the sack and tried to get to sleep. Luckily no children turned up until 5.30a.m., so I did manage a good four hours sleep, but the headache and the sick feeling still lingered which was annoying and not overly conducive to morning exercise.

More rain and grey skies again; where oh where is the summer? Come on sun, it's June for goodness sake. Even though I was early again I sat in the car on the seafront for a bit as I wanted to swim with Bob this morning; also I wasn't feeling well enough to rush. Having swum in the pool yesterday Bob had injured his leg and said he would just want to swim a little, which suited me just fine the way I was feeling. But the sea was calm and flat despite the rain and we were heading for the end of the pier before I really had time to think about it; so much for not doing a big swim! Coming around the head of the pier was splashy and the tide was against us most of the way, but apart from that it was an easy enough swim. The temperature however has dropped yet again; a massive 1-degree drop from the last few weeks, down to just 12.2 degrees - it should be more like 15-16 degrees by now! Coming back to dry land I was a little wobbly....

Day 498 - Thursday 14th June 2012

I managed to get all the kids to bed at a decent hour; 7.40p.m. and all went to sleep. After a mammoth ironing session, dinner and a short gym workout I headed upstairs to my bedroom at 10.45p.m. and look what I found - two kids in my bed. It gets to something when they get into my bed even before I do! They did let me take them back before Sharon got home at 11ish and none returned until about 4a.m., so some sleep was had, thankfully.

The morning started with the sun shining and no rain clouds to be seen; apparently as the day goes on that will change of course. The Arch this morning was once again very quiet in terms of people: eight in total, which seems average these days for the morning sessions between 6a.m. - 8a.m. I think maybe there are another ten who come and go during various times in the day but that still only leaves about twenty in total for the day, which in a city the size of Brighton is not even a recordable percentage. Of course if you had seen the swim Bob and I did this morning you can understand that!

It had really started to chop-up as we were halfway around. By the time we got to the head of the pier we had lost each other a couple of times and were being washed around by a fierce and bumpy westerly tide and wind. Coming around the pier and heading back down the east side we had to swim diagonally just to avoid being dragged into the pier; getting across to the buoy was a challenge in itself. Despite all this action and his age and health, David was still out there with his fishing bamboo, floating around the pier on his back hunting for his breakfast - the man is quite incredible.

As for the rest of today, apart from a short gym at home after work, it is off to City College for a *Hell's Kitchen* event in aid in the Starr Trust - very excited about that.

Then tomorrow, apart from my morning swim and afternoon gym, I was meant to be joining my relay team for a 5.30p.m. swim to the West Pier and back. However the forecast is for the wind to keep picking up and by tomorrow apparently we will have 50m.p.h. winds and rain and crazy waves and tide. The likelihood is that this swim will be cancelled, which will be a real bummer as it was hard enough to get everyone to be able to agree a date in the first place. But that's the point when you are doing a sport that involves the elements; the control is simply not yours; it lays in the hands of a greater force!

Day 499 - Friday 15ᵗʰ June 2012

A magnificent Starr Trust event at Brighton City College, a *Hells Kitchen* event put on by the Starr Trust in partnership with Hilton Hotel Group and City College catering students; just a wonderful night. The trainee chefs were astonishing, the trainee front-of-house staff were wonderful and the guests were all engaged with the evening. One of our patrons, Robin Cousins, was in attendance to meet everyone and hand out the certificates at the end of the night and he was truly a star. Just a great evening for all and a fantastic way to unwind and relax at the end of the week....

Until 3.50a.m. the next morning of course, after being kicked out of my bed yet again by the twins.

7.05a.m. saw me heading into a slightly warmer sea (13.1 degrees), but a sea with high waves. Big Bob and I headed out and around the pier in lots of highs and lows, lots of bumps and a lot of seawater whacking us straight in the face and some sadly finding its way into our mouths as we grabbed a breath. I reckon I swallowed a pint of seawater today. The swim was actually great fun for some reason; a serious shoulder and leg work out as we were being hurled all over the place, especially near the helter skelter way out in the depths of the ocean. Then around the end of the pier the waves got really big and lifted us way up into the air before literally dropping us back down again. As I keep saying, not for the faint-hearted!

8a.m. at the Red Roaster. Wonderful creamy cappuccino with a flavour only the Red Roaster could deliver. Visit them if you can, St James St, Brighton, just the best.

Day 500 – Monday 18th June 2012

Five hundred days of swimming/175,000 words on my blog /hundreds of gallons of seawater drunk. And so, so, so much more in terms of people I've met, experiences in the sea (good and bad), life-changing swims (some literally life-threatening, not just life-changing) and a change in my body shape that I really couldn't have predicted, not to mentioned a whole new lifestyle in terms of what I do before work now (and most likely will always continue to do).

The Channel relay swim is now only eight weeks away and that is both exciting and scary. As a relay, I know I am more than able to complete all my 1-hour swims during the challenge, as will all my team. The only area out of our control is the weather and this year particularly has stayed much colder than previous years and the weather has been unpredictable. However I know for sure that come our week on 8th August that the weather will be very much in our favour and we will get this done .

As for today, I particularly felt strong. All the daily training on my Vasa is starting to pay dividends and I am at last grasping the fact that bending my arms and using my elbow to my wrist rather than a straight arm is so much more powerful. Over the next eight weeks I'll be working on this daily to make sure that come the swim day I am as strong and as quick as I can be.

Day 501 – Tuesday 19th June 2012

7.50a.m. – Sitting in a Starbucks in the heart of the City of London, in a suit, sipping a tepid coffee, is seriously not the way I like to start my days any more. Not that I ever much liked it but since starting my sea swimming and since selling a big part of my business (and hitting my forties) my need for starting and ending the day the way I want has become a necessity. Quality of life and an inner peace are vital nowadays and whilst I haven't quite got there yet, my morning swims go a long way towards it.

The plan today (and the next two days in fact as I have early London starts Wednesday and Thursday as well) is to get back to Brighton by 5ish in the afternoon and get an afternoon end-of-day swim instead. I'm really into using my Vasa swim trainer every night for 15 minutes. It's a great machine and really starting to improve my swimming. Why oh why didn't I start using it properly when I brought it a year ago? Better late than never, I guess.

4p.m. – Back in Brighton, extremely hot from a very warm day. Straight to the Arch and within minutes was walking down a fairly crowded beach in my Speedos and swim cap getting a few odd looks (which is exactly why I like my private, early morning swims from an empty beach!). The sea was completely flat and still and the sun was beating down; a Mediterranean afternoon if ever there was one. The afternoon sea temperature was naturally warmer than the morning would have been, probably about 14 degrees; still chilly but with warm patches around. I did twice around the pier at a decent, regular pace and enjoyed every stroke of it. Walking back up the beach, cap and goggles in hand trying to look a little more normal, I was called over to the lifeguard tent. Wondering what on earth I might have done wrong, it was a nice surprise to see Alex from my relay team and BSC member sitting there. In all his lifeguard finery he looked every bit the Baywatch boy!

Tomorrow is another day when I have a very early start, so no chance to get a morning swim; such a shame. Will try again to head to the beach after meetings and then onto the Vasa in the evening.

Day 502 – Wednesday 20th June 2012

Death in the sea around Brighton; so, so sad. I've just seen on the BBC news website that a 24-year-old man drowned yesterday afternoon in the sea between the piers. His body was washed up at about 5.30p.m., soon after

I left the beach. During my swim I stopped at the head of the pier on my second time around because a helicopter was hovering quite low over me. I looked up and floated a little bit as it was unusual to see a helicopter that low, then I carried on and swam around and then back to shore. The story on the BBC news website shows a picture of the helicopter doing a search. How scary to think that while I was swimming around the pier, someone was drowning near me; it makes me feel a little sick. It also shows how dangerous the sea is, even on a relatively calm and hot day it can still be deadly.

Another 5a.m. start today; certainly earning my salary at the moment! I will hopefully finish my last meeting by 4p.m. and if the weather holds be down on the beach parading my sculptured body in front of the lily-white tourists.

Talking of sculptured bodies, Bob sent me this cool swimming article to read (his way of pretending we look 20 years younger than we are - Bob, even 20 years younger still ain't young, my friend!).

A pool might not be the first place you think of going when you're looking to shape up and slim down – but perhaps it should be. No other workout burns calories, boosts metabolism and firms every muscle in your body (without putting stress on your joints) better than a swimming workout. And you don't have to be an Olympic gold medallist to get the perfect body. When researchers at Indiana University compared recreational fitness swimmers with non-swimmers, they found that swimmers of all ages had more lean muscle and trimmer waists and hips.

While swimming may not offer the lace-up-your-shoes-and-go convenience of running, all you need are three key items — swimsuit, cap, and goggles — and you're set to hit the water.

Why Water Works
The body-shaping benefits of swimming are the result of a perfect storm of calorie burn and muscle recruitment. An easy swim burns around 500 calories an hour, while a vigorous effort can torch almost 700. And because water is

nearly 800 times denser than air, each kick, push and pull is like a mini resistance workout for your entire body — especially your core, hips, arms, shoulders and glutes. So in addition to blasting calories as you swim, you build lean muscle, which ignites your metabolism so that you burn more calories once you've showered and dried off.

The irony is that while swimming makes you lean and mean, it's also kind to your body. Water basically neutralises gravity, so you become virtually weight-less when immersed, giving your joints a much-needed vacation. 'You can swim almost every day without risking injury,' says Joel Stager, Ph.D., director of the Counsilman Center for the Science of Swimming at Indiana University at Bloomington, who has studied the effects of swimming for years. 'You can't say the same for running or strength training.'

And that makes swimming something you can do for your entire life — a major bonus because it can literally help you stay younger. 'Our research shows that habitual swimmers are biologically up to 20 years younger than their actual age,' Stager says. The data, which was presented at an American College of Sports Medicine Conference, revealed that a swimmer's blood pressure, choles-terol levels, cardiovascular performance, central nervous system and cognitive functioning are all comparable to someone far younger.

Day 503 - Thursday 21st June 2012

After work yesterday I headed to the beach and in a much choppier sea did twice around the pier in almost exactly an hour. It was perhaps foolish to do that on my own, especially since the swimming death yesterday but I felt strong enough and confident enough. I like to think that if I were to get to the beach on my own and have any fitness doubts or condition concerns then I would stay closer to shore rather than head out. It was a good, tough swim in a warm sea (around 15 degrees at that time in the day - although some much warmer patches and much colder patched thrown in along the way). Afterwards I headed home and with Sharon out every night this week it was around 8.30p.m. before I got the kids to bed and managed to get up to my gym and do my 15 minutes on the Vasa - particularly hard as

I was rather tired at that point.

Another early start today (6a.m. and in the car to Kent for a board meeting) and then back to Hove for an office meeting and then off to Asher's school for prize giving. No swim this morning (again!), however, despite the rain and general change in the weather, I still aim to hit the beach at 4p.m. Then tonight naturally I shall be back on the Vasa and maybe a stint on the running machine or cycling machine, assuming the kids hit the sack in good time.

Tomorrow - Back to the beach first thing for my 7a.m. swim (way-hay hay hay) before heading off to London for a long but exciting day all about the Starr Trust and my plans for building The Lyrics Leisure/Art Centre - now that is exciting, for sure. I really am wondering now if I can pull this development off, it might actually happen, craziness!

Day 504 - Friday 22nd June 2012

The wind doth bloweth; in fact the wind doth howleth! Luckily it was a very low tide this morning and that meant that we had a playground to enjoy at the beach. Big Bob and I had the sea all to ourselves. The wind was blowing very very strongly from the east and the tide was keeping up with it, which meant that we went in right at the doughnut groyne and attempted to swim west against it. With lots of powerful strokes we eventually made it across our beach onto the next beach and a little way along before turning and literally zooming back to the buoy on our beach. The waves were coming thick and fast and some really did bash you and spin you over, but the low tide meant that they were not full of water and not dangerous. A fantastic Friday morning play and a decent shoulder workout. You really needed to be there to understand the fun, we were playing in the sea like ten-year-old kids in a Funplex, running, jumping and cheering - wonderful to be a kid again.

Day 505 - Monday 25th June 2012

A lovely start to the day, starting the week in the most amazing swimming pool that Mother Nature could have dreamt up. Despite waking up with stomach pains (Crohn's for some reason playing up?) a minute standing still in the sea up to my shoulders soon dealt with that; once again the healing power of the sea amazes me. Big Bob, having not exercised for a few days (unlike me who so far has done 10 consecutive days in the gym as well as all the swimming), decided we needed to do a longer swim today. So we went around all the buoys on our beach, then around the pier, to the furthest buoy the other side, then back through the pier and back around our own buoys and then in. Total swim time about 40 minutes and temperature slightly up (no up enough still) to 14.6 degrees. It was a good strong swim to start the week and really set up the day/week ahead. What was pleasing for me was that all the swimming and excess training is starting to pay off (finally!). Not that I'm so super fast still, but I am finding that Bob and I are pretty much together from start to finish, which for me is great, especially as he is a lot faster than he was last year. I need to keep the pressure up and keep thinking about my technique as much as I think about the physical exercise.

This week I will be in the gym every day at home before bed, do two gym sessions with Ross at Falmer, four sea swims and one pool swim. That's fourteen training sessions this week. With the relay just six weeks away I need to do all I can and them some!

Day 506 – Tuesday 26th June 2012
'Continuous skin friction can produce skin damage or abrasions of variable severity. This starts at the surface involving the epidermis first. If it goes deeper into the dermis, it can produce severe pain - similar to a burn - and/ or bleeding. Below the dermis sits a layer of fat. If the skin is well-padded or the fat layer is thick, the skin protrudes. This exposes more skin to friction and produces more severe "burns". In other words, more slender people report that they are less likely to abrade.'

Ouch! Yesterday after our quick and long swim I had some chaffing under my right arm, caused no doubt by the amount of swimming and training I have been doing lately, mixed in with a choppy sea and me powering along as fast as I can and maintaining the speed throughout. It was really red and felt like sunburn. The plan this morning was to apply some Vaseline to the area and not swim at quite the same pace. Naturally with this in mind all night, I got to the Arch (with sleep deprivation as Mia was next to me all night and coughing and kicking me throughout), got changed, walked into the sea and was two minutes into my swim before I realised, 'Bugger, I forgot the Vaseline!' Oh well, I thought, at least I'll take it easy today which will help; mmm, maybe not. With such a gloriously flat sea and a tide pushing to the west, Bob and I swam at a really good pace; possibly the fastest I've done during the last two years. Ouch, ouch, ouch! The patch under my right arm is literally pulsing and sitting here at my desk it feels like arm and my side are sticking together each time they touch.

Tomorrow is a pool day so no salt water, although I wonder how the chlorine will react to it. Definitely going to smother it is Vaseline though ('I shall not forget, I shall not forget' will be my night time mantra!).

I'm at the gym after work with Ross so will have to also be careful not to do stuff that will aggravate it and I think I'll definitely lay off the Vasa training tonight. Oh the joys of being an athlete !

Day 507 – Wednesday 27th June 2012

It's not often I big myself up, but this morning I am doing just that because I went to the pool and did my best, despite my best being less good than previous days and despite really not wanting to go.

I was almost exhausted physically from all the training I have done over the last three weeks without rest, without much sleep and on top of some major work projects. Then last night, after going to parents evening at school, we joined fellow parents for an Indian meal in Brighton. Even though I have to have the plainest Indian food possible, my Crohn's disease still finds it a struggle. As such this morning I was not only tired from lack of sleep but my stomach was really hurting. Getting up at 6a.m. and having to face the pool was the last thing I wanted to do.

However.... by 6.45a.m. I was in the outside pool with Big Bob (my saviour, as without him being there I really might not have turned up!). We did a 400 metre warm up followed by 100 metre sprints x 10 sets with a few seconds rest between each set, then followed by a punishing ¼ mile, leg-only session with a float - youch on the cramp; followed by a 200 metre cool-down. Despite not being as fast or as strong as I would have liked to have been, it was still job very much done.

A wise man once said, 'Always do your best. Your best is going to change from moment to moment; it will be different when you are healthy as opposed to sick. Under any circumstances, simply do your best and you will avoid self-judgement, self abuse and regret.' I'm not sure what wise man or lady said that, but they are wise words indeed.

Day 509 - Friday 29ᵗʰ June 2012

Another month gone. Another month of work stress done and survived, always a good thing - and another month closer to my Channel swim, which is also a very good thing.

After a week of exhaustion Big Bob and I decided on an easier swim today; easier in terms of no long distances, that is, but not so easy when you see a very wavy and bumpy sea with a high tide and a strong tidal pull to the west. Sea temp up now to 15.9 degrees, which was welcome and air temp about 16 degrees, also welcome. Bob and I battled the waves with some butterfly; a hard stroke, especially in a tough sea.

Day 510 - Monday 2ⁿᵈ July 2012

Thirty-six days to go and counting.... but where is the sun? Yesterday was nice and warm at times but the sun was in and out, as were the rain clouds. This morning the air temperature had dropped again and walking down the beach really felt more like the start of winter rather than the start of the summer.

After another massively busy and tiring weekend and a night of the twins keeping me awake. The sea this morning was an average 15.2 degrees, apart from right at the coast, which was probably just around 12 degrees, and the seaweed was twisting around your limbs and squeezing whenever it wanted to. The waves were big and choppy and the tide was strong to the east.

We swam around the pier, literally being lifted and smacked back down at regular intervals, like being in a wrestling ring with someone far hairier and heavier than you. We swam around the pier, to the buoys and back, Shoichi leading the way as ever (and then staying out a good 10 minutes longer than us), with me next and then Bob on my tail. It's good at the moment because I am now pretty equal with Bob (sometimes a little faster and sometimes a little slower) and it means that I can enjoy swimming with him.

Day 511 – Tuesday 3rd July 2012
Thirty-five days to go (weather permitting).

Yesterday's exercise – I ended up doing four sessions yesterday; (1) sea swim 6.30a.m. (2) Gym session with trainer 1p.m. (3) Home gym session 8p.m. (4) pool swim 9p.m.

Yesterday's food/drink – (1) Strong coffee 8.30a.m. (2) Cheap sausage roll 11.30a.m. (3) Pot noodle 12.30p.m. (4) Noodles, chicken and veg 10.15p.m. (5) Xmas pudding and custard 10.45p.m. Lots of exercise and basically rubbish eating (although the Christmas pudding was nice). I wonder why I was tired this morning?

Today – Changed to the pool this morning for a change; nice to get the pool done early on in the week. Bob and I were in the outside pool by 6.45a.m. and it was relatively warm in the air, but raining constantly. The thing about swimming in the rain (almost an idea for a musical!) is that you're wet anyway. It sounds so much worse than it actually is, which is actually quite pleasant as long as the wind is still, which today it was. We did the same routine as last week, including the ¼ mile leg kicking (lots of cramp on that one).

After work at 5p.m. I'm down at the beach for a swim. I was planning a two-hour swim but the temperature and the conditions are still not great, so I will aim for an hour. I am possibly being joined by some of my relay team, though I'm not sure who, if anyone, is coming. Then tomorrow morning back in the sea and Bob wants us to do an hour as well. Will I be achy by the weekend? I should coco!

Day 512 – Wednesday 4th July 2012

Thirty-four days to go…. and happy Independence Day (for my American brethren out there).

Yesterday after work (and that was after an hour in the pool with Bob in the morning and then a full and very busy day at work) I went to the beach. No-one there but me so I headed into a fairly warmish sea and a low tide and swam up and around Brighton Pier, through it at the middle and then onwards to the West Pier and to the red buoy at the end, then turned back. Total swim time 1 hour 20 minutes. Afterwards I purchased two very hot and wonderfully sugared doughnuts and wandered back down the prom to my car. So far a boring story, you might think. But then the birds turned!! Arrgggh… blooming seagulls dive-bombed me; two straight into my head and the other two nicked my bag of doughnuts and then they all flew off! Seriously, it actually happened. People stopped and watched the theft but no-one called the police. A council worker on street-sweeping duty came over to tell me that the same thing happened to him a few minutes before when they nicked his bag of chips! What's the world coming to when you get mugged by birds?

Back to today. Why has Mia decided that sleeping sideways is a good thing? After joining us around midnight she spent the next five hours turning around like a spinning ball, each turn producing a kick or a poke into my back or head. That's it; tonight I take her back to her room as many times as it takes otherwise I will end up being more bruised than a welterweight against a heavy weight.

At the Arch by 6.45a.m. and in a very bouncy sea again. It's strange because on a low tide with no wind like this morning (and in fact the same as last night's swim) it looks as though it will be calm and easy. However when you are lying flat in the sea, every little movement can feel enlarged by multiples of ten. Heading up and around the pier it was so bumpy I just couldn't get a rhythm going and it seemed no matter which way I turned I was swallowing water and being buffeted around. The temperature was down again to under around 14.8 and the air, whilst warm, was rather dark still. Despite that it was a good workout and I was most pleased when Bob and Dr Sean suggested a coffee at the Red Roaster afterwards; a well deserved mid-week treat, especially after my bird mugging last night!

Day 513 – Thursday 5ᵗʰ July 2012

Thirty-three days to go... Not feeling my best today, which is annoying. I have a pain that goes around my entire middle. It's not a bad tummy pain at all and it only mildly suggests a Crohn's pain, so possibly I have overdone the training and pulled something? I was meant to be swimming in the sea after work, but a meeting in London was called so I had to cancel that, which considering my pain is a good thing. Also I will not use the gym tonight and will cancel both gym sessions tomorrow, so just sea swim in the morning. That way at least I'm giving it a chance to heal before next week's crazy exercise onslaught.

Pain, pain, go away, don't come back another day!!

Day 514 – Friday 6ᵗʰ July 2012

Thirty two days to go.... and the pain, pain didn't go away. The whole night my chest felt tight but there is no sick feeling, so I reckon it must be a strain. This morning, despite it being a completely flat, glass-like sea and very low tide I just swam around the buoys for half an hour and stayed away from fast swimming or crazy depths. Time for a few days rest; hopefully that will do the job and I can start again on Monday. It really frustrates me when these things happen but it's too close to my swim now for me to take any silly chances.

Talking of the swim, the stats so far in the Channel are that only one out of twenty-six solos has made it and only one out of nine relays has made it, which goes to show that both the solo and the relay are massive challenges. The problem this year is that the temperature has just not risen and mid Channel it's under 14 degrees and likely to stay that way now for the whole year. This is a lot lower that it should be and unless one is conditioned to deal with that, then failure will come smashing at the door.

The whole team have to pull off a 2-hour swim this month to enable us to qualify for the team (CSA rules) and while I have done a few in the pool I am personally only up to about 1 hour 45 minutes in the sea. I can definitely do a 2-hour swim though and will do it next week. Fiona has also suggested we add a sixth person to the team for definite now; either as a back-up in case someone can't qualify or drops out and also as a possibility of having a six-person relay, as in these temperatures a five-person team has a lot less chance of success than one with six, which is the norm. A lot for me to contemplate this weekend, as I need to make sure we not only start the swim but also finish it!

Day 515 – Tuesday 10ᵗʰ July 2012

Pain, pain has gone away; whoop whoop! It was definitely a Crohn's pain and not a muscle thing as it went too quickly to be the latter, which is good news as a muscle issue could have been a longer-term problem whilst the Crohn's is already longer term!

This morning I was somewhat reluctant to go to the beach, which always happens when I've missed a couple of days but I dragged myself down there and was extremely pleased I did. The sea was very bumpy, but the tide was slack and the temperature still cold at just 15.3 degrees. A group of us headed off together and we all ended up swimming alone (the bumps in the sea made visibility impossible). A decent swim to start the week.

I had to go for an early gym session today and as Ross is away I trained with Soula; she is a gym devil! Unlike my usual training, which has pretty much been core, strength and stamina, Soula started me on speed training. We did 2,000 metres on the rowing machine at serious speed without slowing down, which was preceded by the cross trainer. This alone made me feel a little sick. Then we spent a whole hour on the TRX, which was back to core and strength, including a lot of leg work. Halfway through and then also near the end I had to excuse myself and stand outside for a minute taking in gulps of air to stop myself throwing up. The last time that happened to me was when I was eighteen and first went to a gym! It was compounded by lack of sleep, zero food, a swim to the West Pier and back in a bumpy sea and two hours of dashing around the office beforehand, but it was still an odd feeling for me considering how much exercise and training I do. Just goes to show that no matter how fit you might be, if all of a sudden you change your routine and try something new you have to accept that to a great degree you are starting from scratch!

Day 516 – Wednesday 11th July 2012

Twenty-six days to go...

A tough day yesterday with exercise. It's been a while since I felt ill from working out. This morning I could really feel my thighs and legs burning but the sea soon took care of that. It was a really bumpy sea again, way more bumpy than yesterday, yet surprisingly unthreatening. Lindy and James were on a monumental West Pier swim; they really are tough cookies those two, how lucky I am to have them on my team. Shoichi was heading out on one of his crazy long swims as we were getting showered, and Alex (another team member) has just finished a pier swim and was getting ready for lifeguard training. Leo meanwhile (now welcomed back on the team officially as the sixth and final starrfish) continues to amaze me with 2-and 3-hour swims regardless of weather and condition– what a team!

As for the rest of the day, it's the twins' fourth birthday today, so a lovely day off with them. Talking of birthdays, a very happy sixty-two years young to Little Bob. A legend amongst men, for sure.

Day 517 – Friday 13th July 2012

Twenty-four days to go... No swimming or gyming yesterday as my little Asher was in hospital for an operation (ears, nose and throat) and I needed to be with him from morning 'til night. Pleasingly, all went well and apart from slight breathing issues which meant an overnight stay, all was good and we were able to bring him home at 10a.m. this morning.

Talking about this morning; back to the sea and a very bumpy day again. Waves were everywhere and of variable height; medium, large and extra large - no XXL thankfully. A lot of fun and a decent workout. Then off to the Red Roaster for a Friday coffee, and then up to the Royal Alex to collect my baby. Now back at home working and absolutely gonna hit the home gym at least twice, lunchtime and evening, and also (before the twins get back from nursery) will get an hour in the pool at home against the jets and in far too hot water. I'm already sweating just thinking about it.

Next Tuesday, I am gonna do a 2-hour swim with the team, with Fiona in her kayak; getting this adjudicated swim done is a major focus, as without that we can't go! I remain hopeful that the entire team (including me) will step up and nail this. Also next week I am going to grab a day where I can do three, 1-hour sea swims in one day (am/afternoon/evening). Leo and Shocihi did it yesterday and it was a big challenge for them, especially in these seas. Lindy was also out this morning in these crazy seas for nearly an hour; a great performance from everyone.

I'm looking forward to a great sea swimming week next week in preparation for the upcoming event.

Day 518 - Monday 16th July 2012

With under a month to go until the swim you'd think that the weather would give us a break but once again this morning the winds were high and the clouds were open. If you know the Saddlescombe Road in Brighton, the one that runs from Devil's Dyke to Henfield, then you can get an idea of what swimming in the sea was like this morning. One minute you are flying down a huge dip and the next you are up high amongst the hills; unbelievable. All in a 14.3 degree sea (1 degree down on last week!). Also the tide, helped by the wind, was racing east, which made going where you wanted harder than you'd like. Bob and I headed out into a massive sea and straight to the second buoy; a straight line it was not! Having got there, being bounced around and having our goggles and hats bashed and pulled, we headed west to go past the doughnut groyne. Twenty minutes of non-stop swimming at full pelt kept us rooted to the spot! Eventually we came back in and were putting on our Crocs when Bob got fidgety and wanted to go back in and try again (a kid in a sweet shop)! So off we went, back into the raging waves and gave it a go; nope, the sea 1, Bob nil! A bloomin' good workout though and despite a crazy sea, we got in and out safely.

Tomorrow was meant to be our 2-hour adjudicated swim but with the conditions as they are, Fiona has called it off. It means we all still have to do it of course, but frustratingly it will be individually rather than together as there is no way six of us, all with different lifestyles and commitments, can get a day together when the weather misbehaves. So it'll be a case of each of us looking out the window and just going for it, and then reporting it back. I guess it's our own fault for choosing to live in a country that refuses to have a summer.

On another note entirely, tomorrow is a *massive* day for my 17-year-old nephew, Zachary Narvaez. He is one of only 8,000 people in the whole country chosen to be an Olympic Torch Bearer, recommended by his school for all his charity work. An amazing honour for him and so well deserved. He will be the first Torch Bearer in Brighton at 7.20a.m. and along with thousands of excited Brightonians we will be cheering him on and celebrating a wonderful and once-in-a-lifetime experience for him. I am so very proud of him.

Day 519 – Tuesday 17th July 2012
Twenty-two days to go... To say we are proud of Zac is an understatement. Chosen as an Olympic beacon in his home town at the age of 17 shows what an amazing man he is turning into. Zac, your Poppa [grandfather] is smiling down on you, my darling, and your uncle could not be prouder.

8.00am - My 2-hour (well, 2.01.34) adjudicated swim all done, thankfully. This morning was great for the team as the sea was a lot calmer than yesterday; still bumpy, but swimmable. Lindy was amazing as she suffers the cold more than the rest of us and for her to do a 2-hour swim in 14.6 degrees was incredible and I am so very proud of her. She did hers at about 6a.m., then at 6.30a.m. James went in and did his 2 hours. Soon after, Shoichi and Leo went in and did theirs. With Alex already done it was just me. I couldn't miss Zac's big moment so I had to wait until 8a.m. to go in. I was not particularly looking forward to it as I was on my own, it was late for me as I prefer 7a.m., I had not eaten or drunk anything at all since 6p.m. yesterday and had only about three hours sleep - so I wasn't in the best frame of mind. However I went in hopeful and before too long I realised why I love swimming.

Being on my own, whilst not particularly safe sometimes, is very good for the mind. It is great thinking-time as long as you can switch your mind off from the actual swimming, which I mostly managed to do today. I swam from Brighton Pier to the red buoy at the end of the West Pier, then back to the Brighton Centre, then turned and went back to the red buoy (trying to fill up the 2 hours), then turned and went back to Brighton Pier, then around the pier and over to the buoy the other side, then through the pier and over and around the three buoys on my side and then back in; total swim time 2 hours, 1 minute and 34 seconds. The tide was quite strong to the east, so it took at least 58 minutes to get to the West Pier and then only 25 minutes back, so I was filling in time with the buoys afterwards, but the swim was done and I was greeted on the beach by Fiona and Little Bob; a very welcome and unexpected greeting, as I thought I was on my own. Little Bob particularly was so fab that he waited for us all to finish. Fiona said she had to call the coastguard at one point because they lost sight of me in the waves! How funny! Apart from my usual morning swims and gyms for the rest of the week, the next big thing will be our boat ride on James' boat this Friday, where we will be doing an hour each from the boat. Not long now and getting excited.

What a great day; Zac doing his torch run and the Channel relay team all being approved. Fantastic!

Day 520 – Wednesday 18th July 2012

Twenty-one days to go... and a big thank-you to those who have gone onto my site and donated recently; almost at £74,000 now!

Despite yesterday's big swim I still managed an hour at the gym after work, which was tiring but good. It wasn't until after the gym that I realised I hadn't eaten anything all day; in fact nothing since 6p.m. the night before. It still amazes me that I am able to pull off a big sea swim (equivalent to around 5 hours in the pool) and then work and then go to the gym and all with no food in me. Blooming bad for the body I would think, but I just keep forgetting to eat!

Having completed the final swim adjudication yesterday it feels much more relaxed today; all we need to do now is keep up the hour-at-a-time swims and then pray for a warm, calm August; please, please let's have an August summer so we can get the swim done and I can then move on!

Day 521 - Thursday 19ᵗʰ July 2012

Twenty days to go... Another treadmill swim today, although only about half as strong as yesterday, thankfully. Bob and I headed straight out past the first buoy (actually we walked all the way to the first buoy) and then headed against the tide (on our virtual treadmill) and did a non-stop, 30-minute, head-straight-down-in-the-water swim. Usually at that pace we would have been well past the Brighton Centre, but with the tide gushing against us we only got as far as the Thistle Hotel. Heading back we reached the groyne in 6 minutes flat; 30 minutes out and 6 minutes back shows you the strength of the tide. The temperature in the sea was 14.6 degrees, making mid Channel something like 13 degrees. Yuck. Tonight, like last night, will also be a short, 20-minute gym session at home. I'm kind of enjoying them now in an odd and tired sort of way.

Day 522 - Friday 20ᵗʰ July 2012

Nineteen days to go... Mid (almost end) July and wearing a sweatshirt after my swim; rubbish weather! The sky was thankfully dry, although chilly, and the sea was flat as a plate but again chilly. The temperature today was down to just 14.1 degrees, a drop of almost half a degree since we did our 2-hour swim on Tuesday. These cold temperatures really do pile on the pressure in terms of our training and our possible success; the success rate for the

CSA swimmers this year still sits at one of the lowest-ever on record, which is pressure for us indeed. Mind you, a wise man once said that pressure is a positive thing as it focuses you and makes you work harder; pressure after all is what creates diamonds!

This morning Bob and I were in the sea by 6.45a.m. and we swam clockwise around the pier, then passed the two fishing buoys that are about 50 metres out further from the head of the pier, then diagonally across to the two buoys at the far end of our beach and then in. Total swim about 40 minutes and we really did work hard to do that. Coffee very deserved!

The forecast for the rest of the day is very clear skies until about 3p.m. and then rain and lots of it. Typical, because at 3p.m. my relay team are meeting at Brighton Marina for a boat ride out into the depths and then a swim from the boat that James owns between 4p.m. and 8p.m. Of course if the sea chops up then the ability to swim from the boat will be limited and it will turn into a 'get thrown around on a boat experience' only!

On the positive side (gotta search out the positive at all times) the weather people, those strange beings who seem to know what the shape of a cloud really means, are still predicting a summer for us. Apparently, if they are to be believed, the summer will start from this weekend and could run throughout August, providing respite for the Olympics and our Relay; both important milestones for the country, of course. Let's please all pray to the weather gods and their earthly disciples that this may come true.

Friday evening, 20th July 2012

Whoa, what an evening. My relay team (minus Leo who couldn't make it tonight) and I met on James's boat at 3p.m. and headed about 4-5 miles out to sea. James, as part of the Relay Team Starrfish, brought along his wife and a friend to act as pilot and co-pilot; cool characters they were as well, undaunted by six of us jumping off their boat.

It was choppy right from the moment we left the Marina and we ended up with Force 6 and Force 7 gales throughout. It turns out that in a Force 7 gale it is much nicer in the sea than on a boat!

We have a new member called Lois, who is acting as our back-up member if anyone can't make it on the day. She is only fourteen and is being trained by Fiona as a sea swimmer; a balls-y kid for sure. Once we were in position, three of the team (Lindy, Alex and Lois) all got changed into their costumes and then launched themselves with a leap off the back of the boat into the ocean. It was particularly impressive watching a slight, fourteen-year-old girl jump from a boat in the middle of the sea straight into a Force 6 storm. Whilst the rest of us hung onto the boat for dear life, they simply got on with the job in hand and swam for an hour.

A short 55 minutes later, myself, James and Shoichi were standing at the back in our trunks, ready to jump. On the hour we jumped in and swam past them and then they clambered out. By this point the gale was at force 7 and the boat was a roller coaster. The actual swim itself was fine, almost enjoyable but it is certainly different swimming in that type of sea way out in the middle of the ocean compared to our swims around the piers.

Due to the crazy conditions it wasn't possible for James, Shoichi and I to stay together and very quickly we became a challenge to the boat; them trying to somehow stay near three of us when we were all literally 150 metres apart in rolling waves. But they did a tremendous job. At times when I could barely see the other two and the boat was a few hundred metres away I did feel very vulnerable and wonder what would happen if they lost me, which in all seriousness would have been easy to do. After an hour they blew the whistle and came to collect us. By the time I was coming out, last of course, the boat was being thrown about so much that I had to keep swimming away from it for fear of it being dropped back down on me. Once safely aboard, the fun and games started. James, Shoichi and I were downstairs in the cabin area trying to get dry and change into warm clothes whilst the boat was doing acrobatics. It took a good 40 minutes to get dressed and in that time I had the pleasure of meeting each wall and corner of the boat several times, each one leaving me with a bruise as a memento. Back on deck I found that out of all the people on board, only Fiona, James, Shoichi and I were not sick or feeling sick. This is no slight on anyone, as it is by no means shameful to feel ill in a boat in a rolling gale force wind, but it shows how much harder it is on the boat than in the sea.

This experience, which was fantastic for us all, really showed me that a Channel Relay is a tough challenge and should not be taken lightly. I have at times felt that changing from a Solo to a Relay was somehow an easy option – I shall now take that right back! A Relay is a massive challenge, hence so far this year only having one successful team. For me, having only been swimming for two years, it is perhaps even more of a challenge, although for my team having me as a novice swimmer is a challenge for them. All of this, and Lois, our youngest member, took it in her stride; impressive to say the very least!

Day 523 – Monday 23rd July 201 2

Just sixteen days to go.... Summer is here; way-hay, way-hay, way-hay (am I excited or what)!

The weekend was beautiful; 22 degrees and sunny. Apparently it's here to stay for the month, through the Olympics and throughout our swimming week. Could we really be that lucky? Could we get a clear day after all this crazy rain?

This morning was bright sunshine by 6a.m. I was at the Arch by 6.45a.m. and in the sea within minutes. I was on my own as Big Bob is not around today, and I did a decent swim this morning; a pier triple which I've never done. Girlie beach around pier to our beach, then back all the way around to start and then back all way around to end on our beach – beach to beach to beach to beach. It was so calm out there that it was really easy just to keep going. Also the temperature was 15.6 degrees, more than 1 degree up from Friday. I am now keeping everything crossed that the temperature keeps rising and the waves keep falling!

Rest of the day is a usual day at work, then an hour with Ross in the gym at the end of the day and then the new Batman film tonight - what a nice day.

There is however some sadness. A 45-year-old chap swimming the Channel at the weekend got within a mile of France and died. I am sure we will learn more as the story unfolds. It is such a sad thing to hear of someone, especially so young, being lost in pursuit of a dream. The sea is a dangerous place to be, even in calm days such as today; so much can happen that could end your life that you have no control over. Should we not follow our dreams because of it? Should we somehow water down our hopes and expectations of our possible achievements? Maybe we should, who knows. But I for one believe that we should always do our best whenever we can and we should always follow our dreams wherever they may take us. The sea is a dangerous place, to be respected, but it is equally as dangerous on the roads and equally as dangerous on the playing fields as it is in the deserts. When your time comes, it comes, and up to then we need to grab life and follow whatever dreams we can. Dare to dream and dare to follow your dream; the rest, they say, is in the lap of the gods.

Day 526 - Thursday 26ᵗʰ July 2012

Thirteen days to go… I was absolutely *exhausted* this morning. Thankfully the boys are now staying in their own beds all night but Mia still insists on ending up with us. She then bullies me to the end and places an elbow in the small of my back all night. Last night she took to slapping me in her sleep until I got so fed up I moved to the floor (really should have gone to the spare room, but I just was too tired to take the walk).

I literally dragged myself out of bed at 6.05a.m., drove to the beach in a semi coma and sat in the car outside the Brighton ferris wheel for a good 10 minutes just trying to get the energy to open the door – I was seriously that exhausted. The radio was playing Lady Gaga's song that I used to hear all the time when I started this swimming journey; funny how it quickly brought back my first day in the sea in April 2010, music can invoke memories from out of nowhere.

Dragging my feet after Bob down the beach I suggested the first buoy and back; like he was ever gonna accept that! He suggested the three buoys, which I naturally had to agree to. Of course he bluffed me and when we got to the second buoy he took off for the pier and dragged me along with him.

By the time we got to the head of the pier my exhaustion had vanished and I was back in the game. We held a good pace all the way and landed back onto a crowded beach in a decent time. I guess without the swimming I would have been exhausted all day, so I'm pleased he pushed me.

Why was the beach crowded at 7.30a.m? Well, as usual a film crew were there and those interested BSC members were hanging around to watch or be filmed. This time it was with Rory Bremner. Bob and I however skipped the theatrics and headed off for a shower and then to the Red Roaster for a Friday cake and coffee – I know it's Thursday but he's away tomorrow so we made Thursday a Friday instead!

Then I headed to the Withdean for an hour with Kim my physio and boy, that hurt! I have been getting some quite bad pains in my left shoulder and Kim reckons it stems from all the swimming and the fact that in the sea I breathe one-sided, thus stretching my neck one way for hour on end. So I paid for it with an hour of pain – no pain, no gain, of course! With two weeks to go until the swim I am seeing Kim again next week to get a top-up session; lovely to see her always as she is just fab, but I never look forward to the torture.

As for the rest of the day; it's a good one today. A couple of business meetings then followed by afternoon meetings with architects and council members regarding our King Alfred project for The Lyrics Centre – exciting day for sure. Nothing is agreed yet of course but I think that we may have a better than even chance of pulling this mad dream off! We even have a website now – www.thelyicshove.com

If energy levels continue I'll also grab half an hour tonight in the gym at home; energy and shoulder permitting.

Day 527 – Friday 27th July 2012

12 days to go... Not a bad night's sleep thankfully; a decent five hours so I was ready to get up and head to the beach. Not as hot today, possibly rain later, but still dry and clear and a very flat sea yet again. A strong tidal pull to the west made the swim a decent exercise and a very clear ocean made

the fish and starfish watching rather pleasant. I had a nice gentle hour's swim. I'm still achy from all the exercise and the physio so this was sensible. Tonight I will grab half an hour in the gym at home, but again on more gentle exercises rather than caning it. Then tomorrow (assuming the wife allows) I'll grab an hour in the sea first thing.

Next week I'll do a couple of West Pier swims if the weather holds and a couple of gym sessions, but then will tail the exercise off to make sure I am not achy or overworked for the big swim. How exciting to think about tailing it off for a while! Jeeze, this swim better happen and better be successful; two-and-a-half years of learning to swim, and aiming for this, is a long time for me. I've been watching a lot of Olympian biogs on TV this month and I am astounded at their dedication to their sport. I know my two-and-a-half years does show some sticking power and is certainly more than I expected I could do, but compared to the Olympians it is less than a weekend's work. These are seriously dedicated people.

Day 528 – Monday 30ᵗʰ July 2012

Nine days to go... After watching an amazing Olympic Games opening ceremony on Friday night into the wee hours I was inspired enough do an early Saturday swim. Only me at the Arch when I got there at 6.20a.m., although when I finished at 7.30 there were a few others there, including yet another film crew. I really don't understand the fascination with filming middle-aged men and women in their swimming gear first thing in the morning. A clear sky, 15.9 degrees in the sea, but it felt colder as the air was colder. I swam for an hour around the pier, the buoys and back again. A nice start to the weekend.

Day 529 – Tuesday 31ˢᵗ July 2012

Eight days to go.... The house last night was busier than the sea this morning, but only just. I was bounced to the end of the bed by Mia, then bounced back to the middle of the bed by Jesse, then kicked to the bottom of the bed by Sharon and then eventually at 2a.m. kicked out altogether by Asher.

By 2a.m. I was alone in Mia's room and whilst it is a kiddie bed it was a lot calmer than my room!

The sea was not much of a contrast. Bob, Shoichi and I headed into quite rough waters - wind blowing, rain dropping, waves rushing - but no tide movement, which was strange. It was bumpy all the way to the Brighton Centre and even bumpier all the way back. We didn't go out too deep, just to the first buoy, but that makes it bumpier as the waves are heading in at a pace and really pick up speed at about that distance. All of a sudden you are hit in the side and spun over and it takes all your strength to stop from completely rolling over and keeping your pace going forward. It's certainly great exercise and each day you learn something from it.

Back at the Arch we found David with the largest bucket of mackerel I've seen in months - he must have caught 25, which in this sea is astonishing. Also Yvo was there with her hand in a bucket of boiling water and the kettle hotting up for the next; she'd been fishing with David and had unknowingly caught a weaver fish. She certainly knew about it when she picked it up to remove the hook - yowch! First time I've seen a weaver sting on a hand! Leo was stung on the foot at the weekend as well and was hobbling for days. You don't get this in hobbies like cake-making or sewing!

The swim is now just eight days away, though there was talk of us possibly going early - even as early as this week, but the weather has now turned again. Not a bad thing as we have all prepared next week with work and social diaries and it would be difficult for the majority of my team if it came early. This from Fiona's father, who apparently understands these things (it's all gobbledegook to me):

Weather update for your coming Channel relay if you went early:
Not very good at the moment.

North Foreland to Selsey Bill:
Strong winds are forecast for coastal areas up to 12 miles offshore from 1800 UTC Mon 30 July until 1800 UTC Tue 31 July

24 hour forecast:
Wind – south-westerly, backing southerly for a time later, 5 or 6, occasionally 7
in east, decreasing 4 for a time
Sea state – slight or moderate
Weather – showers, then occasional rain for a time
Visibility – good, becoming moderate, occasionally poor

Outlook for the following 24 hours 1800 Tues 31st July to 1800 Wed 1st Aug:
Wind – southerly or south-westerly 5 or 6, decreasing 3 or 4 for a time
Sea state – slight or moderate
Weather – mainly fair
Visibility – moderate or good, occasionally poor at first

Dover shipping forecast issued 1625 UTC Mon 30 July:
Wind – south or south-west 5 to 7, decreasing 4 for a time
Sea state – moderate
Weather – rain for a time
Visibility – good, occasionally poor

Whatever that all means, it seems that up to next Monday it'll be rather unpleasant. Tuesday and Wednesday next week look good at the moment though and as such I remain very hopeful, and almost positive, that Wednesday 8th August will be our day .

Day 530 – Wednesday 1st August 2012
Seven days to go... A week today and game on (weather permitting, of course). Everything that can be crossed is being crossed by me at the moment.

Back to reality. Last night was once again busy at home with Jesse for some reason joining Mia in our room – just as we thought he had nailed it! By around 1a.m. I was receiving physio treatment in my back and neck from Mia; thump, thump, dig, dig, thump, dig, push, pull... the full works.

She may only be four years old but boy, can she kick and pull; a true physiotherapist in the making.

I was at the seafront by 6.45a.m. but Big Bob wasn't feeling great and not wanting to push it too much. That suited me, as I am in my last week of training and want to bring it down a bit. So we headed out to the first buoy, rested, then the second buoy, rested, then the third buoy by the pier, rested, and then diagonally back to the first buoy and rested! At the last buoy I raised my goggles and let the sea slowly bring me to shore without any swimming at all. I've never done that before, and it was strange as instinctively you want to kick, but it was nice all the same and very calm. In many places the tide genuinely pulls you in and out but in Brighton you will go left or right (or right to left) rather than out to sea. The lesson is that if you are ever in the sea in Brighton and are too tired to swim in, don't panic; just relax and let the sea do its thing.

Day 531 – Thursday 2nd August 2012

Six days to go… With six days to go, the sea throws a treadmill at us! Great fun actually and superb exercise. Bob and I started at the groyne, swam our hearts out for 20 minutes and were still at the groyne! The tide can be so powerful that sometimes it keeps you still and sometimes it shoots you back; without us swimming like that we would have been shot back across the whole beach and into the pier in a matter of minutes. Our aim was simply to get across the groyne to the next beach and it took three concerted efforts to do it. It was perhaps 2 metres only, but across the line is across the line, job done.

Afterwards I headed off to my final physio appointment before my Relay and had an hour of Kim squashing my shoulder muscles and stretching my neck until I looked like a giraffe.

Tomorrow will be an easier Friday swim and a Red Roaster coffee, plus a gym session later in the day. Then it's a restful weekend awaiting next week. I've got that Christmas feeling: nervous with anticipation but excited about the event approaching!

Fiona decided on our order today, based on who she needs to swim when in terms of speed, endurance and ability to handle the cold. It is:

Lindy Dunlop
Alex Downey
Shoichi Yanagisawa
James Hooper
Leo Santos-Shaw
Rob Starr (me)
The big Six Starrfish, way-hay!

Little Bob isn't able to crew for us as he was so unwell on the trip with James's boat that he felt he could end up being a liability but he will act as our driver by waiting it out in Dover for us to return. Lois, as our back-up, will come on the boat and crew with us – at 14 she is an amazing girl and destined for swimming glory, I think. Having LB as our driver is fantastic as I really can't imagine wanting to drive back as well.

Day 532 – Friday 3rd August 2012

Five days to go... Having been off the sauce for some time I hit the bottle last night; oh dear! Let's just say an incident at work with a member of staff letting me down very badly caused it. Two cold beers and two very large whiskies later I was more relaxed with life. Sleep was fine (I wonder why?), but the head and stomach were a tad shaky this morning. Definitely the last drink until the swim is over.

The sea this morning was nicely warm at 16.4 degrees and actually felt warm for the first time this year. A very low tide and a very high sand bank let me stand with both feet flat on the ground and the sea only to my chest right next to the second buoy. That has never happened before – was I perhaps in a state of such peace and calm that I floated up without realising? Despite the low, almost stationary tide, the waves were very choppy indeed. After leaving the second buoy Bob and I headed around the pier and it was bump, slap, bump, slap, all the way. He and I took completely different routes, with him heading straight to the pier and up along the side and me heading straight out to sea and then along to the pier. We met at exactly the same moment at the head and crashed into each other! With the entire sea before us, and heading in from different places, we converged on exactly the same spot as if it were a target; funny, really, that this happened.

A good, strong swim followed by a very strong coffee made for a good end to a tough week. I know I've still got today ahead, but I have the feeling it'll be OK! I have a gym session with Ross after work (the last before my swim, as I'll leave next week clear until after the Relay) and then I'll head home for a relaxing evening with a good book.

Last night I laid out all the stuff I need to take on the swim. It was really odd getting my bag together after preparing for it for so long. In my bag are:

Sharon's best camera
Three pairs of trunks, three pairs of goggles and three large towels
Tubs of Vaseline
Flashing lights for night swimming
Warm clothes (jumpers, fluffy tracksuit bottoms, T-shirts, waterproofs etc)
Bag of pink swimming caps for everyone
A lot of dry food, tea, coffee, hot chocolate, crisps, biscuits – enough for an army of 10 (which we are with crew).

Butterflies were flittering in my stomach throughout and will probably remain with me until after the swim is completed (please god).

Day 533 – Sunday 5ᵗʰ August 2012

Three days to go... I thought a nice Sunday swim would be good for the mind. I was in the gym at home today at 7.30a.m. and did an exhausting hour and then got to an empty Arch at 8.45a.m. The sun was mostly up and the sea was mostly calm; a strong tide to the west, but hardly any waves. There I was getting changed and about to slip on my Crocs when I noticed something stuck to the inside of the shoe. I figured it was a piece of seaweed that must have been on the ball of my right foot on Friday and which I had trodden into my shoe without knowing. On closer inspection it turned out to be the smallest, most perfectly-formed starfish, completely embedded in my right shoe, in the ball of the heel.

I didn't put the shoe on but repacked them and when I got home after my swim (a gentle hour around the pier and buoys a couple of times) Sharon used a palette knife to gently peel it off and save it. As my Relay team is Team Starrfish I took this as a very good omen indeed – a sign from Dad perhaps saying it'll all be all right?

Another cool thing happened today, totally unrelated to the swim of course. A musical I co-wrote, *Remember Remember* (www.remember-remember.net) is being produced and restaged in Lewes next year (October 2013); how cool is that? It seems that next year may be an interesting one as well after all. Life can be very exciting if you let it.

Day 534 – Monday 6ᵗʰ August 2012

Two days to go... I awoke this morning to the sun and the rain and at 6.30a.m., on the way to the beach, I was met with a wonderful and perfectly-coloured rainbow; yet another sign of the amazing world we live in.
An email from Fiona today:

Hi All,
The CSA have asked me to be the official observer.... Yippee! No cheating on my watch! :)
Our pilot thinks it's a 95% chance we'll be going at 4a.m. on Wednesday. I have confirmed the logistics of this with another pilot whom I trust explicitly and he informs me that he will also be taking a solo at that time. Their feeling is, it's better a flat sea on a spring tide than a choppy sea on a neap tide, which makes sense!
I will know for certain at 8p.m. tomorrow evening.
Fiona xx

So it is all set for Wednesday at 4a.m. We'll be leaving Brighton at midnight on Tuesday and then driving to Dover to get it done!

By the way, what is a neap tide and what is a spring tide? Perhaps I should have looked these up and studied them before I even committed to the swim two-and-a-half years ago. In hindsight, if I wasn't so impulsive, I would have looked into Channel swimming before I decided to learn to swim and take it on. It's such a massive task and there is so much to learn, least of all about swimming and about tides. Anything I take on in future I shall slow down a bit and learn about! Saying that, this Channel swimming journey has changed my life beyond recognition in so many ways, and perhaps if I had understood the task ahead I may never have started on that road; so possibly ignorance was bliss after all!

The following is an explanation of **spring** and **neap tides** in relation to lunar and solar cycles:

'Since antiquity, people have noticed that oceans exhibit a much greater tidal range around the time of the full Moon and new Moon. This is when the Moon and Sun are either together in the sky or are on opposite sides of the heavens. Higher tides occur during these Moon phases because the Sun also exerts a gravitational pull on our oceans, although it is only 46 percent as strong as the Moon's.

When the gravitational effects of the Sun and the Moon combine, we get spring tides, which have nothing to do with the season of spring. The term refers to the action of the seas springing out and then springing back. These are times of high high tides and low low tides.

A week later, during either of the two quarter Moon phases, when the Sun and Moon are at right angles to each other and their tidal influences partially cancel each other out, neap tides occur, and the tidal range is minimal. In fact, because the oceans take a bit of time to catch up to the geometry of the Moon, spring and neap tides usually occur about a day after the respective lunar cycles.'
(Source: Bob Berman on www.almanac.com)

I like the following quote, which I found on the same website:

'Now morn has come,
And with the morn the punctual tide again.'
–Susan Coolidge, American writer (1835-1905)

Due to the volume of water being lower in a neap tide it seems it's a better option for a Channel swimmer. However, we are on a spring tide and that is that; we have no choice, as our window is our window. The dice will be rolled and the result will be the result. We will be successful – I know that for sure – but what we judge as success is a personal thing and it isn't always about crossing the finishing line; it is so very much about the journey.

Day 535 – Tuesday 7ᵗʰ August 2012

Eighteen hours to go… This morning saw the team down at the beach and having a gentle swim in preparation for later on. Big Bob, James and I took a leisurely swim around the pier, nothing strenuous or fast. The sea was an enjoyable 16.5 degrees, the air was a pleasant 14 degrees and the wind was down to a simmer (it was howling last night and clearly wore itself out). We are still on for a 4a.m. start and I am picking up the team en route to Dover from midnight tonight. I can't believe it's almost here! Please god, we have a successful and trouble-free swim and keep all fins and gills crossed for Team Starrfish.

Swimming day 536 – Wednesday 8ᵗʰ August 2012

No hours left… Everyone safely in the car and we got to Dover by 2.30a.m. and met James and Lois in the harbour. We were on the *Louise Jane* by 3.30a.m., all loaded and ready to go. The *Louise Jane* is a fishing boat. It has no niceties about it, no comfort, no chairs; just somewhere for the pilot and his mates, a god-awful toilet and an outside area with fixed boxes for us to store our gear and sit on. Welcome to the world of luxury Channel swimming. It is, however, a decent crew, a fantastic pilot and a safe (if not comfortable) boat. Safety and quality are all of a sudden all that matter. The swimming order was changed slightly by Fiona due to the conditions and was set as follows:

Lindy
Alex
Leo
Shoichi
James
Me

The order was based on various things, the most important being that the two quickest swimmers get us out of Dover as fast as they can, covering as much distance as possible.

As expected and hoped, Lindy just flew from the beach despite a massive sea and pitch blackness, her flashing light adorning her as she glided through the waves.

We had expected, and hoped for, a calm sea throughout and a bright sun once the moon had dropped off. What we got was a gale force 4 from start to finish, a cloud covering that was completely grey, and on/off rain. So this clearly was not going to be an easy Channel swim.

The swim itself was not plagued by jellyfish as we had feared and a force 4 gale, although very choppy and bumpy, was not enough to stop six swimmers who spend every morning in the sea off Brighton, which mirrors Channel conditions so accurately. I would suggest that a lot of the unsuccessful attempts are because people simply do not have the opportunity we have to swim in such a similar sea every day. Saying that, I can easily think of at least three big differences between Brighton beach and the English Channel:

1) Salt content – the moment I jumped into the sea when James was finishing his leg I was shocked not by the cold water (it pretty much averaged

15 degrees the whole time, which was spot on) but by the salt. It was so acrid in the water – a mixture of salt content, natural chemicals that build up, shipping oils and the diesel fumes from the back of our boat – that my throat started to swell up immediately and the inside of my nose started to burn. I had no idea how I was meant to swim for an hour like that. I actually felt the skin peeling off my tongue the moment I got in. I'm not sure if everyone felt it, but no-one else mentioned it, so it may just be the way my body reacted.

2) Water volume – not only is the volume of water in the Channel so much more than the local beach but we were on a spring tide, which I at last understand means that the water is building up for a big tide, adding to the volume. This makes swimming a lot harder and the waves and bumps massively heavier.

3) Shipping – very rarely is one confronted by million-ton tankers on Brighton beach! In the Channel they are like insects; none one minute and dozens the next. Incredible to see but very challenging when they are heading towards you and creating massive waves.

Despite all of this, Team Starrfish rocked. Lindy was a speeding fish and was averaging 84 strokes a minute each time, Alex was hot to trot covering massive ground with an average 74 strokes per minute, crazy Leo and Shoichi were ploughing through with averages of 64 strokes a minute, James was our old stalwart with no fear and no excuses and was averaging around 60 strokes a minute – and me? Well, my average of 52 strokes a minute was good enough for someone who two years ago could hardly swim and had never been in the sea.

The *Louise Jane*, our boat, was perfectly adequate and the crew led by Andy King, was wonderful. They were totally supportive and did everything they could to protect us from the waves by trying to block them with the boat, and by battling a massive tide to keep us as close to our landing destination as possible. The *Louise Jane* is a fishing boat, as are all the pilot boats for the CSA, and it was basic to say the least. There was the wheelhouse for Andy and his two crew, there was a small (elf-sized) toilet outside the wheelhouse and then there was the back of the boat for us! The toilet was so small that every time you went (and you really tried to avoid it) you found your head banging on the wall above the pan; I came out with 20 bruises on my forehead each time. I think only crazy Leo decided to risk going to the toilet for number twos!

An open-backed fishing boat, the *Louise Jane* had large storage containers fixed in place where we put our bags to protect them from the sea and rain and then sat on them for some 20 odd hours. Our plastic food containers were strapped down on deck with bungee cords. In a rough sea the bungee cords did what you would expect them to do: stretch! As such, it was a battle to stop the containers from sliding around and breaking someone's legs each time a big wave hit.

From the moment we boarded the boat and left Dover harbour the sea was sloshing in over the decks and our feet and shoes were sopping wet before the swim even started. Throughout the swim we were in a mixed state of being thrown left, right, up and down and being sluiced by seawater. Getting into the sea was almost a welcome relief (almost!).

It works like this: swimmer one gets in by jumping into the sea from the side of the boat. The pilot offers his preference as to which side to try to protect you from the massive swells but the choice is yours. As our swim started at night time we wore flashing bright lights. The first person (Lindy in this case) swims to the beach at Dover from the boat (a few hundred metres), walks out to the furthest place beyond the sea and then enters the water to start the swim once the pilot sounds his horn. The swimmer then swims as fast as possible for an hour. Five minutes before the hour is up, with the second swimmer now changed into swimming gear and with Vaseline in the appropriate places, a whistle is blown and the current swimmer is given a hand signal to indicate he/she has 5 minutes left. After the five minutes (which feels like another twenty when you're in the sea!), the swimmer hears two sharp whistle blows and then treads water.

The second swimmer then jumps off the boat, landing behind the first swimmer. The first swimmer then swims around the second swimmer, to the back of the boat and climbs out, with help from the crew once you have reached the top step only (you are rather exhausted by then). The next swimmer, who has had to tread water until the first swimmer is safely on board, is signalled to swim for an hour. The process is then repeated throughout the swim, with each swimmer doing an hour at a time exactly and following the same swim order as was started.

If during this process any of the swimmers in the sea touch the boat you all go home; if any of the swimmers touch another swimmer who just came in, you all go home; if any of the swimmers swim out of the agreed order you all go home; and if any swimmer refuses to go back in, you all go home! Oh yes, and the pilot can call off the swim at any time if he fears for your health or if he believes you cannot make it to France. Lots of regulations and rules. As I've said before, wetsuits are not allowed, men must wear Speedos or trunks that are just below their bits and women can only wear small swimsuits.

While the boat is rocking madly and the sea is sloshing on the floor, the swimmer who just got out has to somehow get out of their costume with as much dignity as possible (not easy in a force 4 gale I can tell you), get dried, into their warm clothes, get as warm as possible, consume a hot drink and get some food down. Everyone else is simply sitting around on the boxes trying to stay warm and dry and not to be sick.

This is not a challenge for everyone; it takes a decent level of swimming ability (which I have only just about got), a stomach that can take the boat rolling around for 20+ hours, a mental toughness to get in again and again, and a passionate desire to complete the task. If you have all those, plus a small amount of eccentricity, then maybe you can give it a go! Most Soloists and Relay teams simply do not successfully make it and there must be a reason for that.

Our swim went as well as we could have hoped for and we reached our almost finishing point in amazing time; passing a number of other Channel swimming boats who mostly ended up going back home without success. I believe that there were eight attempts on our day and we were one of only three that were successful. By the time we could see our destination up ahead the tide had turned and we spent the next 90 minutes swimming in completely the wrong direction.

This was not an accident, I should add. You cannot swim against the tide, it is simply not do-able. Therefore the boat has to lead you with the tide, even if it is completely the wrong way, and then if you are lucky the tide will change when you still have some energy left and it will bring you back around. Thankfully for us the tide did change back and the last two swimmers - myself and then Lindy - had the tide behind us. This enabled me to get us within half a mile or so of the coast of France, and then Lindy roared in like a mermaid possessed! With her safely on the beach in France a dinghy was launched to collect her and bring her back to the boat. We had taken 12 hours and 55 minutes exactly, an amazing time and one we were all thrilled with.

Job done we packed up and stored everything as best we could and then settled on our boxes whilst Andy King put his foot down and darted the *Louise Jane* back to Dover at top speed. About two-and-a-half hours later, after having swum the Channel and then having once again been thrown around on the back of a fishing boat in a force 4 gale, we were back at Dover and had the welcome sight of Little Bob waiting to drive us back to Brighton. His smile was a lovely welcome after an exhausting journey.

After dropping everyone except Fiona home, Little Bob and Lindy got back to their house and I then drove Fiona back to her house. This was probably the longest 30-minute each-way drive I have ever done. I was exhausted from being up for over 36 hours, exhausted from the whole Channel trip and my head was banging like a steel drum; I literally had to hold my hair by my temple as tight as I could to reduce the headache pain I had, as close to a migraine as I have had in a long, long while. I was amazed I got home safely having driven an hour like that; I almost pulled over to the side of the road half a dozen times as it got so bad. I eventually rolled into bed (in the spare room to avoid the kids coming in at same mad hour) and fell into what I can only describe as a coma-like sleep! I had been up from 6a.m. on the Tuesday and finally got into bed at about midnight on the Wednesday.

For me, this journey – which started on Sunday 26th April 2010 and ended on day 536, Wednesday 8th August 2012 – saw me manage to learn to sea swim, battle the sea, survive sleep deprivation, run a marathon, have too many Crohn's and rheumatism moments, eat too little and moan too much. Eventually, though, I did conquer the English Channel and Team Starrfish did triumph!

So many people encouraged and helped me, but a few in particular gave way above what one could expect or hope. My wife Sharon particularly put up with two-and-a-half years of me training for stupid amounts of hours every week and then coming home and moaning and complaining and worrying all the time; she is without a doubt my Starr. Big Bob Bicknall was my training partner for two years and has probably put up with as much of my madness as Sharon has – he really is a wonderful person. What can I say about Fiona? She is a Wonderwoman in almost every sense, and without her I doubt I would ever have been able to take on this challenge. Then finally there are my BSC friends, all of them new friends to me and, I hope, friends for a long time. Little Bob Phipps and Lindy Dunlop in particular are two very special people and I am honoured to now count you as my friends – friends for life, I hope.

Huge thanks to my brother-in-law Darren Abrahams, my partner in the Starr Trust and The Lyrics Centre (to be built one day, I swear), for being my 'mind' coach – I love you to bits. I could not survive without my sister Tracey, simple as that. My mum, Trish, continues to amaze me with her strength and her capacity to continue life with a smile despite the loss of Dad, and her inspirational ability to keep seeing the good in the world should be a lesson to all. And to all those who encouraged me, sponsored me and helped me on my way, I salute and thank you all.

The Swim4Smiles campaign raised a total of £75,342.67 for the Starr Trust, and this was given out to the twenty-one projects we chose. We included Childhood First, a pioneering charity that helps children and young people at risk of a lifetime in and out of the justice and psychiatric systems as a result of severe emotional trauma suffered through neglect and abuse. Among others, we also included the Royal Alexandra Hospital for Sick Children in Brighton and Naomi House children's hospice near Winchester.

It left £2,100 each for two scholarships, funded by us so that two children could achieve their dream. Both were teenagers aged sixteen who had an opportunity that could change their lives - one to train as a stage manager in a top theatre school and the other to go from junior to senior in her chosen sport - but both came from families who could not financially support them to do this.

So what has my experience taught me? Well, that every challenge one takes on has to be about the journey. The end result certainly seems important but it is the journey that shapes us and it is ultimately the journey that we remember. It has taught me that when things get tough we can still do our best; our best may change from day to day but we must always still do our best. It has taught me that if life changes the direction in which we are heading then maybe we should be big enough to let it happen and see where it takes us, rather than fight for something that perhaps is not for us after all. It has also taught me that getting up at 6a.m. and putting your face into a freezing sea is nuts!

To sum up, I have to repeat Henry T. Ford's words that I used at the start of this book: 'Whether you think you can, or you think you can't - you're right.'

Finally I have to thank my father, Edward Lawrence Starr (1945-2006). You may not be with us in body, Dad, but you have inspired me all my life and you have continued to inspire and teach me every day since your death. The day we meet up again will be nothing but joy for me, but in the meantime, like you did, I will always try to live life to the full and I will always do my best to make you proud.

If, having read this story, you feel moved and inspired to contribute to the Edward Starr Charitable Trust, please log onto www.starrtrust.com and help us help a child smile. Thank you.

The End...

Until the next challenge that is... a cycling one, I think, as 2013 is the hundredth anniversary of the Tour De France. Do I dare?
Maybe time to buy a bike and find out!

Afterword - Sunday 26th Jan 2013

The super competitive Fiona will not be pleased I have added this; but I feel it's worth her wrath for me to have it documented in print.

Today was the UK Cold Water Swimming Championships in Tooting Bec, London. The water was a chilling 0 celsius (32 degrees faranheit). The fastest times achieved by Fiona, Big Bob and me over the 30 metres was:

Fiona 25.3 seconds
Bob 24.54 seconds
Me 23.81 seconds

I was fastest over the 30 metres than both of them. It's taken me 3 years to do it, but I got there in the end.

My job here is done!